ECONOMIC ISSUES, PROBLEMS AND PERSPECTIVES

THE MUNICIPAL SECURITIES MARKET

OVERVIEW, CONCERNS AND IMPROVEMENT RECOMMENDATIONS

Economic Issues, Problems and Perspectives

Additional books in this series can be found on Nova's website under the Series tab.

Additional e-books in this series can be found on Nova's website under the e-book tab.

ECONOMIC ISSUES, PROBLEMS AND PERSPECTIVES

THE MUNICIPAL SECURITIES MARKET

OVERVIEW, CONCERNS AND IMPROVEMENT RECOMMENDATIONS

MICHAL N. WILSON
EDITOR

nova publishers
New York

For permission to use material from this book please contact us:
Telephone 631-231-7269; Fax 631-231-8175
Web Site: http://www.novapublishers.com

NOTICE TO THE READER

Additional color graphics may be available in the e-book version of this book.

LIBRARY OF CONGRESS CATALOGING-IN-PUBLICATION DATA

ISBN: 978-1-62417-295-3

Published by Nova Science Publishers, Inc. † New York

CONTENTS

PREFACE

The mission of the SEC is to protect investors, including investors in municipal securities, maintain fair, orderly, and efficient markets, and facilitate capital formation. This book provides an overview of the municipal securities market, the regulatory structure and the roles of key market participants, with a focus on two key areas of concern: disclosure and market structure.

Chapter 1 - The mission of the SEC is to protect investors – including investors in municipal securities – maintain fair, orderly, and efficient markets, and facilitate capital formation. In furtherance of that mission, Chairman Mary L. Schapiro announced in May 2010 that Commissioner Elisse B. Walter, along with staff from across the agency, would lead an effort to examine the municipal securities market.

In 2010 and 2011, Commissioner Walter and the Commission staff ("Staff") held public field hearings in San Francisco, California; Washington, DC; and Birmingham, Alabama. At each of the hearings, the Staff invited individuals representing many different perspectives to participate in panels on specific topics, including disclosure, accounting, pre-trade price transparency, and other investor and municipal issuer concerns. In addition to the field hearings, the Staff held meetings and conference calls with market participants and public comment was invited by email, by mail, through the Commission's web-based comment submission form, or through a dedicated telephone line.

The development of this Report on the Municipal Securities Market ("Report") included consideration of the transcripts of the field hearings, the comment letters received, academic studies, other publicly available materials, Staff-generated statistics based on certain data sources, and the input received during meetings and conference calls with market participants.

This Report commences with an overview of the municipal securities market, the regulatory structure and the roles of key market participants. Next, the Report focuses on two key areas of concern in the municipal securities market: disclosure and market structure.

Finally, the Commission provides a number of recommendations for potential further consideration, including legislative changes, Commission rulemaking, Municipal Securities Rulemaking Board ("MSRB") rulemaking and enhancement of industry "best practices." These recommendations are designed to address the various concerns raised by market participants and others and to provide avenues to improve the municipal securities market, including transparency for municipal securities investors. While the authors believe, based on our review of the market as described in this Report, that these recommendations could help improve the municipal securities market, the authors recognize that further action on specific recommendations will involve further study of relevant additional information, including information as applicable related to the costs and benefits of the recommendations and the consideration as applicable of public comment.

Chapter 2 - The MSRB was created by Congress in 1975 as the principal regulator for the municipal securities market with the mandate to protect investors and the public interest. By adopting a principles-based approach to regulating municipal securities dealers, operating retail-oriented information disclosure systems and establishing professional standards for municipal securities professionals, the MSRB has effectively created protections for retail investors in the $3.7 trillion United States municipal securities market.

The MSRB also acts as an independent resource and expert on the municipal securities market for policymakers such as Congress and the U.S. Department of the Treasury as well as other federal and state regulators including the Board of Governors of the Federal Reserve and the Internal Revenue Service.

The Dodd-Frank Wall Street Reform and Consumer Protection Act (the Dodd-Frank Act) included multiple provisions that affect the municipal market and the MSRB. The provisions relating to the MSRB's rulemaking and related activities became effective on October 1, 2010. Specifically, Section 975 broadened the mission of the MSRB to include the protection of state and local governments, as well as certain private sector obligated persons — such as universities and hospitals — that access the capital markets through the issuance of municipal bonds. The MSRB, of course, also continues to pursue its original mission of protecting investors and the public interest.

Section 975 of the statute expanded the MSRB's responsibilities to include the regulation of municipal advisors. Municipal advisors include businesses and individuals that advise municipal entities concerning municipal financial products and municipal securities, as well as businesses and individuals that solicit certain types of business from municipal entities on behalf of unrelated broker-dealers, municipal advisors or investment advisors. Municipal securities dealers performing municipal advisory services were previously subject to MSRB regulation because of their municipal securities dealer activities. Under the new law, however, other municipal advisors are subject to MSRB regulation for the first time.

The MSRB's Board of Directors was reorganized under our amended authorizing statute to be made up for the first time of a majority of public, independent members and to include municipal advisor representatives. Previously, the Exchange Act required that the MSRB be governed by a board with a majority of industry members. Under the new structure, effective October 1, 2010, the MSRB is required by statute to maintain a balance of regulated and non-regulated Board members, with investors, municipal entities, securities dealers, bank dealers and municipal advisors each having representation on the MSRB Board of Directors.

In: The Municipal Securities Market
Editor: Michal N. Wilson
ISBN: 978-1-62417-295-3

Chapter 1

REPORT ON THE MUNICIPAL SECURITIES MARKET*

U.S. Securities and Exchange Commission

EXECUTIVE SUMMARY

Background on Report on the Municipal Securities Market

The mission of the SEC is to protect investors – including investors in municipal securities – maintain fair, orderly, and efficient markets, and facilitate capital formation. In furtherance of that mission, Chairman Mary L. Schapiro announced in May 2010 that Commissioner Elisse B. Walter, along with staff from across the agency, would lead an effort to examine the municipal securities market.

In 2010 and 2011, Commissioner Walter and the Commission staff ("Staff") held public field hearings in San Francisco, California; Washington, DC; and Birmingham, Alabama. At each of the hearings, the Staff invited individuals representing many different perspectives to participate in panels on specific topics, including disclosure, accounting, pre-trade price transparency, and other investor and municipal issuer concerns. In addition to the field hearings, the Staff held meetings and conference calls with market participants and public comment was invited by email, by mail, through the Commission's web-based comment submission form, or through a dedicated telephone line.

The development of this Report on the Municipal Securities Market ("Report") included consideration of the transcripts of the field hearings, the comment letters received, academic studies, other publicly available materials, Staff-generated statistics based on certain data sources, and the input received during meetings and conference calls with market participants.

This Report commences with an overview of the municipal securities market, the regulatory structure and the roles of key market participants. Next, the Report focuses on two key areas of concern in the municipal securities market: disclosure and market structure.

---

* This is an edited, reformatted and augmented version of U.S. Securities and Exchange Commission, dated July 31, 2012.

Finally, the Commission provides a number of recommendations for potential further consideration, including legislative changes, Commission rulemaking, Municipal Securities Rulemaking Board ("MSRB") rulemaking and enhancement of industry "best practices." These recommendations are designed to address the various concerns raised by market participants and others and to provide avenues to improve the municipal securities market, including transparency for municipal securities investors. While we believe, based on our review of the market as described in this Report, that these recommendations could help improve the municipal securities market, we recognize that further action on specific recommendations will involve further study of relevant additional information, including information as applicable related to the costs and benefits of the recommendations and the consideration as applicable of public comment.

Overview of the Municipal Securities Market

The municipal securities market is critical to building and maintaining the infrastructure of our nation. State and local governmental entities issue municipal securities to finance a wide variety of public projects, to provide for cash flow and other governmental needs, and to finance non-governmental private projects (through the use of "conduit" financings). As of December 31, 2011, there were over one million different municipal bonds outstanding, in the total aggregate principal amount of more than $3.7 trillion.

Depending on the type of financing, payments of the principal and interest on an issue of municipal securities may come from general revenues of the municipal issuer, specific tax receipts, revenues generated from a public project, or payments from private entities or from a combination of sources. In addition to being issued for many different purposes, municipal securities are also issued in many different forms, such as fixed rate, zero coupon or variable rate bonds. The interest paid on municipal securities is typically exempt from federal income taxation and may be exempt from state income and other taxes as well.

Municipal bonds also may be accompanied by a form of credit enhancement, such as a letter of credit issued by a bank, a governmental guarantee, or an insurance policy issued by a bond insurance company. Credit enhancements were common during 2000-2007, with more than half of the municipal principal issued supported by at least one type of credit enhancement during that period. However, private sector credit enhancement in the form of bond insurance in particular has decreased since 2008 due to the effect of the financial crisis on banks and municipal bond insurers. This decline has impacted the market for municipal securities and renewed investor focus on the disclosure practices and underlying credit quality of municipal securities, municipal issuers, and conduit borrowers.

Historically, municipal securities have had significantly lower rates of default than corporate and foreign government bonds. Studies indicate that the risk of ultimate non-payment for municipal debt historically has been low, both when compared to total municipal debt outstanding and total municipal debt in default. Nevertheless, municipal bonds can and do default, and these defaults can negatively impact investors in ways other than non-payment, including delayed payments and pricing disruptions. Reports indicate that a majority of defaults in the municipal securities market are in conduit revenue bonds issued for non-governmental purposes, such as multi-family housing, healthcare (hospitals and nursing homes), and industrial development bonds (for economic development and manufacturing purposes).

Overview of the Federal Regulatory Structure for the Municipal Securities Market

Despite its size and importance, the municipal securities market has not been subject to the same level of regulation as other sectors of the U.S. capital markets. The Securities Act of 1933 ("Securities Act") and the Securities Exchange Act of 1934 ("Exchange Act") were both enacted with broad exemptions for municipal securities from all their provisions, except for the antifraud provisions of Section 17(a) of the Securities Act, Section 10(b) of the Exchange Act, and Rule 10b-5 promulgated thereunder.

Congress, as part of the Securities Acts Amendments of 1975 ("1975 Amendments"), created a limited regulatory scheme for the municipal securities market at the federal level in response to the growth of the market, market abuses, and the increasing participation of retail investors.

The 1975 Amendments required firms transacting business in municipal securities to register with the Commission as broker-dealers, required banks dealing in municipal securities to register as municipal securities dealers, and gave the Commission broad rulemaking and enforcement authority over such broker-dealers and municipal securities dealers. In addition, the 1975 Amendments created the MSRB and granted it authority to promulgate rules governing the sale of municipal securities by broker-dealers and municipal securities dealers.

The 1975 Amendments did not create a regulatory regime for, or impose any new requirements on, municipal issuers. Pursuant to provisions commonly known as the "Tower Amendment," the 1975 Amendments expressly limited the Commission's and the MSRB's authority to require municipal securities issuers, either directly or indirectly, to file any application, report, or document with the Commission or the MSRB prior to any sale of municipal securities by the municipal issuer.

The 1975 Amendments do not, by their terms, preclude the Commission from promulgating disclosure standards in municipal offerings, but there is no express statutory authority contained in the Exchange Act over disclosure by municipal issuers.

The Dodd-Frank Wall Street Reform and Consumer Protection Act ("Dodd-Frank Act") did not change these provisions, but required a study and review by the U.S. Comptroller General of municipal securities disclosure, possible recommendations for municipal issuer disclosure requirements and the advisability of the repeal or retention of the Tower Amendment. In addition, the Dodd-Frank Act contained other provisions that affected the municipal securities market. Among other things, it amended Section 15B of the Exchange Act to require the registration of municipal advisors with the Commission and provide for their regulation by the MSRB. Additionally, the Dodd-Frank Act expanded the MSRB's authority by explicitly requiring it to protect municipal entities and obligated persons.

In the absence of a statutory scheme for municipal securities registration and reporting, the Commission's investor protection efforts in the municipal securities market have been accomplished primarily through regulation of broker-dealers and municipal securities dealers, including through Exchange Act Rule 15c2-12, Commission interpretations, enforcement of the antifraud provisions of the federal securities laws, and Commission oversight of the MSRB. The existing regulatory scheme for broker-dealers and municipal securities dealers can significantly impact municipal entities' and obligated persons' business practices and the availability of information about them in the marketplace.

Overview of Disclosure Practices in the Municipal Securities Market

Disclosure practices in municipal securities offerings and on an ongoing basis have developed as a result of the antifraud provisions of federal and state securities laws, Exchange Act Rule 15c2-12, Commission interpretive guidance, MSRB rules, and voluntary guidelines published by various industry groups.

Some field hearing participants noted significant improvements over time in the disclosure practices of issuers in the municipal securities market, including the widespread use of the Internet, the creation of the MSRB's Electronic Municipal Market Access system ("EMMA"), and implementation of rule changes such as recent amendments to Rule 15c2-12.

Other market participants and investors emphasized an interest in greater and timelier disclosures in several key areas. The disclosure issues discussed arise in the primary offering and continuing disclosure contexts. In the primary offering context, many participants raised specific concerns, particularly with respect to smaller, less sophisticated issuers and non-governmental conduit borrowers.

These concerns related to content and timeliness of financial information in primary offerings. The major challenge in secondary market disclosure, according to many market participants, is the timeliness and completeness of filings as well as compliance with continuing disclosure agreements.

In addition, the Report discusses several key areas (highlighted below) in which market participants and others have raised concerns and called for expanded and timelier disclosure.

The Report notes concerns about access to issuer information; the presentation and comparability of information; and the existence/adequacy of disclosure controls and procedures. At the same time, the Report notes concerns raised by issuers about the potential burdens that could result from increased regulation. Some emphasized that a "one size fits all" approach would not be appropriate.

- Financial Statements and Financial Information
- Timeliness of Financial Information. The timeliness of financial information in primary offerings and on an ongoing basis is an area of concern. Studies have shown that disclosure of audited annual financial statements by many municipal issuers is particularly slow. By the time annual financial statements are filed or otherwise publicly available, many municipal market analysts and investors believe the financial information has diminished usefulness or lost relevance in assessing the current financial position of a municipal issuer. Market participants have not only called for more timely disclosure of annual financial information, but also for disclosure of interim financial information, such as budgets and cash flow reports.
- Comparability of Financial Information. There are no uniformly applied accounting standards in the municipal securities market and the Commission generally lacks authority to prescribe the accounting standards that municipal issuers must use. The

Governmental Accounting Standards Board ("GASB") establishes generally accepted accounting principles ("GAAP"), which are used by many state and local governments of widely varying size and complexity. Market participants noted that adherence to GASB standards promotes consistency and comparability of financial information among municipal issuers and differing municipal securities.

- Disclosure by Conduit Borrowers. Historically, conduit borrowers in many types of conduit municipal financings have provided substantially less continuing information than issuers of municipal securities involving non-conduit financings. Some market participants thought that the same registration requirements and disclosure standards should apply to non-governmental conduit borrowers that apply to other non-governmental issuers selling securities directly into the corporate securities market.
- Pension Funding Obligations and Other Post-Employment Benefits ("OPEBs") Disclosure. Obligations to provide pension and OPEBs can significantly affect a municipal issuer's financial health and may impact the issuer's ability to make debt service payments on municipal securities. The accuracy and adequacy of disclosure regarding pension and OPEB funding obligations by municipal securities issuers is a focus of legislators, the Commission, issuers, investors, and other market participants.
- Exposure to Derivatives. Some municipal issuers use derivative products in connection with their municipal securities offerings. Although the use of derivatives can provide municipalities with benefits, such as the potential to reduce borrowing costs and/or manage interest rate risk, derivatives also pose special risks to municipalities. Additionally, several field hearing panelists noted conflicts of interest and other factors that may cause some municipal issuers to enter into disadvantageous derivatives transactions. We note, however, that some market participants stated that, in their experience, risks, including credit risk, interest rate risk and termination risk, were carefully explained to issuers and understood by them. The increased use of derivative instruments by municipal issuers has underscored the benefits of enhanced disclosure to provide investors and issuers a clear understanding of the terms and risks to the municipal issuer.
- Disclaimers of Responsibility for Information Included in Official Statements and Other Disclosures. Some municipal market participants attempt to disclaim responsibility for information included in official statements and other disclosure documents. We are also aware that some counsel have encouraged the use of disclaimers in official statements and other disclosure documents in an attempt to protect against liability under Section 10(b) of the Exchange Act for portions of offering documents that have been prepared by "experts" and, in part, to avoid common law liability for implied warranties.
- Disclosure of Conflicts of Interest and Other Relationships or Practices. As highlighted in the 1994 Interpretive Release and Commission enforcement actions, information concerning certain financial and business relationships or practices, such as undisclosed payments, political contributions, and bid rigging, by offering participants and municipal entity decision makers may be critical to investors. The role of advisors to issuers, such as swap advisors and other municipal advisors, also has raised questions regarding undisclosed conflicts of interest.

Overview of the Municipal Securities Market Structure

Individuals, or "retail" investors, directly or indirectly hold more than 75% of the outstanding principal amount of municipal securities. The municipal securities market traditionally has been described as a "buy-and-hold" market because many investors hold municipal securities until maturity. Indeed, following the initial distribution period, municipal securities trade infrequently.

Those municipal securities that trade do so in a decentralized over-the-counter dealer market that is illiquid and opaque. Brokers, dealers, and municipal securities dealers (collectively, "municipal bond dealers") execute virtually all customer transactions in a principal capacity, with a portion of these principal trades effected on a "riskless principal" basis. A handful of these intermediaries account for the majority of trading in municipal securities. The relatively high transaction costs in the municipal securities market have been attributed the market's illiquidity, opacity, and fragmentation.

A retail investor wishing to buy municipal securities would typically request that its municipal bond dealer identify bonds with credit, payment, tax, maturity, and other characteristics that meet the customer's investment needs. The municipal bond dealer may recommend municipal securities that it holds in its inventory or that are available in the over-the-counter market, either from another municipal bond dealer or through a broker's broker or an alternative trading system ("ATS"). Although investors tend to hold these bonds to maturity, they may decide to sell their bonds for a variety of reasons. An investor wishing to sell municipal securities would typically contact its municipal bond dealer, who may offer to purchase the municipal securities from the customer and take them into its inventory, or may find a buyer by contacting other municipal bond dealers directly or using a broker's broker or an ATS. When finding a buyer, these municipal bond dealers would execute the customer's transaction on a riskless principal basis.

Although there have been improvements in the availability of pricing information about completed trades (*i.e.*, post-trade information), the secondary market for municipal securities remains opaque. Investors have very limited access to information regarding which market participants would be interested in buying or selling a municipal security, and at what prices (*i.e.*, pre-trade information). Firm bid and ask quotations are generally unavailable and municipal bond dealers typically do not widely display firm quotations electronically. To the extent there is pre-trade price transparency, it tends to be provided through electronic networks operated by broker's brokers, ATSs, or similar trading systems. This information, however, is not broadly accessible by the public, but rather is generally available only to participating municipal bond dealers.

Market participants have developed alternative means to value municipal securities. The necessity for market participants to undertake a more exacting analysis to value municipal securities has been made more apparent due to the declining use of bond insurance and other types of credit enhancement, as well as concerns about the reliability of credit ratings. Credit enhancements and credit ratings previously had been viewed as serving to "commoditize" assessments of the credit quality of disparate municipal securities and often led market participants to make more simplified pricing judgments.

Municipal bond dealers may look at recent trades in "comparable" bonds for insight into the price at which market participants may be willing to transact in a municipal security that has not traded recently.

They may also rely on benchmark yield curves to assist in valuing a bond. Independent professional pricing services that estimate the current market price of a particular municipal security are also available to municipal bond dealers and their evaluated prices are often included in account statements provided to individual investors.

Market participants have varying access to pricing information. Municipal bond dealers, particularly those with significant order flow, have access to the broadest range of pricing information. Larger institutional investors also tend to have access to a variety of sources of pricing information. Retail investors, on the other hand, have access to relatively little pricing information about municipal securities, and generally have limited knowledge about the execution options that are available to them.

Within this market structure, municipal bond dealers owe their customers certain duties. In general, MSRB rules require municipal bond dealers effecting transactions with customers, whether as principal or agent, to trade at a fair price and to exercise diligence in establishing the market value of the municipal security and the reasonableness of the compensation they receive. Many municipal bond dealers face challenges in fulfilling these duties due to a market structure that provides uneven transparency and access to the best prices.

Recommendations

The Commission recommends that Congress, the Commission, and other market participants such as the MSRB could consider several potential approaches to improve the municipal securities market. We believe that improvements in the municipal securities market could involve a combination of approaches, including legislative, regulatory, and industry-based initiatives.

While we believe these recommendations could potentially help improve the municipal securities market and enhance investor protection, we are sensitive to changes in legal or regulatory standards that could lead to certain costs and believe that such costs should be considered in connection with the economic analysis conducted as appropriate in the context of specific proposals, including when evaluating the appropriateness of pursuing such proposals.

Recommendations Relating to Disclosure

First, in light of the Commission's limited regulatory authority, we recommend a number of potential legislative changes which, if implemented by Congress, would provide the Commission with additional authority to initiate changes to improve municipal securities disclosures made by issuers. The legislative changes would not result, however, in the repeal or modification to the existing proscriptions on the SEC or the MSRB requiring any presale filing of disclosure documents, known as the "Tower Amendment" (discussed in more detail in the Report).

The legislative recommendations would nonetheless give the Commission the authority to take regulatory steps that it determines to be appropriate to meaningfully enhance disclosure practices by municipal issuers, which could be accomplished in a short period of time. Second, there are a number of regulatory approaches that the Commission could consider pursuing under its existing authority. Although such measures could effect improvements, they may not be sufficient, on their own, to address the concerns discussed in this Report. Also, we recognize that further action on specific recommendations will involve further study of relevant additional information, including information as applicable related to the costs and benefits of the recommendations and the consideration as applicable of public comment.

Third, we recommend that market participants continue to strive for high-quality disclosure practices through development and enhancement of best practices guidelines.

Legislative

The following are possible legislative approaches that could be considered in order to provide the Commission authority to establish improved disclosures and practices in the municipal securities market.

- Authorize the Commission to require that municipal issuers prepare and disseminate official statements and disclosure during the outstanding term of the securities, including timeframes, frequency for such dissemination and minimum disclosure requirements, including financial statements and other financial and operating information, and provide tools to enforce such requirements.
- Amend the municipal securities exemptions in the Securities Act and Exchange Act to eliminate the availability of such exemptions to conduit borrowers who are not municipal entities under Section 3(a)(2) of the Securities Act, without differentiation based on the size of the financing due to the continuing availability of other exemptions, including those available for small businesses, private offerings, and non-profit entities that take into account different types of offerings and issuers.
- Authorize the Commission to establish the form and content of financial statements for municipal issuers who issue municipal securities, including the authority to recognize the standards of a designated private-sector body as generally accepted for purposes of the federal securities laws, and provide the Commission with attendant authority over such private-sector body.
- Authorize the Commission, as it deems appropriate, to require municipal securities issuers to have their financial statements audited, whether by an independent auditor or a state auditor.
- Provide a safe harbor from private liability for forward-looking statements of repeat municipal issuers who are subject to and current in their ongoing disclosure obligations that satisfy certain conditions, including appropriate risk disclosure relating to such forward-looking statements, and if projections are provided disclosure of significant assumptions underlying such projections.
- Permit the Internal Revenue Service to share with the Commission information that it obtains from returns, audits, and examinations related to municipal securities offerings in appropriate instances and with the necessary associated safeguards, particularly in instances of suspected securities fraud.
- To provide a mechanism to enforce compliance with continuing disclosure agreements and other obligations of municipal issuers to protect municipal securities bondholders, authorize the Commission to require trustees or other entities to enforce the terms of continuing disclosure agreements.

Regulatory

There are a number of possible actions that the Commission could pursue under its existing regulatory authority to improve disclosures and practices in the municipal securities market.

- The Commission could host market participants, regulators, and academics at an annual conference on the municipal securities markets.
- The Commission could consider issuing updated interpretive guidance regarding disclosure obligations of municipal securities issuers and others.
- The Commission could consider amendments to Exchange Act Rule 15c2-12 to further improve the disclosures made regarding municipal securities.
- The Commission should continue to work with the MSRB to strengthen its rules and further enhance EMMA.

Municipal Market Initiatives

We also recommend that municipal issuers and other market participants continue to work together on initiatives to improve municipal securities market disclosures and other practices.

- Municipal market participants should follow and should encourage others to follow existing industry best practices and expand and develop additional best practices guidelines in a number of areas to enhance disclosures and disclosure practices in the municipal securities market.

Recommendations Relating to Market Structure

Transparency is a vital aspect of promoting competition, and it enables customers and regulators to assess whether market professionals are providing best execution. Enhancing price transparency and promoting fair access to those prices could improve market efficiency, promote competition, and ultimately facilitate the best execution of retail customer orders in municipal securities. There are a number of recommendations that could achieve these goals. As these possible recommendations are examined in more detail, consideration as applicable should be given to the potential impacts on investor protection, liquidity and dealer participation in the market.

Improve Pre-Trade Price Transparency

- The Commission could consider amendments to Regulation ATS to require an ATS with material transaction or dollar volume in municipal securities to publicly disseminate its best bid and offer prices and, on a delayed and non-attributable basis, responses to "bids wanted" auctions.
- The MSRB could consider rules requiring a brokers' broker with material transaction or dollar volume in municipal securities to publicly disseminate the best bid and offer prices on any electronic network it operates and, on a delayed and non-attributable basis, responses to "bids wanted" auctions.

Improve Post-Trade Price Transparency

- The MSRB could consider requiring municipal bond dealers to report "yield spread" information to its Real-Time Transaction Reporting System to supplement existing interest rate, price and yield data.
- The MSRB should promptly pursue enhancements to its EMMA website so that retail investors have better access to pricing and other municipal securities information.

Buttress Existing Dealer Pricing Obligations

- The Commission and the MSRB should consider initiatives to improve the understanding of retail investors as to the various ways in which they might buy or sell a municipal bond, and the relative advantages and disadvantages of each.
- The Commission and the MSRB could consider ways to encourage the use of ATSs or similar electronic networks that widely disseminate quotes and provide fair access.
- The MSRB should consider encouraging or requiring municipal bond dealers to provide retail customers relevant pricing reference information in connection with any municipal securities transaction a municipal bond dealer effects for such customer.
- The MSRB should consider issuing more detailed interpretive guidance to assist dealers in establishing the "prevailing market price" for a municipal security, for purposes of determining whether the price offered a customer (including any markup or markdown) is fair and reasonable.
- The MSRB should consider requiring municipal bond dealers to disclose to customers, on confirmations for riskless principal transactions, the amount of any markup or markdown.
- The MSRB should consider a rule that would require municipal bond dealers to seek "best execution" of customer orders for municipal securities.

I. INTRODUCTION

A. Overview of the Municipal Securities Market

Over the past 30 years, the municipal securities market has grown significantly[1] and now represents an increasingly important part of the U.S. capital markets. The municipal securities market is also an extremely diverse market, with close to 44,000 state and local issuers, and with a total face amount of $3.7 trillion (face amount is hereinafter referred to as "principal").[2]

Depending on the type of financing, payments of the principal and interest on an issue of municipal securities may come from general revenues of the municipal issuer, specific tax receipts, revenues generated from public projects, payments from private entities, or from a combination of sources. The interest paid on municipal securities is typically exempt from federal income taxation and may be exempt from state income and other taxes.

The municipal securities market is critical to building and maintaining the infrastructure of our nation. The municipal securities market raises hundreds of billions of dollars each year[3] on behalf of states, localities, and other public and private entities. Many individuals play a dual role in the market – not only as taxpayers and residents of the states and localities that borrow through the municipal securities market, but also as the source of those funds as purchasers of municipal securities. Individual (or "retail") investors hold as much as 75% of outstanding municipal securities both directly and indirectly, through mutual funds, money market funds, and closed-end funds.[4]

Although the municipal securities market is often characterized as a "buy-and-hold" market, significant secondary market trading occurs.[5] Almost $3.3 trillion of municipal securities were traded in 2011 in close to 10.4 million transactions.[6] Customer trades of retail size (up to $25,000) accounted for less than $58 billion of principal traded in more than 3.8 million transactions.[7]

Despite its size and importance, the municipal securities market historically has not been subject to the same level of regulation as other sectors of the U.S. capital markets. Except with respect to securities fraud, the Securities and Exchange Commission's (the "SEC" or "Commission") authority over the disclosure practices of municipal issuers is significantly constrained under existing laws. Investors in municipal securities are often not afforded access to the types of timely and accurate information available to investors in other securities.

Additionally, because of the decentralized, dealer-intermediated over-the-counter market in which municipal securities trade, investors do not typically have access to the same types of pricing information as investors in other markets.

B. Review of the Municipal Securities Market

The mission of the SEC is to protect investors – including investors in municipal securities – maintain fair, orderly, and efficient markets, and facilitate capital formation. In furtherance of that mission, and with the specific goal of promoting enhanced transparency for municipal securities investors, Chairman Mary L. Schapiro announced in May 2010 that Commissioner Elisse B. Walter and Commission Staff (the "Staff") from across the agency would lead an effort to examine the municipal securities market.8 Commissioner Walter and the Staff held a series of public field hearings designed to elicit the analyses and opinions of a broad array of municipal market participants.

Ultimately, the initiative helped to inform the preparation of this Report on the Municipal Securities Market ("Report") concerning the state of the municipal securities market, which includes recommendations for further action that Congress, the Commission, and municipal market participants should consider.

In 2010 and 2011, the Staff held public field hearings in San Francisco, California;[9] Washington, District of Columbia;[10] and Birmingham, Alabama.[11] At each of the hearings, the Staff invited individuals representing many different perspectives to participate in panels on specific topics, ranging from disclosure and accounting to pre-trade price transparency and investor concerns, among others.[12] Transcripts of all three hearings and archived webcasts for two of the hearings are available on the Commission's website.[13] In addition to the field hearings, the Staff held more than 35 meetings and conference calls with market participants to gather further information, analyses, and opinions on the municipal securities market.[14]

The team of staff members from across the agency participating in these meetings and calls included staff from the Office of Municipal Securities, the Division of Trading and Markets, the Division of Corporation Finance, the Office of the Chief Accountant, the Division of Risk, Strategy, and Financial Innovation, the Division of Enforcement, the Office of Investor Education and Advocacy, and the Office of Compliance Inspections and Examinations, in addition to Commissioner Walter and members of her staff.

Public comment was invited by email, by mail, through the Commission's web-based comment submission form,[15] or through a dedicated telephone line.[16]

The development of this Report included consideration of the transcripts of the field hearings, the comment letters received, academic studies, other publicly available materials, Staff-generated statistics based on certain data sources, and the input received during meetings and conference calls with market participants.

C. Summary of Report

Section I of this Report provides an overview of the municipal securities market, the regulatory structure, and the roles of key market participants. Section I incorporates, where relevant, the views of market participants gathered during the field hearings.

Section II addresses issues relating to disclosure, with a particular emphasis on the observations of market participants. Section II begins with a summary of voluntary industry initiatives and guidelines, followed by an overview of initial disclosure, continuing disclosure, and market participant views. Next, Section II discusses in detail several key substantive disclosure areas: financial statements and financial information, including governmental accounting; pension and OPEBs; exposure to derivatives; disclaimers of responsibility for information included in official statements and other disclosure; and conflicts of interest and other relationships or practices.

Finally, it summarizes other issues raised by market participants pertaining to disclosure, including issues relating to access to and presentation of information and issuer disclosure controls and procedures.

Section III of this Report examines the structure of the municipal securities market and issues related to price transparency. Section III begins with an overview of the secondary market for municipal securities, including a discussion of how transactions occur in this market.

Next, it addresses specific market structure topics, including price transparency and a summary of relevant literature concerning transaction costs in the municipal securities market. Finally, Section III discusses the pricing and best execution obligations of municipal bond dealers.

Section IV of this Report sets forth a number of recommendations for further consideration concerning potential legislative changes, Commission rulemaking, MSRB rulemaking and enhancement of industry "best practices." These recommendations are designed to address the various concerns raised by market participants and others and to provide avenues to improve the municipal securities market.

II. OVERVIEW OF THE MUNICIPAL SECURITIES MARKET

A. The Municipal Securities Market

1. Municipal Securities Issuers

State and local governmental entities issue municipal securities to finance a variety of public projects, to meet cash flow and other governmental needs, and to finance non-governmental private projects (through the use of "conduit" financings on behalf of private organizations that obtain lower-cost tax-exempt financing).[17] Issuers of municipal securities consist of a diverse group of entities that includes states, their political subdivisions (such as cities, towns, counties and school districts), and their instrumentalities (such as housing, health care, airport, port, and economic development authorities and agencies). State and local laws, including state constitutions, statutes, city and county charters, and municipal codes govern these public bodies.[18]

Such constitutions, statutes, charters, and codes impose on municipal issuer's requirements relating to governance, budgeting, accounting, and other financial matters.[19] The governing bodies of municipal issuers are as varied as the types of issuers, ranging from state governments, cities, towns, and counties with elected officials to special purpose entities with appointed members.[20]

In 2011, there were over one million different municipal bonds outstanding[21] compared to fewer than 50,000 different corporate bonds.[22] These municipal bonds totaled $3.7 trillion in principal, while corporate (and foreign) bonds and corporate equities outstanding totaled $11.5 trillion and $22.5 trillion, respectively.[23]

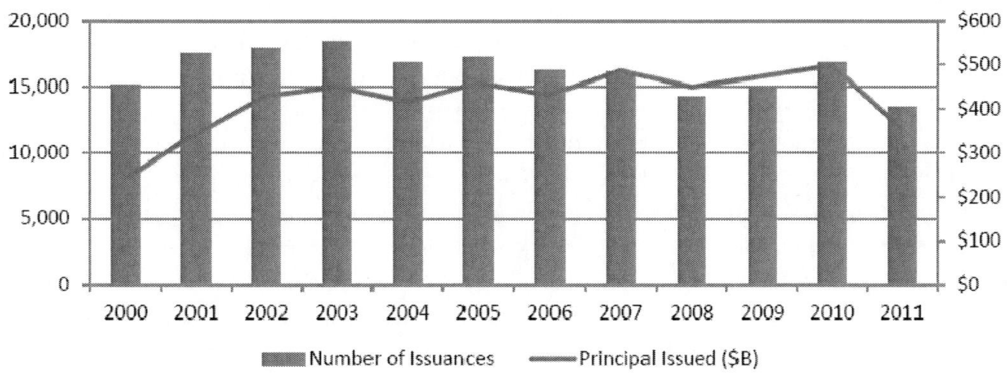

Staff generated statistics. Data source: Thomson Reuters' SDC Platinum, Global Public Finance module ("SDC Platinum").

Newly Issued Municipal Securities.

As shown above, the primary market for municipal securities is large both in terms of number of issuances and principal amount of securities issued. While municipal securities issuances slowed following the onset of the 2008 financial crisis, they appeared to rebound in 2010, in part due to the popularity of Build America Bonds ("BABs"), as discussed in more detail below.[24] In 2011, there were only 13,463 municipal issuances totaling $355 billion of principal, down from 16,848 issuances and $499 billion of principal in 2010.[25] Some attributed the drop in issuances to budget pressures and the rise of fiscal austerity;[26] the end of the BABs program at the end of 2010;[27] and new governors in more than half of the states.[28]

2. Description of Municipal Securities

a. Types of Municipal Securities

Municipal entities primarily issue securities that are generally classified as either general obligation bonds or revenue bonds.[29] General obligation bonds are backed by the taxing power and/or "full faith and credit" of the issuing entity. A holder of a general obligation bond may look for repayment to all sources of revenue received by the municipal entity that may legally be used for such payments or, for example, the receipts of unlimited *ad valorem* taxes levied for that purpose. Revenue bonds may be backed by specific non-*ad valorem* revenues, such as sales and use taxes or the revenues of the specific project or enterprise being financed (*e.g.,* a utility system, a toll road, or an airport or port facility).

Conduit revenue bonds are issued by a municipality or an agency or instrumentality of a municipality on behalf of a third party (often called a "conduit borrower" or "obligated person").[30] If certain requirements in the federal Internal Revenue Code ("IRC") and Internal Revenue Service ("IRS") regulations are met, conduit revenue bonds may be tax-exempt. Tax-exempt conduit revenue bonds include industrial development bonds on behalf of private entities, as well as financings for both non-profit and for-profit borrowers: such as hospitals; colleges and universities; power and energy companies; resource recovery facilities; multi-family housing projects; hotels; and sports stadiums. In a conduit revenue bond financing, the bondholder cannot look to the municipal issuer for payment of the bonds but rather must rely on payment from the conduit borrower.[31]

As discussed later, reports indicate that a majority of defaults in the municipal securities market are in conduit revenue bonds issued for nongovernmental purposes, such as multi-family housing, healthcare (hospitals and nursing homes), and industrial development bonds (for economic development and manufacturing purposes).[32]

Derivative products are used by both municipal issuers and investors for financial and risk management.[33] Municipal market derivatives often must be structured in accordance with the provisions of the IRC and other laws that apply to the issuance of tax-exempt financings.

The most common use for derivatives by municipal issuers is the execution of interest rate swaps in connection with new, anticipated, or outstanding debt.[34] Municipal issuers enter into interest rate swaps, caps, or collars either to create a synthetic fixed interest rate or to attempt to manage their exposure to interest rate risk.[35] Municipal securities investors and dealers may use credit-focused derivatives to hedge risks or increase returns.[36]

Another common type of municipal security is a college savings plan that complies with Section 529 of the Internal Revenue Code. These plans, known as "529 Plans," involve offerings of interests in state tuition programs and qualified savings plans that are public instrumentalities of the particular state and provide tax advantages designed to encourage saving for future college costs.

b. Different Features of Municipal Securities

In addition to being issued for many different purposes, municipal securities are issued in many different forms, such as fixed rate, zero coupon, or variable rate bonds.

Fixed rate municipal securities pay a fixed interest rate over the term of the security, with interest payments made periodically, typically semi-annually. Historically, most municipal securities were fixed rate securities. With zero coupon bonds, interest accrues and compounds, but is paid only on the maturity date of the bond.[37]

Finally, variable rate municipal securities pay interest based on an interest rate that changes periodically, either as a result of changes in a reference rate, in a commonly followed index, or as a result of regular resets by the issuer or a third party.

The two main types of variable rate municipal securities are variable rate demand obligations ("VRDOs") and auction rate securities ("ARS"). VRDOs are long-term municipal securities with a floating interest rate that resets periodically - often daily or weekly - and provide investors the option to sell (with a "put" or "tender" right) the securities back to the issuer at par, typically with seven days' notice.[38]

They usually are additionally secured by either a letter of credit or a standby bond purchase agreement.[39] Variable rate municipal securities with put rights arose to satisfy the needs of money market funds that must maintain portfolios with short durations.[40] The issuance of variable rate municipal securities spiked in 2008, but then decreased to historic lows in 2011.[41] In 2011, VRDO issuance totaled $18.7 billion, representing approximately 5.3% of the aggregate principal amount of municipal securities issued.[42]

ARS are long-term municipal bonds with interest rates that are periodically reset through an auction process, sometimes referred to as a "Dutch" auction, which allows the municipal issuer to issue long-term debt but pay short-term interest rates.[43] ARS were introduced into the municipal market in 1988.[44] In early 2008, municipal ARS outstanding totaled approximately $200 billion.[45] Beginning in February of 2008, the auctions for these municipal securities began to fail when the auctions attracted too few bidders to establish a clearing rate.[46] Following the failed auctions, a number of municipal issuers either changed to another interest rate mode, such as a fixed rate, or refunded and redeemed the securities.[47] There were no new issues of ARS in 2011.[48]

As discussed in more detail below,[49] the issuance of municipal securities is also affected by the availability of credit enhancement, which often takes the form of a letter of credit issued by a bank,[50] a governmental guarantee, or an insurance policy issued by a bond insurance company. Municipal bond insurance was first introduced in 1971 and letter of credit-supported municipal bonds became very popular after the introduction of variable rate municipal bonds in the early 1980s.[51]

Credit enhancements were common during 2000-2007, with more than half of the municipal securities principal issued supported by at least one type of credit enhancement during that period. This trend was reversed in 2008 due to the effect of the financial crisis on banks and municipal bond insurers.[52] Since 2008, the availability of private sector credit enhancement, including bond insurance, has declined significantly: only 17% of the municipal securities principal issued in 2009, 2010, and 2011 had a credit enhancement (*e.g.*, bond insurance, guarantees, letters of credit, or standby bond purchase agreements[53]).[54]

c. Tax Treatment of Interest

Tax-exempt municipal securities have traditionally comprised the vast majority of municipal securities.[55] Interest payable on such securities is not subject to federal income tax if certain requirements imposed by the IRC and IRS regulations are met.[56] In 2008, taxable municipal securities accounted for 11% of the aggregate principal amount of municipal securities issued; that number rose to 18% in 2009 and 32% in 2010.[57]

The increase in taxable municipal securities in 2009 and 2010 was due to the passage of the American Recovery and Reinvestment Act of 2009 ("ARRA"), which authorized the issuance of BABs[58] and other taxable municipal bonds.[59] The BAB Program expired on December 31, 2010. After the expiration of the BAB Program, taxable issuance returned to its historical levels: 9.4% in 2011.[60]

3. Investors in Municipal Securities

Municipal securities, particularly tax-exempt municipal securities, are largely held by individual or "retail" investors. Retail investors usually buy and hold municipal securities until maturity.[61] Prior to the enactment of the Tax Reform Act of 1986, commercial banks were the primary holders of municipal securities because they were allowed to deduct 80% of the interest expense associated with acquiring tax-exempt securities.[62] The Tax Reform Act of 1986 significantly reduced the tax benefits to banks for purchasing tax-exempt municipal securities.[63] As a result, commercial bank holdings of municipal securities declined from a high of 51% of municipal securities outstanding in 1971-1972[64] to 7.6% in 2011.[65]

Households as a group have represented the largest single owner of municipal securities outstanding for the past six consecutive years, as shown in the graph below. As of December 31, 2011, they accounted for nearly $1.9 trillion of municipal securities holdings, which is a 12% increase relative to 2006.[66] The years since 2008 have also seen a decline in money market funds' holdings of municipal securities and an increase in mutual funds' holdings. Approximately 50.2% of the outstanding principal amount of municipal securities was held directly by individuals and up to 25% was held on behalf of individuals by mutual, money market, closed-end, and exchange-traded funds.[67]

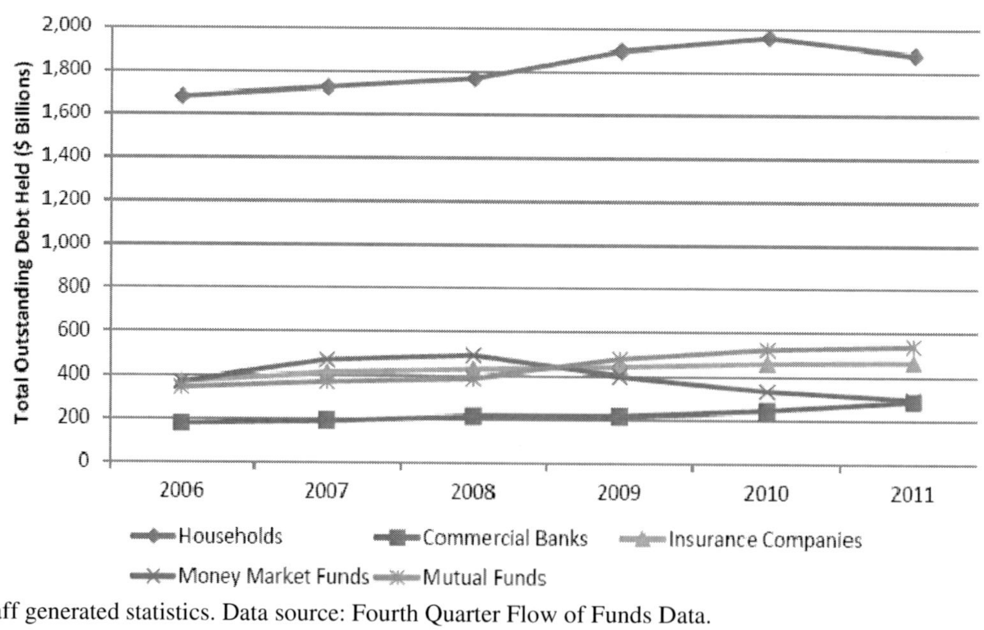

Staff generated statistics. Data source: Fourth Quarter Flow of Funds Data.

Primary Holders of Municipal Securities (2006 - 2011).

The municipal security holdings by category of investor are presented in the graph below. With respect to bank holdings currently, some banks may still favor municipal securities because of their low default rate as well as their tax-exempt status and relative yield.[68] In addition to purchasing municipal securities through traditional public offerings, commercial banks have begun to increase their purchases of municipal securities through private placements (also known as "direct purchases") and increase their provision of conventional loans to state and local governments and other municipal issuers (also known as "direct loans").[69]

Recent articles have indicated that these commercial bank activities have increased for a variety of reasons.[70]

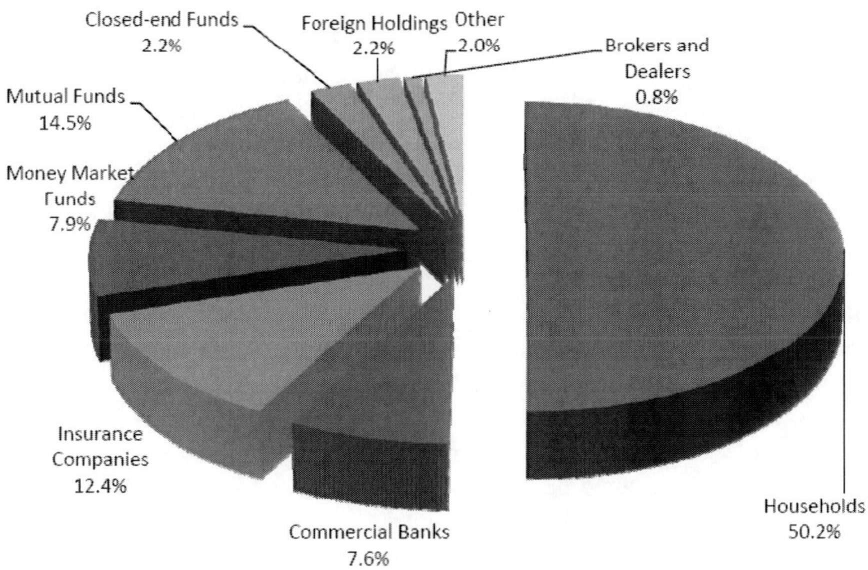

Staff generated statistics. Data source: Fourth Quarter Flow of Funds Data.

Municipal-Security Holdings by Investor Category (Fourth Quarter 2011).

4. Municipal Securities Offerings

Municipal securities typically are issued through an underwriting process in which one or more broker-dealers or municipal securities dealers (referred to in this section as "underwriters") purchase the securities directly from the issuer and reoffer them to investors. When underwriters form a group to purchase the securities and share the risks of underwriting the issuance, the group is called a "syndicate."[71]

The underwriters' fee from the sale of the municipal securities typically is the difference between the price the underwriter pays the issuer for the securities and the price at which the securities are reoffered to investors. This fee is called the underwriter's discount or the gross underwriting spread.[72] Once the broad terms of the transaction are agreed upon, a preliminary official statement typically is prepared for distribution to prospective investors. Some underwriters and issuers also may arrange a "road show" presentation to investors as part of their marketing efforts,[73] in which investors may ask questions about the financing.[74]

The two primary means of underwriting municipal securities are negotiated sales and competitive sales. During 2011, 54.4% of the 13,463 municipal securities issuances were done through underwritings that were negotiated sales and 42.4% were through competitive sales;[75] the remaining 3.2% were sold through private placements – representing a record high of approximately $15 billion.[76] This is an increase from only $3 billion of private placements in 2010.[77] The increase in private placements is generally attributed to an overall decline in the issuance of variable rate bonds and the refunding of outstanding variable rate debt backed by letters of credit.[78]

a. Negotiated Sale

In a typical negotiated sale, an issuer selects an underwriter to be the senior manager before the date the securities are sold to investors.[79] The issuer may permit the senior manager to be the sole manager of the issue, or the issuer may select one or more senior co-managers or one or more co-managers.[80] These selections may be made by means of a formal request for proposals ("RFPs") or by other means.[81] The senior manager determines the size and composition of the underwriting syndicate.[82]

Depending on various factors, including the size of the issue and its potential profitability, the senior manager may decide to price and market the securities with the other managers instead of forming a syndicate.[83] In some cases (typically in smaller offerings), a "selling group" may be included as part of the offering.[84] Members of a selling group are brokers and dealers that are permitted by the senior manager to buy underwritten municipal securities for resale on the same terms offered to underwriters. These members neither share in the underwriting profits nor share the risk of any losses incurred by the underwriters or of the purchase of any unsold securities.[85]

Negotiated underwritings are not as risky for underwriters as competitively bid underwritings because the price of the municipal securities is based on how the securities sell during the offering, and the underwriter can adjust the sale date and yields (and prices) in accordance with market conditions.[86] Negotiated offerings appear to be more expensive for issuers than competitive offerings both in terms of bond yields and underwriter gross spreads.[87] The experience of New Jersey, which restricted the use of negotiated offerings, suggests that issuers may be able to realize borrowing-cost savings by switching to competitive offerings.[88] Finally, negotiated offerings create opportunities for municipalities to allocate underwriting business on the basis of political contributions rather than on the price and quality of underwriting services. Indeed, negotiated offerings brought to the market by contributing underwriters are underpriced by 2.3% on average, while there is no underpricing effect from choosing a contributing underwriter through a competitive process.[89]

b. Competitive Sales

In a competitive sale, the issuer publishes a notice of sale setting forth the terms and conditions of the offering and the underwriters submit to the issuer at a specific time and date a sealed bid to buy the issuer's securities at a specific price. The underwriters then reoffer the municipal securities to investors.[90] The winning bidder typically is the underwriter that offers the lowest interest cost for the securities.[91] Underwriters can either bid alone, or can group together into two or more competing syndicates to bid on the securities. The formal award of the securities occurs in a much more expedited fashion than in a negotiated underwriting – normally within minutes of the bid submission deadline and the determination of the winning bid. Competitively bid underwritings are more risky for underwriters because bids are final and the underwriters are committed to a set price for the securities regardless of market conditions.[92]

c. Certain Primary Market Practice: Reporting of Not Reoffered Bonds

One problematic practice that has been identified relating to municipal securities offerings is the reporting of "not reoffered" bonds. Broker-dealers and municipal securities dealers generally are required to report to the Municipal Securities Rulemaking Board ("MSRB") pricing information for each purchase and sale transaction effected in municipal securities in the secondary market within 15 minutes of the time of trade.[93] Additional MSRB requirements that delay the reporting of pricing information apply to new issues of municipal securities.[94] Underwriters generally are not required to report trade information for primary market sale transactions until the end of the day on the date of the formal award of the bonds.[95] Underwriters only are required to submit complete information about offering prices or yields to the MSRB, not to other parties, such as third-party information vendors.[96]

Market participants and the MSRB have indicated that it is common for underwriters to provide real-time reporting of primary market price information to third-party information vendors, such as Bloomberg, L.P. and Ipreo Holdings, L.L.C., substantially in advance of the time this information is required to be reported to the MSRB.[97] However, when the entire issue, or one or more maturities of an issue, is fully subscribed or sold, or purchased by the underwriter for its own account prior to the general reoffering of the issue by the underwriter to the public, such issue or maturity or maturities, as the case may be, may be considered to be "not reoffered" or "NRO."[98] In these instances, real-time reporting of the pricing data by underwriters to information vendors is limited to an NRO designation. As a result, pricing data disseminated by dealers through information vendors about a maturity designated as NRO typically does not include the price or yield at which the maturity was sold. Thus, investors and other market participants may not have access to the initial offering price and yield information until it is reported as required by MSRB rules (which may be end-of-day).[99]

Issuers and market analysts have criticized this practice for inhibiting price discovery in both the primary and secondary markets because the use of the NRO designation denies the market important information about primary market prices and makes accurate pricing of comparable bonds trading in the secondary market more difficult.[100] One commenter further noted that the practice of NRO reporting can lead to "suspicions of less commendable practices."[101]

To address this issue, the MSRB recently requested comment on a proposed change to MSRB Rule G-34 that would prohibit a broker, dealer, or municipal securities dealer from using the term "not reoffered" or other comparable term or designation in any communication about a new issue of municipal securities without also including the applicable initial offering price or yield information about such securities.[102]

5. The Secondary Market for Municipal Securities

Municipal securities trade in an over-the-counter dealer market.[103] There is no central exchange for municipal securities. Municipal bond dealers execute nearly all municipal securities transactions for customers in a principal capacity,[104] with a portion of these principal trades effected on a "riskless principal" basis.[105] Market participants who want to trade municipal securities buy from or sell to intermediaries, including broker-dealers and banks registered as municipal securities dealers. These intermediaries trade in the inter-dealer market amongst themselves, through broker's brokers, or by participating on electronic trading platforms such as alternative trading systems ("ATSs"). Broker's brokers and many ATSs serve only institutional market professionals and not the general public. Currently, there are more than 1,800 municipal bond dealers that trade municipal securities.[106] However, trading activity is heavily concentrated among a few institutions. As the pie chart below shows, in 2011, the top ten most-active municipal bond dealers in terms of par amount of municipal securities traded accounted for approximately 75% of the par amount of customer trades. The dominant firms in the municipal securities market generally are large full-service securities firms that offer and sell many different types of securities.

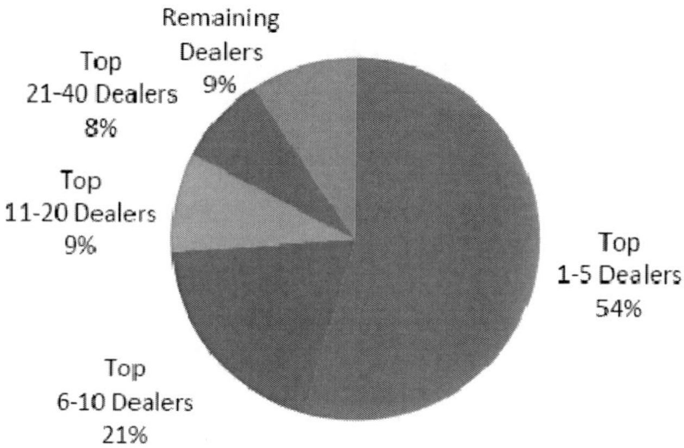

Source: MSRB 2011 Factbook, *supra* note 6.

Distribution of Customer Trades Traded (based on par amount traded).

As noted above, significant secondary market trading occurs, despite the tendency of municipal securities investors to "buy and hold" bonds until maturity.[107] The tables below show the total number of secondary market trades that occurred during 2006-2011 and the total par amount of municipal securities traded during this period. Although the par amount traded in 2011 is, in total, approximately 54% of that traded in 2006, the number of trades has generally increased over time. This suggests that secondary market trading in municipal securities is increasingly characterized by small-size trades.[108]

Secondary Market Transactions

Transaction Summary Total Number of Trades						
	2006	2007	2008	2009	2010	2011
	8,467,987	9,182,124	10,976,658	10,359,611	10,497,319	10,392,855
Transaction Summary Total Par Amount Traded ($millions)						
	2006	2007	2008	2009	2010	2011
	6,081,093	6,685,128	5,514,420	3,791,271	3,749,730	3,278,679

Source: MSRB 2011 Factbook, *supra* note 6; MSRB 2010 Factbook, http://www.msrb.org/msrb1/pdfs/MSRB2010FactBook.pdf; MSRB 2009 Factbook, http://www.msrb.org/msrb1/pdfs/MSRB2009FactBook.pdf.

Despite the large number of trades and principal of outstanding bonds discussed above, the municipal securities market is characterized by relatively low liquidity. In 2011, average daily trading volume ("ADTV") in the more than one million municipal bonds outstanding was $11.3 billion, compared to $20.6 billion ADTV in the fewer than 50,000 corporate bonds outstanding.[109] Most active trading occurs in newly issued municipal bonds, as trading declines significantly in the months following issuance.[110] As noted above and discussed in more detail below, municipal bond dealers are generally required to report to the MSRB pricing information for each transaction in the secondary market within 15 minutes of the time of trade.[111] For a more detailed discussion of the municipal securities secondary market, see Section III of this Report.

6. Default and Bankruptcy Risk

a. Rates of Default

Historically, municipal securities have had significantly lower rates of default[112] than corporate and foreign government bonds.[113] A study by Moody's Investor Services, Inc., ("Moody's") and data provided by Standard & Poor's Ratings Services ("S&P") in 2007 and 2008 of defaults of debt issues that they rate support this historical pattern, showing that municipal bonds rated "Baa/BBB"[114] or higher all have lower default rates than "Aaa/AAA"[115] rated corporate bonds.[116] Moreover, studies indicate that the risk of ultimate non-payment for municipal debt historically has been low, both when compared to total municipal debt outstanding and total municipal debt in default.[117]

Nevertheless, municipal bonds can and do default, and these defaults can negatively impact investors in ways other than non-payment, including delayed payments and pricing disruptions.

Municipal bond default rates have varied considerably in recent years. For example, according to S&P, at least 917 municipal bond issues went into monetary default during the 1990s.[118] These issues had a defaulted principal amount of over $9.8 billion, an average of just under $1 billion per year. In 2007, a total of $226 million in municipal bonds defaulted (including both monetary and technical defaults).[119] However, municipal bond default rates spiked in 2008 as 162 issuers defaulted on $8.2 billion in municipal bonds.[120] Nevertheless, despite speculation about the arrival of a large wave of municipal defaults as a result of the financial crisis,[121] municipal bond default rates since 2009 have begun to return to historical average rates.[122]

Municipal bond default rates also vary considerably depending on the types of bonds issued, ratings on the bonds, and whether the ultimate obligor is a municipal entity or a non-municipal entity (*i.e.,* a conduit borrower). In the S&P study of municipal bond defaults in the 1990s, non-rated bonds accounted for 85% of all defaults.[123] That same study noted that bonds for the three major types of conduit bond issues (healthcare, multifamily housing, and industrial development) accounted for more than 70% of defaulted principal.[124] More recent reports have also indicated that non-governmental conduit borrowers account for more than 70% of municipal bond defaults.[125]

A similar conclusion was reached in a 2011 report that stated that the largest share of modern era defaults consists of industrial development revenue bonds, followed by bonds supporting health care and housing. The report states that these three sectors accounted for 67% of all defaulting issues during the period 1980 to 2011.[126]

b. Municipal Bankruptcy

Although relatively rare, municipal bankruptcies, state law receiverships, and similar proceedings also occur. The number of municipalities that have formally filed for bankruptcy protection pursuant to Bankruptcy Code Chapter 9 has to date remained limited. Since 1980 there have been, on average, only about 7.5 municipal bankruptcy filings per year, with the majority originating from municipalities located in Nebraska (51), California (38), Texas (37), and Colorado (22).[127]

The low number of bankruptcies in the municipal sector can be attributed to several factors, both legal and practical, including: the negative effects of a bankruptcy filing on the credit ratings of not only the municipalities themselves, but also the states in which they are located, which means that bankruptcy is often used only as a last resort;[128] the public nature of bankruptcy; state restrictions against filing under Chapter 9; and the negative effects on access to future capital markets, which motivates financially distressed municipalities to rely on mechanisms other than Chapter 9 (including state refinancing authorities, receiverships, and commissions)[129] to restructure debt.

Nonetheless, municipal bankruptcies can and do occur, as evidenced by high profile bankruptcies by municipalities such as: Orange County, California (1994); the City of Bridgeport, Connecticut (1991; withdrawn); the City of Camden, New Jersey (1999; withdrawn); the City of Vallejo, California (2008); the City of Central Falls, Rhode Island (2011); the City of Harrisburg, Pennsylvania (2011);[130] Jefferson County, Alabama (2011);[131] the City of Stockton, California;[132] and the Town of Mammoth Lakes, California.[133] Bankruptcy has also been contemplated by officials of the City of Miami, Florida;[134] the City of Detroit, Michigan;[135] and the City of San Bernardino, California.[136] Bankruptcies can have significant consequences for municipalities that have outstanding municipal securities, both for the issuers of the securities and their investors.[137]

c. Market Participant Observations and Other Commentary

The issues related to issuer default or financial distress suggested to some field hearing participants the potential need for consideration of additional primary and secondary market disclosure to investors. Some field hearing participants noted the potential importance of primary market disclosure regarding default-related issues including, for example, disclosure about whether Chapter 9 bankruptcy is authorized by the state; what rights and remedies the investors may have in the event of a default; what options the municipality will possess; and what options for assistance the issuer may have in the event of financial distress.[138]

Market participants also suggested that because of the inconsistent nature of municipal securities disclosure in the secondary market and the lack of routine rating agency review, investors may not have information that could allow them to identify an issuer's deteriorating financial condition.

One participant suggested consideration of an "early warning system" to alert investors and other market participants to potential signs of issuer financial distress.[139] The participant provided a number of examples of such "early warnings," such as budget deficits and imbalances, service cuts, furloughs, layoffs, high unfunded pension liabilities, and decreases in property value and per capita income.[140]

It has also been suggested that once an issuer has defaulted, it may stop providing continuing disclosures, exacerbating opacity for defaulted bonds in the secondary market.[141]

B. Regulatory Structure

1. Federal Securities Laws

a. Overview

The Securities Act of 1933 ("Securities Act")[142] and the Securities Exchange Act of 1934 ("Exchange Act")[143] were both enacted with broad exemptions for municipal securities from all of their provisions except for the antifraud provisions of Section 17(a) of the Securities Act, Section 10(b) of the Exchange Act, and Rule 10b-5 promulgated thereunder.[144] Congress, as part of the 1975 Amendments,[145] created a limited regulatory scheme for the municipal securities market at the federal level in response to the growth of the market, market abuses, and the increasing participation of retail investors.[146]

The 1975 Amendments required firms transacting business in municipal securities to register with the Commission as broker-dealers, required banks dealing in municipal securities to register as municipal securities dealers, and gave the Commission broad rulemaking and enforcement authority over such broker-dealers and municipal securities dealers.[147] In addition, the 1975 Amendments created the MSRB and granted it authority to promulgate rules governing the sale of municipal securities by broker-dealers and municipal securities dealers.[148]

The 1975 Amendments did not create a regulatory regime for, or impose any new requirements on, municipal issuers. Pursuant to provisions commonly known as the "Tower Amendment,"[149] the 1975 Amendments expressly limited the Commission's and the MSRB's authority to require municipal securities issuers, either directly or indirectly, to file any application, report, or document with the Commission or the MSRB prior to any sale by the issuer.[150] The 1975 Amendments do not, by their terms, preclude the Commission from promulgating disclosure standards in municipal offerings, but there is no express statutory authority contained in the Exchange Act over disclosure by municipal issuers.[151] The Dodd–Frank Wall Street Reform and Consumer Protection Act ("Dodd-Frank Act") did not change these provisions,[152] but required a study and review by the U.S. Comptroller General of municipal securities disclosure, possible recommendations for municipal issuer disclosure requirements, and the advisability of the repeal or retention of the Tower Amendment.[153]

In the absence of a statutory scheme for municipal securities registration and reporting, the Commission's investor protection efforts in the municipal securities market have been accomplished primarily through regulation of broker-dealers and municipal securities dealers pursuant to Exchange Act Rule 15c2-12, Commission interpretations,[154] enforcement of the antifraud provisions of federal securities laws,[155] and Commission oversight of the MSRB.[156] The Commission first recommended, over 15 years ago, that for-profit conduit borrowers utilizing industrial development financings through municipal entities and their agencies and instrumentalities be subject to the registration and disclosure provisions of the Securities Act.[157]

b. Antifraud Authority

In light of the national scope of the municipal securities market and its importance to the economy and state and local governments, there is an overriding federal interest in assuring that there be adequate disclosure of all material information by issuers of municipal securities.[158] As noted above, Congress did *not* exempt transactions in municipal securities from the coverage of the antifraud provisions of Section 17(a) of the Securities Act, Section 10(b) of the Exchange Act, and Rule 10b-5 promulgated thereunder.[159] The antifraud provisions of the federal securities laws prohibit any person, including municipal issuers[160] and dealers, from making any untrue statement of material fact, or omitting any material facts necessary to make statements made, in the light of the circumstances under which they were made, not misleading, in connection with the offer, purchase, or sale of any security.[161] Municipal issuer disclosures, such as disclosures in official statements and ongoing annual, periodic and event-related disclosure, are subject to these prohibitions.[162] In addition, broker-dealers, municipal securities dealers, and municipal advisors are subject to regulations adopted by the Commission, including those regulations adopted to define and prevent fraud.[163]

Municipal issuers and other market participants also are subject to the antifraud provisions in connection with statements made after the securities have been sold. In fact, whenever a municipal issuer releases information to the public that is reasonably expected to reach investors and the trading markets, such disclosure is subject to the antifraud provisions.[164]

c. Rule 15c2-12

Exchange Act Rule 15c2-12 was adopted in 1989 to establish standards for the procurement and dissemination of disclosure documents by underwriters as a means of enhancing the accuracy and timeliness of disclosure to municipal securities investors.[165] Rule 15c2-12 also was designed to assist underwriters in meeting their responsibilities under the antifraud provisions of the federal securities laws by requiring them to review issuer disclosure documents before commencing sales to investors.[166]

In 1994, the Commission amended Rule 15c2-12 to improve disclosure practices in the secondary markets by prohibiting underwriters from purchasing or selling municipal securities in connection with a primary offering unless the issuer had committed to providing continuing disclosure regarding the security and issuer, including its financial condition and operating data.[167]

In 2008, the Commission amended Rule 15c2-12 to establish a single centralized disclosure repository for the electronic collection and availability of information about municipal securities. The Commission's rulemaking was intended to improve the availability of information about municipal securities to investors, market professionals, and the public generally.[168] This repository, established and maintained by the MSRB, is its Electronic Municipal Market Access system, known by the acronym EMMA, and is freely accessible to all investors on the Internet.[169]

On May 26, 2010, the Commission again amended Rule 15c2-12 to make significant changes to the material event notice requirements and to make the continuing disclosure requirements of the Rule applicable to variable rate demand obligations.[170] These amendments apply to municipal securities issued on or after December 1, 2010.[171]

d. Enforcement Actions

The Commission has pursued a significant number of enforcement actions involving municipal securities over the past 20 years. These enforcement cases have involved materially misleading statements and omissions in disclosure relating to municipal securities as well as many other improper activities of municipal securities market participants. Generally, the allegations in these enforcement actions have focused on (a) offering and disclosure fraud;[172]

(b) tax or arbitrage-driven fraud; [173] (c) pay-to-play and public corruption violations;[174] (d) public pension accounting and disclosure fraud;[175] and (e) valuation/pricing issues.[176]

2. Internal Revenue Service

In addition to the Commission, Congress has provided oversight and enforcement powers with respect to the municipal securities industry to the IRS. The IRS and the Commission entered into a Memorandum of Understanding ("MOU") in March 2010, in which each acknowledges the other's need for, and interest in, sharing information, and agrees, within the confines of existing law, to communicate with each other regarding, among other things, market risks, practices, and events relating to tax-exempt bonds and municipal securities. Although this MOU has generally led to a successful working relationship between the IRS and the Commission, certain provisions of existing law have hindered the IRS's efforts to cooperate with the Commission.[177] As a result, the Commission is generally not aware of IRS audits and investigations of municipal bond issues unless they become public.

Similarly, the IRS cannot alert the Commission to potential fraud involving municipal securities by broker-dealers or other entities under the Commission's jurisdiction. For example, the Commission's investigation concerning the Neshannock Township School District, which ultimately led to the precedent-setting decision concerning bond counsel by the D.C. Circuit Court of Appeals in Ira Weiss v. SEC,[178] had to be delayed until the IRS had completed its investigation and come to the preliminary determination that the School District's 2000 notes were taxable. Additionally, the Commission's investigation into bid-rigging schemes involving the investment of tax-exempt municipal securities from at least 1997 through 2005, although conducted in parallel with similar investigations by the Department of Justice and the Office of the Comptroller of the Currency ("OCC"), could not be easily coordinated with the IRS. These investigations ultimately resulted in a number of criminal indictments and guilty pleas as well as settlements in 2010 and 2011 with five financial institutions that, among other things, included $117 million in payments to the IRS and aggregate payments of nearly $745 million.[179] Had the IRS been able to communicate with the Commission, these investigations could have been conducted in a more efficient and timely fashion.

3. Self-Regulation

a. Municipal Securities Rulemaking Board

Created by the 1975 Amendments, the MSRB is a self-regulatory organization ("SRO") subject to Commission oversight. The MSRB has authority, as expanded by the Dodd-Frank Act, to adopt rules regulating: transactions in municipal securities by broker-dealers and municipal securities dealers; advice provided to or on behalf of municipal entities (including but not limited to issuers of municipal securities) and conduit borrowers and other obligated persons by municipal advisors[180] with respect to municipal financial products[181] or the issuance of municipal securities; and solicitations[182] for compensation of certain business on behalf of broker-dealers, municipal securities dealers, and municipal advisors from municipal entities and obligated persons.[183] The Dodd-Frank Act also changed the composition of the membership on the MSRB (or the "Board") to require a majority of public representatives.[184] The Board has the power to determine all matters relating to the operation and administration of the Board.[185]

The MSRB rules, among other things, establish appropriate standards for broker-dealers, municipal securities dealers and municipal advisors[186] and are designed, among other things, to prevent fraudulent and manipulative acts and practices and promote just and equitable principles of trade.[187] The MSRB does not, however, have the authority to enforce its rules. Rather, Congress divided enforcement responsibility among multiple regulatory agencies.[188] Currently, in addition to the Commission, the Financial Industry Regulatory Authority ("FINRA"), the Federal Deposit Insurance Corporation ("FDIC"), the Federal Reserve System ("FRS"), and the OCC (OCC together with the FDIC and FRS, the "bank regulators")[189] all play a role in the enforcement of MSRB rules.[190] The MSRB, in turn, facilitates the enforcement efforts of these agencies through regulatory coordination and enforcement support programs, which provide the agencies with market information and reports of potential violations as they become known, and consultation concerning its rules.

The Commission's 2008 amendment of Exchange Act Rule 15c2-12 designating the MSRB as the central repository for continuing municipal securities disclosure[191] and the MSRB's establishment in 2009 of the EMMA website[192] significantly improved the availability of both primary market and continuing disclosure documents to investors.[193] EMMA now serves as the official repository of municipal securities disclosure, providing the public with free access to relevant municipal securities data, and is the central database for information about municipal securities offerings, issuers, and obligors.[194]

In addition to final official statements and advance refunding documents submitted by underwriters under MSRB rules and continuing disclosures submitted by municipal entities and obligated persons to EMMA pursuant to continuing disclosure agreements, the MSRB is authorized to accept disclosure that issuers of municipal securities, on a voluntary basis, submit to EMMA, including a number of additional categories of continuing disclosures such as quarterly or other interim financial and operating data, preliminary official statements, and other related pre-sale documents, official statements and advance refunding documents, as well as information relating to the preparation and submission of audited financial statements and/or annual financial information and hyperlinks to other information available from the issuer's website.[195]

This issuer disclosure, in addition to real-time trade data, education resources, current interest rate information, liquidity documents, and other information for most variable rate municipal securities, as well as credit ratings from Fitch Ratings ("Fitch") and S&P,[196] is available on EMMA at http://emma.msrb.org. The MSRB recently published its Long-Range Plan for Market Transparency Products, which includes its vision for enhancing EMMA to, among other things, expand the universe of information available and improve search functionality.[197]

b. Financial Industry Regulatory Authority

FINRA is an SRO that oversees more than 4,400 securities firms and nearly 630,000 registered securities representatives in the United States.[198] FINRA's responsibilities include:

- regulating broker-dealers and their registered persons;
- providing market information;
- adopting and enforcing rules to protect investors and the financial markets;
- examining broker-dealers for compliance with FINRA rules as well as federal securities laws, including the rules and regulations thereunder, and MSRB rules;

- informing and educating the investing public;
- providing industry utilities; and
- administering the largest dispute resolution forum for investors and registered firms.[199]

While its responsibilities extend well beyond the municipal securities market, FINRA plays an instrumental role in overseeing the registration and examination process for municipal dealer professionals and encouraging, examining, and enforcing compliance with MSRB rules by non-bank municipal dealers. However, FINRA's rules explicitly do not apply to transactions in and business activities relating to municipal securities[200] because transactions in municipal securities effected by municipal bond dealers, and municipal advisory activities engaged in by municipal advisors, are subject to the rules of the MSRB.[201]

Approximately 1,800 MSRB-registered broker-dealers are members of and examined by FINRA, with the remaining dealers registered with the SEC as municipal securities dealers and examined primarily by the various federal bank regulators.[202] The Commission recently approved a change to MSRB Rule G-16 (Periodic Compliance Examination) to provide for risk-based examinations for FINRA member brokers and dealers.[203]

In addition to examinations, FINRA surveils the marketplace with respect to the pricing of bond transactions and markups. In recent years, FINRA has conducted sweeps and targeted exams in the area of municipal sales practices;[204] issued guidance reminding firms of their sales practice and due diligence obligations when selling municipal securities in the secondary market;[205] and conducted an informal look at new-issue retail order periods to address concerns about the potential for "flipping" municipal bonds.[206]

4. Federal Bank Regulators

As noted above, federal banking regulators enforce MSRB rules for registered municipal securities dealers that are not members of a registered securities association.[207] However, FINRA oversees the vast majority of entities that are registered with the MSRB as either brokers or dealers.[208] MSRB Rule G-16 requires municipal securities dealers to be examined every two years.[209]

5. State Laws

The issuance of securities by states, local governments, and their agencies and instrumentalities is controlled by the constitution of the relevant state and the laws of the relevant state and local government.[210]

The scope of these laws is broad, covering matters from the lending of credit, permitted use of public funds, tax and debt limitations, public records and open meeting laws to specific conditions for, and restrictions on, the manner and purposes for which bonds may be issued. In some cases a referendum is required to authorize the issuance of bonds, particularly those payable from *ad valorem* taxes revenues.[211] Generally, bonds issued in violation of such requirements or limitations are void. In some states, judicial or legislative validation is available to immunize bonds from challenges to their validity.

In addition to the federal securities laws, municipal securities are also subject to state securities laws, commonly known as "blue sky laws." The goal of these laws is to protect investors from offerings that are fraudulent or worthless.[212]

C. Municipal Securities Market Participants

As discussed above, the primary participants in a municipal securities offering are the issuers of the securities (such as states, cities, counties, school districts, and limited-function state and local agencies and authorities such as housing or health facilities authorities and water and sewer authorities), the investors, and the market intermediaries who purchase the securities and sell them to investors.

In addition to these central participants, other municipal market participants play significant roles in municipal securities transactions and have responsibilities under the federal securities laws when they participate in municipal securities offerings.[213] The availability of a wide variety of financing options has led to an increasing reliance on financial advisors by municipal entities that issue municipal securities to assist them in deciding among the multiplying array of structural choices for their debt issuances[214] and to help them negotiate with the range of market intermediaries.[215] Many of these entities are subject to registration requirements and related regulation under the federal securities laws, in addition to the antifraud provisions, as discussed below. Some of the entities are also subject to state registration requirements.

1. Broker-Dealers, Municipal Securities Dealers, and Related Market Participants

a. Overview

As discussed above, municipal bond dealers play a key role in the distribution of municipal bonds through their underwriting activities. Municipal bond dealers also play a key role in the secondary market for municipal securities.[216] Municipal bond dealers trade among themselves in the interdealer market. They may do so by contacting each other directly. Alternatively, they may use the services of broker's brokers that arrange transactions for these intermediaries through a combination of voice and electronic brokerage services.[217] Trading in the interdealer market may also be effected through other electronic trading platforms such as ATSs. Municipal bond dealers trade in this market to obtain securities desired by customers or to manage their inventories.[218] A small number of municipal bond dealers dominate the market.[219] These firms execute almost all customer transactions in a principal capacity (with a portion of these principal trades effected on a "riskless principal" basis) and customers typically purchase and sell municipal securities through them.[220]

b. Registration and Regulation

All brokers-dealers that underwrite, trade, and sell municipal securities must register with the Commission.[221] The Exchange Act defines a "broker" broadly as "any person engaged in the business of effecting transactions in securities for the account of others"[222] and a "dealer" as "any person engaged in the business of buying and selling securities for such person's own account through a broker or otherwise."[223] If a person engages in the activities of a broker or dealer in municipal securities and does not satisfy an exception from the registration provisions of the Exchange Act, such person must register with the Commission and must join an SRO such as FINRA.

Banks transacting business in municipal securities are excluded from the general definitions of a broker-dealer.[224] But banks can be "municipal securities dealers" because the term is defined to include any person engaged in the buying or selling of municipal securities for its own account, including a separately identifiable department or division of a bank. Bank municipal securities dealers are required to register with the Commission.[225]

All municipal bond dealers that engage in municipal securities transactions also must register with the MSRB and may not act in contravention of its rules.[226] The Exchange Act designates the agencies responsible for overseeing compliance with the provisions in the Exchange Act relating to municipal securities and the rules of the MSRB. The Commission has broad inspection and enforcement authority over municipal bond dealers with respect to MSRB rules, Commission rules, and the federal securities laws.[227] FINRA has inspection and enforcement responsibility over its broker-dealer members and bank regulators have this responsibility for municipal securities dealers that are banks under their respective jurisdictions.[228]

Municipal bond dealers are subject to a variety of sales practice, disclosure and due diligence obligations[229] under the federal securities laws and MSRB rules.[230] Several of the more significant obligations applicable to transactions with customers in municipal securities are discussed below:[231]

i. Fair Dealing and Duty of Disclosure to Customers

MSRB Rule G-17, which the MSRB refers to as the "core" of its investor protection rules,[232] provides that, in the conduct of its municipal securities or municipal advisory activities, each broker-dealer, municipal securities dealer, and municipal advisor shall deal fairly with all persons and shall not engage in any deceptive, dishonest, or unfair practice. Rule G-17 includes an antifraud provision similar to that of Rule 10b-5 under the Exchange Act, and also establishes a general duty of fair dealing, even in the absence of fraud.[233] The MSRB views all activities of the entities it regulates in light of these basic principles, even where other MSRB rules impose more particular requirements.[234]

The MSRB has interpreted Rule G-17 to require a municipal bond dealer to disclose to its customer, at or before the time of trade, all material information concerning the transaction in municipal securities known by such firm, as well as material information about the security when such facts are reasonably accessible to the market.[235] This disclosure obligation under MSRB Rule G-17 applies regardless of whether the municipal bond dealer has made a recommendation to the customer, and such disclosure does not relieve the firm of its suitability obligations (discussed below) if the firm has recommended transactions in municipal securities.[236] The MSRB also has interpreted Rule G-17 as imposing on municipal bond dealers an obligation to make certain that the information they provide to their customers, whether under an affirmative obligation imposed by MSRB rules or otherwise (such as in response to a question from customer), is correct and not misleading.[237]

In addition to establishing these broad disclosure principles, some MSRB rules also impose specific disclosure obligations. For example, MSRB Rule G-22 requires a municipal bond dealer that has a control relationship[238] with the issuer of a security purchased, sold, or exchanged for a customer to disclose this relationship to the customer before effecting the transaction.[239] If the disclosure is made orally, it must be supplemented by written disclosure at or before completion of the transaction.[240]

ii. Suitability for Customer

In general, broker-dealers have an obligation to recommend only those specific investments or overall investment strategies that are suitable for their customers. The concept of suitability appears in specific SRO rules, such as MSRB Rule G-19, and has been interpreted as an obligation under the antifraud provisions of the federal securities laws.[241] Commission actions against broker-dealers for making unsuitable recommendations are typically brought under Exchange Act Section 10(b) and Rule l0b-5 thereunder and under Securities Act Section 17(a).[242]

MSRB Rule G-19(c) provides that a municipal bond dealer shall have reasonable grounds for believing that a recommendation to a customer[243] is suitable (i) based upon information available from the issuer of the security or otherwise, and (ii) based upon the facts disclosed by such customer or otherwise known about such customer.[244] MSRB Rule G-19(b) imposes on municipal bond dealers the obligation to collect certain suitability-related financial and other information from non-institutional customers.[245]

iii. Fair Pricing and Compensation

As discussed in more detail below in Section IV.B.3.a (Fair Prices), MSRB Rule G-30 requires that municipal bond dealers trade with customers in principal transactions at prices that are fair and reasonable, taking into consideration all relevant factors. Similarly, MSRB Rule G18 requires that a municipal bond dealer executing an agency trade with a customer make a reasonable effort to obtain a price for the customer that is fair and reasonable in relation to prevailing market conditions. Compensation of the municipal bond dealer on a principal transaction is a mark-up or a mark-down computed from the prevailing market price of the municipal security.[246] The mark-up or mark-down is not required to be disclosed to the customer.

In contrast, compensation on an agency transaction is a commission, which is required to be disclosed.[247] In both cases, MSRB Rules G-18 and G-30 require a municipal bond dealer to exercise diligence in establishing the reasonableness of compensation received on a transaction.[248]

iv. Fair Dealing and Duty of Disclosure to Issuers

MSRB Rule G-17 requires dealers to deal fairly with municipal entities in connection with the underwriting of municipal securities.[249] With the passage of the Dodd-Frank Act, the MSRB was expressly directed by Congress to protect municipal entities and obligated persons.[250] Accordingly, the MSRB recently issued interpretive guidance that provides additional guidance as to how MSRB Rule G-17 applies to dealers in their interactions with municipal entities as underwriters of municipal securities, as well as other activities, such as interest rate swap transactions.[251] This guidance will become effective August 2, 2012.[252]

2. Alternative Trading Systems

An ATS provides a marketplace for bringing together purchasers and sellers of securities.[253] If registered as a broker-dealer and in compliance with certain rules, an ATS is exempt from the definition of an exchange and thus is not required to register as a national securities exchange.[254]

There are a number of ATSs that provide municipal bond dealers with access to electronic pools of liquidity[255] and these ATSs account for a substantial portion of municipal securities transactions.[256] ATSs play an important role in the municipal bond market by aggregating liquidity in a generally illiquid marketplace. Participation in an ATS generally is limited to municipal bond dealers.

3. Municipal Advisors

Another market participant involved in the issuance of securities is the municipal advisor. The Exchange Act defines the term "municipal advisor" to mean, in part, a person "that (i) provides advice to or on behalf of a municipal entity or obligated person with respect to municipal financial products or the issuance of municipal securities, . . . or (ii) undertakes a solicitation of a municipal entity."[257] Municipal advisors include financial advisors who assist municipal issuers with both competitive and negotiated bond sales, reinvestment of bond proceeds, and the structuring and pricing of related products such as derivatives.[258] Historically, municipal financial advisors and municipal financial advisory activities have been largely unregulated.[259]

Section 975 of Title IX of the Dodd-Frank Act amended Section 15B of the Exchange Act to, among other things, make it unlawful for "municipal advisors" to provide certain advice to, or to solicit, municipal entities or certain other persons without registering with the Commission as a municipal advisor.[260] The registration requirement for municipal advisors established by the Dodd-Frank Act became effective on October 1, 2010.[261] The Commission has received approximately 1,000 confirmed registrations of municipal advisors, including approximately 300 registered broker-dealers, as well as approximately 700 other firms.

In addition, the Exchange Act, as amended by the Dodd-Frank Act, grants the MSRB regulatory authority over municipal advisors[262] and imposes a fiduciary duty on municipal advisors when advising municipal entities.[263] Since the passage of the Dodd-Frank Act, the MSRB has extended its existing Rules G-5 (disciplinary actions) and G-17 (fair dealing) to cover the activities of municipal advisors.[264] The MSRB expects to propose additional rules governing the conduct of municipal advisors after the Commission adopts a final registration rule.[265]

4. Trustees

Bond trustees play an important role in representing municipal bondholders after the securities are issued. Prior to default, bond trustees have specific duties and responsibilities as agreed and set forth in the relevant trust indenture, including administrative duties such as establishing the accounts and holding the monies relating to the debt issue, maintaining a list of bondholders, and passing through principal and interest payments on the bonds.[266] Upon default, the trustee is the party that takes actions to protect the rights of the bondholders.[267]

For bond issues subject to continuing disclosure requirements, trustees can play a key role in the dissemination of the issuer's or obligated person's required disclosure obligations, while not assuming any disclosure obligations themselves.[268] Trustees can also enforce the undertaking of the issuer or obligated person on behalf of the bondholders, depending upon the structure of the continuing disclosure agreement.[269]

5. Attorneys

Lawyers, such as bond counsel, disclosure counsel, issuer's (or borrower's) counsel, trustee's counsel, and counsel to the underwriters, also perform important roles in municipal securities offerings and have certain obligations.

Bond counsel play a unique role in the municipal marketplace.[270] They are engaged to provide an expert and objective opinion with respect to the validity of the municipal securities being offered and other subjects, including the tax treatment of interest on the municipal securities.[271] The bond opinion is intended to be relied upon by the purchasers of the municipal securities, is referred to in the notice of sale for competitive bid transactions, and is always referenced in official statements, which usually describe the opinion in detail and often include the text of the opinion as an exhibit.[272]

The provision of an "unqualified" approving opinion of nationally recognized bond counsel is typically required by underwriters as a precondition to closing in a public offering, and the transfer of municipal securities without such an opinion is generally not considered good delivery unless identified as such at the time of the trade.[273]

Bond counsel frequently perform other functions, such as guiding issuers through the bond authorization requirements under state or local law, preparing documents and supervising the transactional process. Bond counsel generally represents the issuer although bond counsel can also be retained by the conduit borrower.[274]

The Commission brought an enforcement action against a bond counsel who did not conduct a reasonable investigation into the facts underlying his opinion as to the tax-exempt status of interest on the relevant notes, such that the substantial risk that the IRS would find the notes to be taxable was not adequately disclosed to prospective note purchasers.[275]

Typically, issuer's counsel is expected to render a separate opinion as to the organization and good standing of the issuer; the issuer's corporate or governmental power to enter into the transaction; the incumbency of the issuer's officials; the due adoption, execution, and effectiveness of the pertinent documents; pending or threatened litigation (or the absence thereof); the absence of conflicts between the bond documents; and other issuer contracts; and other matters related to the issuer.[276]

Increasing focus on the disclosure duties of issuers has drawn issuer's counsel into a more active role in the disclosure process and, increasingly, issuers hire special disclosure counsel to assist them in understanding and complying with their disclosure responsibilities in primary offerings and in complying with their secondary market disclosure undertakings and responsibilities.

Trustee's counsel, if present in a transaction, typically reviews the bond documents to ensure, among other things, that the appropriate payment and default provisions and accounts are established; that the trustee's continuing disclosure obligations, if any, are clearly defined; and that the bond documents generally minimize potential future risk for the trustee. Counsel to the trustee also reviews the offering document to ensure that it includes information regarding the trustee and any appropriate or necessary disclaimers.[277]

Underwriter's counsel has many responsibilities in a municipal financing, including (1) assisting in structuring the financing and ensuring compliance with the securities laws; (2) assisting with due diligence; (3) reviewing or assisting in drafting the relevant transaction and disclosure documents (*e.g.*, official statement, bond purchase agreement, continuing disclosure agreement, remarketing agreement, and an agreement among underwriters); (4) reviewing and commenting on the bond documents prepared by other counsel; (5) preparing a blue sky survey, if necessary; and (6) providing an opinion addressing the accuracy and completeness of the official statement (known as a "10b-5 opinion"[278]).[279]

6. Credit Enhancers

As discussed above, municipal bonds may be accompanied by a form of credit enhancement, which is usually in the form of a letter of credit issued by a bank, a governmental guarantee, or an insurance policy issued by a bond insurance company.[280] For many years prior to 2007, more than half of all new issues of municipal securities were credit-enhanced. However, as evidenced in the chart below, the prevalence of credit enhancements – bond insurance in particular – has decreased dramatically since the onset of the financial crisis of 2008. In 2008 and shortly thereafter, the major bond insurers suffered ratings downgrades. More recently, rating agencies have modified their ratings criteria for bond insurers requiring higher capital charges for insuring most types of bonds and reducing the likelihood that any bond insurer would be rated "AAA" using the traditional bond insurance business model.[281]

In addition to the immediate effects of the 2008 financial crisis, there may be follow-on effects. Commentators have suggested that banks may move away from providing secondary credit and liquidity facilities to municipal borrowers in anticipation of Basel III provisions[282] that require banks to maintain a liquidity coverage ratio of at least 100% of all lines of credit used for liquidity purposes.[283]

Although the private bond insurance market has contracted, a significant portion of municipal securities issuances are enhanced by a form of governmental guarantee.[284]

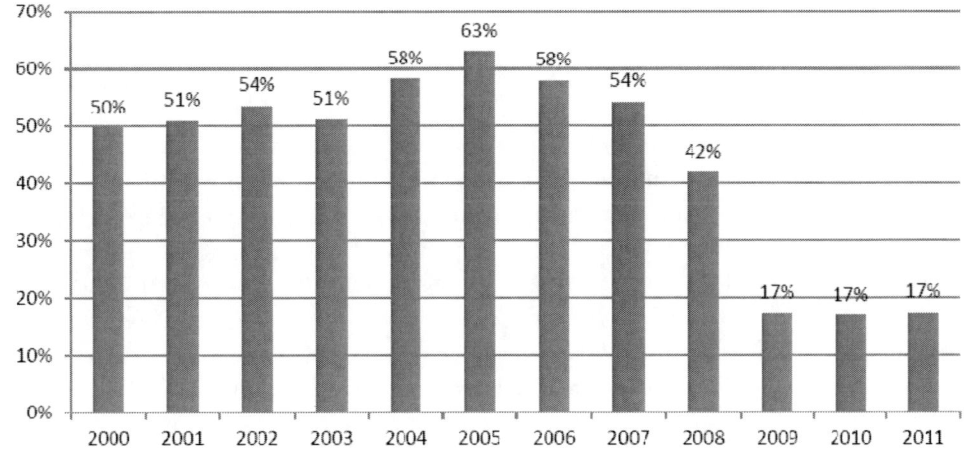

Staff generated statistics. Data source: SDC Platinum.

Credit-enhanced Principal as a Percentage of Annual Principal Issued.

a. Market Participant Observations and Other Commentary

The overall decline in the use of credit enhancement, particularly bond insurance, has impacted the market for municipal securities[285] and renewed investor focus on the disclosure practices and underlying credit quality of municipal issuers.[286] When the majority of new issues of municipal securities were "wrapped" by bond insurance, default risk was viewed as being reduced, municipal bonds received their credit ratings based on the ratings of the bond insurer,[287] and similar types of issues were treated similarly in terms of price.[288] Post-2008, individual credit decisions became more important to market participants in determining whether to purchase a particular bond.[289]

The relationship between bond insurance, default risk, and the need for disclosure was discussed at several field hearings. Bond insurance – and the resulting commoditization of the municipal bond market – was considered by some to be an alternative to a compulsory municipal securities disclosure regime.[290] As a result of the existence of insurance, some market participants viewed disclosure on the underlying credit as "redundant and unnecessary."[291] Bond insurance companies were described as "super-bond-holders," because the bond insurers monitored the financial condition of issuers as part of the insurance agreement.[292] A representative of a bond insurer expressed the view a significant benefit of bond insurance was that the insurer not only guarantees the bonds but also plays the role of investor, identifying financial difficulties with insured issuers and protecting against defaults.[293] Another panelist, however, stated that the commoditization of the municipal market prior to 2008, where 60% of the market was AAA insured, resulted in hidden risk.[294]

7. Nationally Recognized Statistical Rating Organizations ("NRSROs")

Credit ratings for municipal securities are generally provided by one or more of three NRSROs - Moody's, Fitch, and S&P and reflect a professional assessment of an issuer's ability to meet its financial obligations.[295] Ratings issued by these organizations are ordinarily paid for by the issuer (known as "issuer pay" models).[296]

Rating agencies generally assign ratings upon the issuance of the security and periodically review and update the ratings to reflect changes in the issuer's credit status.[297] Municipal credit ratings are also impacted by credit enhancement such as bond insurance, letters of credit, governmental guarantees, or standby bond purchase agreements.[298] Municipal securities with these enhancement features might carry two ratings; the credit-enhanced rating and the unenhanced rating.[299] As noted above, however, the use of bond insurance and most types of credit enhancement has declined significantly in recent years.

Although issuers disclose financial information in various disclosure documents available to investors, market participants noted that many investors nonetheless rely on municipal credit ratings.[300] The Commission staff has been told by market participants that this reliance on credit ratings has changed over the last few years. Institutions rely on credit ratings less often to determine credit quality of the borrower,[301] whereas retail investors may continue to look to those ratings in making investment decisions.[302]

As of November 21, 2011, investors have access to Fitch and S&P's ratings on EMMA.[303] However, Moody's ratings and proprietary reports, such as the underlying analytical reports on a particular rating or class of ratings, by each of the NRSROs, are not readily accessible to retail investors.[304]

a. Regulation of NRSROs

In 2007, the Commission adopted rules implementing a registration and oversight program for credit rating agencies registered as NRSROs.[305] However, the Commission is limited by statute in its ability to regulate the ratings methodology of NRSROs.[306]

The Dodd-Frank Act mandates that the Commission adopt further rules relating to credit ratings and NRSROs.[307] The Commission has adopted a new rule that requires NRSROs to make certain disclosures for asset-backed securities they rate.[308] The Commission also has proposed the removal of other references to credit ratings or NRSROs in additional releases.[309] The Commission proposed the remaining new rules and rule amendments related to NRSRO oversight required under the Dodd-Frank Act in an additional release.[310]

b. Market Participant Observations and Other Commentary

At the field hearings, some panelists suggested that municipal bonds suffer from ratings "discrimination" as compared to corporate issuers[311] and that this discrimination results in increased borrowing costs for issuers.[312] One panelist cited an S&P study, which found that

0.33% of municipal bond issues rated A minus defaulted during the last 15 years, while corporate issuers rated A minus had an average default rate of 3.16%, nearly ten times higher than similarly-rated municipal issues.[313] Another panelist stated that an AAA-rated corporate bond had 15 times more risk of default than an A-rated municipal bond.[314]

The major credit rating agencies take the position that they have either always maintained or now use common ratings definitions for corporate, municipal, and other classes of credit ratings (commonly referred to as a "global" rating scale).[315] Several panelists in the field

hcarings supported the notion of a global rating scale, whereby investors can compare the credit quality of municipal securities against the credit quality of corporate bonds.[316] However, some panelists argued that global rating scales are a move in the wrong direction because municipal bonds and corporate securities are not comparable and the global scale complicates the evaluation of individual bond safety, thereby diluting the value of ratings.[317]

The Staff has also heard various concerns related to quality and consistency of credit ratings in the municipal securities market. One panelist suggested that rating agencies may not be doing adequate due diligence when assessing their ratings.[318] Another panelist stated that rating agencies do not use proper procedures and methodologies to ensure that ratings accurately reflect default risk.[319] One suggested that the rating agencies should more closely examine the risks of pensions, OPEBs, and debt service obligations, and add these liabilities into their calculations of debt-to-income and other metrics.[320] Another stated that the "core of any such government rating methodology should contain verifiable metrics correlated to default risk and that the remainder of the subjective analysis or the making of finer credit distinctions should be left to investors."[321] Another concern among some market participants is that credit rating agencies do not review credits with sufficient frequency, and that some credits are reviewed only once every three years.[322]

Some field hearing panelists suggested that the Commission should have increased authority over NRSROs, urging the Commission to require rating agencies to use procedures and methodologies that ensure ratings accurately reflect default risk[323] and generally, to disclose more information regarding ratings methodologies and practices.[324]

III. DISCLOSURE

A. Overview of Disclosure Practices and Issues

Disclosure practices in municipal securities offerings and on an ongoing basis have developed as a result of the antifraud provisions of federal and state securities laws,[325] Exchange Act Rule 15c2-12,[326] Commission interpretive guidance,[327] MSRB rules,[328] and voluntary guidelines published by various industry groups.[329] In addition, investors' informational needs have had a role in shaping disclosure practices for municipal securities.[330]

To gauge the credit risk of different types of municipal securities, analysts and investors have historically needed information that depends on the type of issuer and credit involved. Thus, disclosure practices differ for major types of municipal securities (*e.g.*, general obligation bonds, revenue bonds, and conduit bonds) and various subsectors of those major types.

1. Voluntary Disclosure Initiatives and Disclosure Guidelines

Participants in the municipal securities market have worked together to develop voluntary disclosure guidelines and best practices designed to improve the level and quality of disclosure in primary offerings of municipal securities and continuing disclosure in the secondary market. This guidance is in the form of voluntary disclosure guidelines and best practices relating to the municipal securities market, both with regard to primary offerings and secondary market disclosure.[331]

Involved industry groups include the Government Finance Officers Association ("GFOA"), National Federation of Municipal Analysts ("NFMA"), National Association of State Auditors, Comptrollers and Treasurers ("NASACT"), the National Association of Bond Lawyers ("NABL"), and the American Bankers Association, Corporate Trust Division.[332] The existing industry guidelines and best practices relate to, among other matters, the content and timing of financial statements and financial information,[333] disclosure of pension liabilities,[334] industry and financing specific guidelines (discussed below),[335] disclosure controls and procedures of a municipal issuer,[336] and methods of providing disclosure.[337]

Individual industry groups have developed disclosure and operational guidance that affect municipal participants. For example, the GFOA publishes procedural statements and guidelines for continuing disclosure that provide a framework for municipal issuers in providing information to the secondary market.[338] In 2003, NASACT released a proposal discussing minimum quarterly disclosure by state and local governments of certain information, including budget to actual operations, cash receipts and disbursements, and changes in long- and short-term debt.[339]

The NFMA has prepared recommended disclosure practices that divide general obligation bonds, revenue bonds, and conduit bonds into fourteen major sectors based on variations in the nature of the security.[340] The NFMA has noted that these sector-specific disclosure practices reflect the need of investors for information about particular issues that may change the pricing of municipal securities in a given credit sector.[341] The stated purpose of these best practices is to enhance the ability of investors to differentiate among different types of bonds and among specific types of issuers.[342]

In addition to industry group disclosure guidelines, there are also a variety of legal publications aimed at providing disclosure guidance to municipal securities market participants. These publications include "The Securities Law of Public Finance,"[343] "Making Good Disclosure – the Roles and Responsibilities of State and Local Officials Under the Federal Securities Laws,"[344] and "Disclosure Roles of Counsel in State and Local Government Securities Offerings."[345]

These publications provide extensive guidance to municipal market participants regarding their disclosure and other responsibilities in municipal securities offerings and on an ongoing basis.

Moreover, partly as a result of open government laws and similar public accountability measures, state and local governmental bodies routinely make publicly available a large amount of information about issuers of municipal securities.[346] The practices of market participants in voluntarily providing such additional information to investors are not, however, consistent.

Large repeat issuers generally have more comprehensive disclosure than small, infrequent or conduit issuers, who may voluntarily provide little ongoing information to investors.[347]

2. Initial Disclosure

As discussed above,[348] Rule 15c2-12 obligates municipal securities underwriters in most offerings to obtain, review, and distribute to investors copies of the issuer's disclosure documents. Commission interpretations issued in connection with Rule 15c2-12 emphasize the underwriter's duty to have "a reasonable basis for belief in the truthfulness and completeness of the key representations made in any disclosure documents used in the offering" and to review these documents for omissions and misstatements.[349] Additionally, Rule 15c2-12 requires that official statements "set forth information concerning the terms of the proposed issue of securities, including financial information or operating data, concerning such issuers of municipal securities and those other entities, enterprises, funds, accounts, and other persons material to an evaluation of the Offering."[350]

Although the official statement may be prepared by counsel to the underwriter, bond counsel, the issuer's disclosure counsel or financial advisor, the Commission has clearly stated that the official statement is legally the issuer's document.[351] Although market participants that assist the issuer are subject to the antifraud provisions of the federal securities laws, the issuer has ultimate responsibility for ensuring that its official statements meet the disclosure standards of the securities laws and has primary liability for failure to meet them.[352]

In this regard, the Commission has pursued numerous antifraud enforcement actions against municipal issuers for materially misleading statements or omissions in offering materials.

For example, the Commission has brought enforcement actions against: Orange County, California, for failing to disclose the risks relating to, among other things, the County's investment pools and its financial condition;[353] Maricopa County, Arizona, for failing to disclose known material declines in its financial condition and operating cash flow;[354] the City of Syracuse, New York, for falsely claiming a surplus for its general and debt service funds, materially overstating its ending fund balances in those funds, and misleading investors by describing certain financial information as audited;[355] the City of Miami, Florida, for failing to disclose cash flow shortages that the city attempted to hide by using proceeds of issued bonds for operating costs;[356] the Massachusetts Turnpike Authority for failing to disclose substantial cost overruns from the "Big Dig" road and tunnel project in Boston;[357] the City of San Diego, California, for failing to disclose adequately the city's looming pension fund crisis in connection with five municipal bond offerings between 2002 and 2003;[358] and the State of New Jersey for misleading disclosure concerning the underfunding of its public pension funds, and the creation of the illusion that the public pension funds were being adequately funded.[359]

Issuer officials who approve the issuance of bonds or the form of disclosure documents also have responsibilities under the federal securities laws.[360] The Commission has brought numerous cases against underlying obligors or their chief executive officers for materially misleading statements or omissions in offering materials.[361] Municipal securities underwriters have also been pursued by the Commission in enforcement actions regarding false and misleading disclosure.[362]

The parties to Commission enforcement proceedings involving municipal securities include national and regional investment banks, the heads of public finance departments at several investment banks, as well as individual investment bankers at various levels of seniority, issuers, issuer officials, financial advisers, attorneys and accountants.[363]

3. Continuing Disclosure

As a result of the operation of Rule 15c2-12,[364] the application of the antifraud provisions of the federal securities laws, Commission interpretive guidance,[365] and industry initiatives,[366] a continuing disclosure scheme for municipal securities issuers and obligated persons has developed.

Under Rule 15c2-12, underwriters are required to *reasonably determine* that either the issuer of municipal securities or an obligated person (obligated to pay all or some portion of the principal and interest on the municipal securities) has undertaken in a written agreement or contract (commonly called a "continuing disclosure agreement") to provide specified annual information and "material event" notices to certain information repositories (now, to EMMA, as discussed above).[367] These requirements with respect to the content of continuing disclosure obligations for issuers and obligated persons were further broadened by the Commission in 2010 in an amendment that required all event notices to be filed within ten business days, modified the events that are subject to a materiality determination before triggering a requirement to provide notice to the MSRB, and amended the list of events for which a notice is to be provided.[368]

These disclosure obligations arising as a result of Rule 15c2-12 are enhanced by existing industry disclosure guidance. For example, the GFOA best practices related to continuing disclosure recommend that municipal issuers or obligated persons make public already prepared interim financial information that is of interest to investors.[369] Nevertheless, the level and frequency of continuing disclosure continues to vary depending on the type and size of the municipal issuer or obligated person.

Similarly, while continuing disclosure obligations arising under Rule 15c2-12 have existed since 1995, compliance with such obligations is inconsistent.[370] In 2002, the NFMA released an informal survey of approximately 100 obligors subject to the continuing disclosure requirements under Rule 15c2-12 that was undertaken to evaluate disclosure practices in the secondary market and to consider the quality and completeness of the information being provided, particularly with respect to the inclusion of operating data mandated by the Rule.[371] The NFMA Survey concluded that the annual financial information filed by 59.1% of the obligors within the sample was found to contain information deemed to be either complete or near complete, and that the annual financial information filed by 40.9% of the sample was found to be either somewhat inadequate or substantially inadequate.[372] With respect to the entities found to provide less than adequate information, the survey determined that 58.1% failed to deliver all information contained in their continuing disclosure undertaking, 27.9% did file reports, but had inadequate undertakings, and 14.0% were found to be deficient both in terms of the undertaking itself and in subsequently delivering all information promised in the undertaking.[373]

4. Market Participant Observations and Other Commentary

a. General Observations

Panelists at the field hearings noted the significant improvements over time in the disclosure practices of issuers in the municipal market due to Commission enforcement actions, private actions, and regulatory initiatives with respect to the primary market, as well as improvements through the efforts of industry participants, the SEC, and the MSRB.[374] A number of improvements in disclosure were noted, including widespread use of the

Internet, the creation of EMMA, and implementation of rule changes such as recent amendments to Rule 15c2-12. Government official panelists, in particular, felt that the existing disclosure system has served issuers and investors well.[375] Several panelists argued either that additional disclosure requirements are not necessary or that any additional regulation should be limited in scope.[376]

Market participants, including analysts, issuers, and counsel to issuers, expressed the view that, given the size and diversity of issuers in the municipal securities market, a "one-sizefits-all" approach to disclosure is neither necessary nor practicable.[377] Some emphasized that the amount and type of disclosure needed depends, in part, on the type of credit involved and the different risks associated with different issues.[378] With regard to a sales tax revenue bond, for example, updated information concerning the level of sales tax collections would be of paramount concern to an investor.[379] Other market participants noted a possible limitation of resources available for small issuers to comply with increased disclosure obligations.[380] One market participant stated that although standardization is an important part of good disclosure, the challenge is in providing guidance that will address the different nature of local issuers.[381] One field hearing participant objected specifically to increased disclosure requirements for conduit borrowers.[382] Others expressed concern that additional disclosure may create potential legal risks for issuers.[383]

Conversely, investors and other market participants have emphasized a need for greater and timelier disclosure in several key areas.[384] Market participants noted that the need for improved disclosure is underscored by the decline of commoditization achieved through the use of credit enhancement.[385]

b. Initial Disclosure

As noted above, some field hearing participants highlighted improvements to municipal market disclosure practices – particularly initial disclosure practices.[386] However, many participants raised specific concerns about disclosure in primary offerings of municipal securities, particularly with respect to smaller, less-sophisticated issuers and non-governmental conduit borrowers.[387] Commenters have expressed concern about the lack of detailed information in official statements about municipal issuers' outstanding debt, including liens, security, collateral pledges, etc.[388] Market participants also have recently raised concerns that municipal entities may not properly disclose the existence or the terms and conditions of bank loans, particularly when the terms of the bank loans may affect the payment priority from revenues in a way that adversely affects bondholders.[389] Additionally, it was suggested that official statements include disclosure of the number of delinquent taxpayers in a given jurisdiction and material deficiencies in project returns for revenue or project bonds.[390] Comments regarding disclosure of financial information are discussed in detail below.

Market participants have also expressed concern about disclosure practices in circumstances where additional information may need to be provided to investors after a preliminary official statement has been prepared.[391] Market participants have indicated that issuers often make changes between the preliminary official statement and the final official statement of which investors may not be aware. This disclosure could relate to new or additional information on the underlying credit, alterations of security provisions, or the correction of mistakes or omissions.[392] Bond counsel have suggested ways in which municipal issuers could provide this information.[393]

c. Continuing Disclosure

One field hearing participant, representing an industry association of municipal analysts, noted that despite achievements in the municipal market since the adoption of Rule 15c2-12, municipal securities secondary market disclosure continues to trail substantially continuing disclosure in other financial markets.[394] Commenters suggested that the municipal market has become large and complex enough to warrant a more comprehensive and streamlined approach to the disclosure process.[395]

According to many market participants, the major challenge in secondary market disclosure continues to be the timeliness and completeness of filings.[396] As a result of the requirements of Rule 15c2-12, issuers must agree to provide the same type of financial information and operating data as included in the final official statement. In practice, many issuers undertake to include in secondary disclosure filings certain items of information which were included in the official statement.[397]

Market participants have indicated that many issuers comply with their written obligations under their continuing disclosure agreements for a period of time, but that over time, as a result of staffing changes or otherwise, compliance with these contractual obligations weakens. After the passage of time, compliance may be limited solely to annual audited financial statements, and the other ongoing financial information or operating data may not be provided.[398]

Further, some market participants have indicated that they believe that material events notices for some issuers may be filed weeks or months after the event, and that some issuers do not comply with these obligations at all.[399]

Market participants are concerned that some issuers may be failing to report adverse tax information[400] and that issuers may not be filing applicable material event notices even when their financial stress is reported in newspapers.[401]

One market participant stated that it is well known that many issuers simply do not comply with continuing disclosure agreements.[402] Some market participants expressed concern that the use of the comprehensive annual financial report ("CAFR") by some issuers to satisfy the annual disclosure filing obligation under their continuing disclosure agreements does not provide sufficient information.[403]

Additionally, some commenters expressed concern about a lack of enforcement for non-compliance with such continuing disclosure agreements.[404] Some market participants have indicated that in instances of poor disclosure they will choose not to purchase, or insist on more spread or higher yield.[405] However, others argue that the idea of "market discipline" – simply not buying the bonds of an issuer with disclosure deficiencies is an impractical solution in a market with such a retail-heavy composition.[406] Two panelists at the field hearings suggested that improvements in continuing disclosure in the secondary market can be achieved in the same manner as the improvements made in the primary market, through the concerted efforts of all participants and without additional regulation of issuers.[407]

d. Disclosure by Conduit Borrowers

Many types of conduit municipal financings historically have provided substantially less continuing information than municipal securities involving non-conduit financings. However, market participants have noted that since 1994, the health care sector in general, and hospitals in particular, have improved continuing disclosure compliance.

Such hospitals, in fact, may be providing more timely disclosure than other municipal issuers and obligated persons.[408] Some market participants believed that the same registration requirements and disclosure standards should apply to non-governmental conduit borrowers that apply to other non-governmental issuers selling securities directly into the corporate securities market.[409]

B. Substantive Disclosure Topics

1. Financial Statements and Financial Information

a. Overview

As the Commission stated in the 1994 Interpretive Release, sound financial statements are critical to the integrity of the primary and secondary markets for municipal securities, just as they are for corporate securities.[410] Municipal issuer financial statements provide investors with critical information to assess the financial condition of municipal issuers and to enable investors to analyze their investments. This information is also important to other stakeholders, such as government agencies and taxpayers. Additional financial information, such as budgetary information, can be used by investors and creditors to identify future demands on government resources that could negatively impact the ability of governments to repay their obligations. That same information can be used by citizens and citizens groups to assist them in analyzing whether tax dollars were spent in accordance with budgetary restrictions.[411]

As the Governmental Accounting Standards Board ("GASB") has explained, there are differences between the purposes of financial reports of governmental entities and those of private-sector business enterprises.[412] Consequently, financial statements prepared in accordance with accounting principles applicable to governments differ in certain fundamental ways from financial statements prepared in accordance with accounting principles applicable to for-profit business enterprises. These differences derive from several factors, principal among them the differing needs of end users of the financial information provided.[413] In the case of financial report of business enterprises, users demand information that will allow creditors and equity holders to make decisions with respect to their financial investments. In the case of governmental accounting, on the other hand, the principal focus frequently is on public accountability for resources entrusted to the stewardship of the government (*i.e.*, taxes), including how public resources such as taxes are acquired and used; whether resources are sufficient to meet current and future costs; and whether the government's ability to provide services improves or deteriorates on a period-to-period basis.[414]

As noted above, the financial disclosure practices of municipal issuers are influenced by a variety of factors, including the demands of market participants, voluntary/industry guidelines, general antifraud considerations, and the continuing disclosure provisions relating to financial information in Rule 15c2-12. Rule 15c2-12, and specifically the definition of "final official statement," does not establish the form and content of financial information and operating data required to be disclosed in an official statement for a primary offering of municipal securities. In the 1994 amendments to Rule 15c2-12, the Commission did not adopt requirements mandating the use of audited financial statements, recognizing that not all issuers prepared such audited financial statements. The Commission recognized the need for flexibility in determining the content and scope of disclosed financial information given the diversity among types of issuers, types of issues, and sources of repayment.[415]

Annual financial information is intended to be comprised of financial information and operating data of the type included in the final official statement.[416] Rule 15c2-12 also requires that audited financial statements be provided, when and if available, if such financial statements have not been submitted as part of the annual financial information.[417] Consequently, annual submissions should include: (1) financial information and operating data of the type included in the official statement; and (2) audited financial statements, when and if available.

Many of the Commission's enforcement actions regarding materially misleading statements or omissions in official statements involved deficient financial statements or financial information provided by issuers or underlying obligors. For example, the Commission has brought enforcement actions alleging the use of stale audited financial statements,[418] the inaccurate labeling of summary financial information as "audited,"[419] the false representation that auditors had consented to the inclusion of their audit report in an official statement,[420] and misleading language contained in notes to the audited financial statements.[421] The Commission has also brought enforcement actions alleging materially misleading financial statements by virtue of accounting fraud,[422] and has brought enforcement actions against both outside auditors[423] and in-house accountants.[424]

b. Content of Financial Statements - Governmental Accounting Standards

There are no uniformly applied accounting standards in the municipal securities market, and the Commission generally lacks authority to prescribe the accounting standards that municipal issuers must use.[425] However, the GASB[426] establishes generally accepted accounting principles ("GAAP"), which are used by many states and local governments of widely varying size and complexity.[427]

Although there has been no comprehensive study to determine the exact number of municipalities that prepare financial statements on a basis other than GASB standards,[428] generally speaking, larger governments are more likely to adhere to GASB standards than smaller governments. A 2011 study undertaken by GASB, for instance, found that the vast majority of annual financial reports ("AFRs") of 350 larger governments surveyed (991 AFRs out of 1,050 AFRs, or 94%, of the large government AFRs surveyed) were prepared using GASB standards.[429] In contrast, of the 193 smaller governments surveyed by GASB, 81% of the AFRs collected were prepared using GASB standards.[430]

As of December 2010, 38 states compel some or all of their political subdivisions, including counties, cities, and school districts, to prepare their financial reports in accordance with GASB standards.[431] Along with these mandates, certification programs, such as those sponsored by the GFOA and the Association of School Business Officials International, promote the use of GASB standards by recognizing governments that prepare high-quality GAAP financial reports (based on GASB standards).[432] Nonetheless, the absence of a uniform requirement on the part of municipal entities to adhere to GASB standards means that municipal entities that issue municipal securities can (and some do) prepare their financial reports on a basis other than GASB standards. On rare occasion, some governments that otherwise are compliant with GASB standards may not be permitted to, or may choose not to, apply certain GASB standards.[433]

As the Commission noted in the 1994 Interpretive Release, for financial statements that are not either prepared in accordance with GASB standards or accompanied by a quantified (if practicable) explanation of the differences, investors need to be informed of the basis of financial statement presentation (*i.e.,* a full explanation of the accounting principles followed).[434] Rating agencies[435] and organizations such as the GFOA[436] are broadly supportive of GASB standards.

c. Market Participant Observations and Other Commentary Regarding Content of Financial Statements – Governmental Accounting Standards

Participants in the field hearings expressed a range of opinions concerning GASB standards and the use of uniform accounting standards by municipal issuers. One participant noted that GASB has imposed strict accounting standards, and that the requirements of GASB standards as well as other federal and state requirements have resulted in substantial amounts of disclosure.[437] Market participants appear to be in general agreement that adherence to GASB standards promotes consistency and comparability of financial information among municipal issuers and differing municipal securities,[438] although one participant noted that there is flexibility within GASB standards – as there is in some places in FASB standards – that allows issuers to choose alternative presentations and hence diminishes comparability to some degree.[439] Another participant made the observation, however, that adherence to GASB standards can be costly, particularly for smaller issuers, and that even issuers that do not follow GASB standards do in fact follow some other accounting standards.[440]

d. Timeliness of Financial Information

The Commission noted in the 1994 Interpretive Release that timeliness of financial information is a major factor in its usefulness.[441] Timely financial reporting,[442] including timely issuance of audited annual financial information, not only aids market participants in making informed investment decisions, but is critical to the functioning of an efficient trading market.[443] The GASB has identified timeliness of financial reporting as "perhaps the most frequent and common concern expressed to the GASB by the users of state and local government financial reports."[444] Market participants have expressed similar views.[445]

Despite the importance of timely financial statements, some municipal issuers continue to make financial information available significantly after the end of their fiscal year or fiscal period. By the time many annual financial statements are filed or otherwise publicly available, many municipal market analysts and investors believe the financial information has lost relevance in assessing the current financial position of the municipal issuer or obligated person.[446] Municipal issuers are not required, except with respect to certain limited state-imposed or statutory requirements or pursuant to contractual obligations, to issue financial reports within any specific timeframe.[447]

As a consequence, the deadline for making financial information (such as audited annual financial statements) available is often established by agreement between municipal issuers and the underwriters of the municipal securities. Timing requirements vary widely.[448] Market participants have indicated that most municipal issuers are able to file on EMMA their annual financial information, including financial statements, within the deadlines set forth in their continuing disclosure agreements, but that these deadlines may be 270 days after the end of the issuer's fiscal year.[449]

Industry guidelines and initiatives also influence the timing for making audited financial statements public. The MSRB allows municipal issuers to comply with a voluntary deadline of 120 days after fiscal year end for filing annual financial information (including audited financial statements) on EMMA.[450] The fact that an issuer or obligated person has entered into this voluntary annual filing undertaking is prominently disclosed on EMMA as a distinctive characteristic of the securities to which such undertaking applies, although the MSRB does not review or confirm compliance with this voluntary annual filing undertaking.[451] Additionally, the GFOA encourages issuers as part of its Certificate of Achievement for Excellence in Financial Reporting program to submit a CAFR within 180 days of their fiscal year end.[452]

i. Recent Studies of Timeliness of Annual Financial Information

Many issuers do not file or make public their audited financial statements within the MSRB or GFOA voluntary guideline timeframes. In March 2011, the GASB undertook a study of the timeliness of financial reporting by state and local governments. The GASB reviewed the audited AFRs of the 50 states; the 100 largest counties and localities; the 50 largest independent school districts and special districts; and a random selection of smaller counties, localities, school districts, and special districts.[453] The GASB Timeliness Study examined timeliness of financial reporting for a three-year period from 2006 to 2008.[454] The GASB Timeliness Study found that although 73% of the largest governments (regardless of type) issued[455] their audited AFR within six months, only 46% of smaller governments issued their audited AFR within such timeframe. Although the majority of the larger issuers filed within six months, roughly two percent of issuers took longer than one year to issue their audited AFR.

A second study based upon audit completion times of audits covering the period from 2007 to 2009 indicated that timeliness also appears to vary significantly by type of issuer. This study examined a much broader range of entities than the GASB Timeliness Study and found that state and local governments (excluding their agencies and authorities as well as school and special districts) generally took the longest to complete their audit reports.[456] Wholesale electric utilities and hospitals generally took the shortest time to complete their audit reports.[457] This study found that although credit quality was not necessarily a factor in how fast or slow an audit was completed, weaker or more distressed entities were often more likely to be found on the list of entities surveyed that had later audit completion times.[458]

The findings of the GASB Timeliness Study are consistent with data regarding CAFR preparation times compiled by NASACT showing a wide disparity in CAFR completion times among states.[459] The 50-state average of time to complete a CAFR was: 204 days for fiscal 2006, 205 days for fiscal 2007, 204 days for fiscal 2008, 206 days for fiscal 2009, and 188 days for fiscal 2010. States differed widely in their completion times and among fiscal periods. New York, for instance – which is required by law to issue its CAFR within 120 days of its fiscal year end – completed its CAFR in times ranging from 112 days (fiscal 2006) to 116 days (fiscal 2008). Similarly, the CAFR completion times for Michigan ranged from 89 days (fiscal 2007) to 181 days (fiscal 2006).[460] At the other extreme, Illinois took between 237 days (fiscal 2006) and 376 days (fiscal 2008) during the five years surveyed, while New Mexico took between 215 days (fiscal 2008) and 731 days (fiscal 2006).[461]

The findings of the GASB Timeliness Study are also consistent with other recent studies.[462] The 2011 Merritt Report, containing an analysis of over 25,500 audits on more than 6,600 different municipal bond issuers, over a four year period, found that the average time for an audit report to be completed after the close of the fiscal year is nearly five months.[463] While municipal market participants often anticipate a six-month time span before an audit is completed, the range of time to complete an audit can vary dramatically by sector and by individual governmental bodies or agencies.[464] The 2011 Merritt Report found, for example, that entities in the public power sector (the fastest reporting sector) had a 90-day median for completion of an audit in 2010, compared to an average of 141.3 days for 2010 audits across all sectors. Additionally, the 2011 Merritt Report found that the fastest city had its audit completed in 53 days while the slowest took 427 days, while states took as long as 365 days in Illinois to as short as 114 days in New York.[465]

The 2011 Merritt Report and 2011 GASB Timeliness Study both support the view that passage of time diminishes significantly the usefulness of financial information in the hands of investors, analysts and other market participants.[466] The 2011 GASB Timeliness Study found, for example, that over 43% of persons surveyed stated that audited financial statements received within 90 days after the end of an issuer's fiscal year are "very useful."[467] This same survey reported that less than 9% of respondents considered information received within 6 months to be "very useful," and less than 2% of respondents considered information received within 12 months or longer than 12 months to be "very useful."[468] The 2011 GASB Timeliness Study evaluated the time-to-issuance of audited AFRs for various municipalities in light of when the data is most useful and found that there is a noticeable gap between when the financial information is most useful to the users of the AFRs and when governments provide that information.[469]

ii. Interim Financial Information

Although the continuing disclosure provisions in Rule 15c2-12 require the submission of annual financial information and audited financial statements, if available, there is no requirement to provide interim financial information (other than such information as may be event notices under Rule 15c2-12). Some issuers provide interim financial information, including monthly budget or cash flow reports, on their websites or through other means.[470] While some issuers may voluntarily provide some interim financial information, such disclosure is not provided by many issuers or may not be provided in a manner that is readily accessible to market participants.[471]

According to press reports, investors have limited, if any, access to interim financial information.[472] The Staff understands that some issuers and other entities are reluctant to file or otherwise make available interim financial information due to potential liability.[473]

Some market participants have suggested ways in which such interim financial information may be made more readily available. For example, NASACT has supported the use of websites for disclosures of interim financial information.[474] In addition, the GFOA encourages issuers to make available interim financial information.[475] NASACT also has stated, however, that because most state and local governments are subject to public information laws, investors have access to all information pertaining to their investments and that investors should be responsible for obtaining and understanding this information.[476]

There are voluntary initiatives underway by the NFMA and the GFOA to develop guidelines for the issuance of more frequent, unaudited financial information by issuers, such as quarterly disclosure of issuers' balance sheets, income statements, and minimal financial notes.[477]

Quarterly disclosure appears to be most common with respect to health care issuers;[478] it has been speculated that this more frequent disclosure occurs because of the limited market for health care bonds, which gives investors more leverage.[479] Currently, some issuers and other entities voluntarily file certain interim financial information on EMMA. According to the MSRB, between July 2009 and June 2011, issuers and other entities voluntarily filed the following types of interim financial information:

- quarterly or monthly financial information;
- notice of a change in fiscal year or a change of the date specified in the continuing disclosure undertaking for submitting financial information and operating data;
- change in choice of accounting standard used;
- additional financial information or operating data supplementing annual financial information provided on an interim basis;
- budget documents or other information relating to budgets;
- policies on investment activities, debt incurrence, or financial matters;
- information provided to rating agency, credit provider, or other third party;
- consultant reports; and
- other financial or operating data.[480]

Of the 258,162 continuing disclosure documents filed on EMMA between July 2009 and June 2011, approximately 11.9% of them related to interim financial information.[481] Quarterly or monthly financial information was the category of interim financial information that issuers and other entities filed the most during that time period, and this category only represented approximately 5.7% of the total number of EMMA filings during the period.[482]

iii. Market Participant Observations and Other Commentary Regarding Timeliness of Financial Information

•

– Annual Information

Issuer representatives participating in field hearings expressed concern regarding the necessity, or even the feasibility, of a mandated shorter timeframe for dissemination of financial information. One field hearing participant warned that creating shorter deadlines could diminish the value of the financial information and persuade many governments to abandon the high-quality reporting produced from following GASB standards in favor of a greatly reduced set of basic financial statements.[483] This participant expressed doubt whether larger localities and counties can feasibly reduce their timelines below 180 days after the closing of the fiscal year, even with more personnel and preplanning.[484] Another participant expressed a similar sentiment, highlighting that technical requirements for producing audited financial statements are not capable of being accelerated.[485]

As noted above, the MSRB allows municipal issuers to comply with a voluntary deadline of 120 days after fiscal year end.[486] At the time that such provision was under consideration, the GFOA submitted a comment letter suggesting that implementation of a more stringent timeframe would cause issuers to provide information that is far less comprehensive than that found in CAFRs, and would force governments to rely upon auditors that do not have the extensive governmental accounting background needed to review such statements.[487] One commenter pointed to the requirements of GASB itself as an impediment to providing information on a timelier basis.[488] Another noted that a 120-day standard would be unattainable by the overwhelming majority of issuers.[489]

According to market participants, a number of factors contribute to municipal issuers' historical delay in releasing their audited financial statements publicly. Some market participants have noted that a state following GASB standards must include financial data for legally separate entities over which the state has little practical control. For example, a state may be required to wait for financial results from its state universities over which the state has little control. These entities may have divergent accounting standards and different auditors. Market participants noted that these differences make it difficult for the state to incorporate, reconcile, and complete its own financial report in a timely fashion.[490] Market participants also pointed to the fact that an audit opinion is often issued at the level of each major fund, not just at the total financial reporting level.

Some market participants noted that an increased use of estimates, rather than actual amounts, could improve timeliness of financial reporting but could result in less accurate financial statements.[491] Market participants noted other factors that contribute to untimely financial reporting, including the limited number of auditing firms that are capable of completing governmental audits,[492] the lack of resources needed to prepare financial information,[493] and the slow legal process of adopting government budgets.[494]

– Interim Financial Information

Many market participants have called for more timely disclosure of quarterly, unaudited financial information, as well as prompt disclosure of other information that has already been prepared by issuers and thus can be made available without a substantial outlay of time or cost.[495] These include:

- budget information;[496]
- budget-to-actual operations, showing major categories of revenues and expenditures, for the general fund and major governmental and enterprise funds, year-to-date, and an explanation of the major variances;[497]
- internal month-to-month cash flow reports;
- monthly retail sales information and quarterly occupancy numbers;[498]
- statements of monthly balances (*i.e.*, cash on hand), which would be helpful for assessing solvency;
- an annual demonstration of compliance with financial covenants contained within the bond indenture or resolution, such as debt service and liquidity coverage;[499]
- quarterly unaudited financial updates (a practice now largely limited to the health care sector and to many large and frequent issuers), including information specifically related to the pledged source of revenues and up-to-date collection information for the revenues which are securing the bonds in question;[500]
- cash receipts and cash disbursements in the general fund and major governmental and enterprise funds, year-to-date, compared to the previous fiscal year;[501]
- balances and changes in long-term and short-term debt, year-to-date;[502]
- tax assessor reports (for general obligation credits) used to determine localities' budgets for the coming year;[503] and
- significant events (*e.g.*, loss of a major employer or taxpayer, a natural disaster, change in the tax laws that would have a substantial effect on its financial condition, etc.).[504]

One market participant suggested that interim financial information is not feasible not only because of the cost involved, but also because state and local governments operate on an annual timeframe and are not equipped to close their books on a quarterly basis.[505]

In their monitoring and rating activities, certain market participants have indicated that, in lieu of having access to unaudited interim financial information, they instead look at publicly available interim and budget disclosure (including from public websites), budgets, census demographics, and other unaudited information. One market participant observed that municipal issuers are often subject to various laws that require them to make public documents available to anyone that requests them, and are frequently required to file their financial statements and budgets with other government agencies.[506]

2. Pension Funding Obligations and Other Post-Employment Benefits Disclosure

Disclosure regarding pension funding obligations of states and other municipal entities is at the forefront of discussions regarding the municipal securities market. Obligations to provide pension and OPEBs can significantly affect a municipal issuer's financial health and may impact its ability to make debt service payments on municipal securities. There are over 3,400 state and local pension systems in the United States, according to the most recent Census Bureau Survey of State and Local Public-Employee Retirement Systems.[507] The GAO has reported that over 27 million employees and beneficiaries are covered by state and local pension plans.[508] Recently, there has been much debate about the appropriate accounting treatment and disclosure relating to the pension funding obligations of state and local governments to such plans.[509]

a. Enforcement Actions

The Commission has brought enforcement actions regarding inadequate disclosure by municipal entities as to the difficulty they were facing in meeting their funding obligations to their public pension systems. In 2006, the Commission brought an action against the City of San Diego, California, for making false and misleading statements regarding the city's looming crisis in funding its pension obligations in disclosure documents for five bond offerings between 2002 and 2003 totaling $260 million.[510]

In October 2010, the Commission also settled injunctive actions against former San Diego officials for their roles in providing misleading disclosure about the city's fiscal problems related to its pension and retiree health care obligations.[511] This settlement represents the first time that the SEC has secured financial penalties against city officials in a municipal bond fraud case.[512]

Also in 2010, the Commission brought charges for the first time against a state for violations of the federal securities laws when it charged the State of New Jersey with securities fraud for misrepresenting and failing to disclose to investors in municipal bond offerings that it was underfunding the state's two largest pension plans by billions of dollars, masking the fact that New Jersey was unable to make contributions to those pension plans without raising taxes, cutting other services, or otherwise affecting its budget.[513]

b. Calculation of Funding Levels

There are a number of issues affecting disclosures of pension plan liabilities and the funding obligations of state and local governments to such plans. Over the past few years, studies have noted that the underfunded portion of state and local pension liabilities has steadily increased, especially since the collapse of market asset values in 2008.[514] It has been estimated recently that aggregate underfunding of state and local defined benefit pension plans may exceed $4 trillion.[515] Another study found that in 2011, these state and local pension liabilities amounted to $3.6 trillion, compared with an estimated $2.7 trillion in actuarial assets, representing a funded ratio of 75%.[516]

While it has been reported that many state and local pension funds are underfunded,[517] the method of calculating the funding level is the subject of much discussion. Funding levels represent the actuarial value of assets divided by actuarial accrued liabilities. There is significant debate regarding the appropriate investment return assumption (or "discount rate") for measuring public pension liabilities.

Currently, GASB standards require that, for financial reporting purposes, an actuarial valuation should be performed in order to measure the annual pension cost and net pension obligation of a plan.[518] In calculating the annual pension cost, GASB standards require the use of a discount rate based upon an estimated long-term investment yield for the plan.[519] Although there is no specified rate to be used, most state and local pension funds have generally settled on the use of a discount rate of 8%, which reflects their estimate of the rate of return on plan assets.[520] The financial statement calculations of pension plan liabilities may differ from the actuarial computations used to recommend funding for the plans.[521] As discussed below, the GASB is working on revisions to its standards applicable to pension liabilities.

Academics have advocated measuring the underfunding liability using a "fair-value approach," which they argue is a more realistic measure of the extent of underfunding.[522] The "fair-value approach" discounts assets and liabilities based upon what an investor would be willing to pay for assets and receive to assume responsibility of the liabilities.[523] For public pension liabilities, the discount rate reflects the low likelihood – or risk – that the liabilities will not be honored, and hence the discount rate is often referred to as "risk-free" or "riskless."[524] The fair-value or risk-free approach generally results in a significantly lower discount rate than the median rate of 8% used by many state and local government pension plans, which could result in a higher estimated present value of future benefits payments, and consequently, a higher "unfunded" liability.

Some argue that GASB standards may substantially understate the true economic magnitude of these liabilities and create perverse incentives for fund managers.[525] Others argue that using a risk-free investment return assumption presents conceptual as well as pragmatic issues.[526] According to the GAO, many experts consider 80% or better funding levels to be sound for government pensions because states and localities can use tax revenues to make up a shortfall if necessary.[527]

The Boston College Report concluded that using a 5% discount rate, rather than the more widely used 8% discount rate would increase aggregate state and local pension liabilities from $3.6 trillion to $5.4 trillion, and decrease the funded ratio from 75% to 50%.[528]

c. OPEBs

Concerns about unfunded liabilities for OPEBs are similar to the concerns about unfunded pension liabilities. The extent of these types of obligations was, in the past, difficult to ascertain, because the obligations were accounted for on a "pay-as-you-go" basis, under which the cost of the benefit to an employee was not recognized by the state until after the employee had retired and the payments were made.[529] With the implementation of GASB

Statement No. 45,[530] state and local governments that follow GASB standards are now required to measure the annual OPEB cost and a net OPEB obligation. A recent study found that as of fiscal year 2010, only 5% of the $660 billion liability for state retirees' health care and other non-pension benefits had been funded.[531] However, according to one market participant, the unfunded actuarial liability for OPEBs is "inherently and significantly more volatile" than the unfunded liability for pension benefits for several reasons.[532] For example, unlike pension benefits, in many jurisdictions healthcare benefits are not guaranteed by state law and can be more easily reduced or modified.[533]

d. Disclosure of Pension and OPEB Funding Obligations

Regardless of the methodology used for measuring pension and OPEB liabilities, the accuracy and adequacy of disclosure regarding pension and OPEB funding obligations by municipal securities issuers is a focus of legislators,[534] the Commission,[535] issuers,[536] and investors alike.[537] With respect to disclosure regarding pension funding obligations, the Staff has heard from issuers and pension plan experts about a number of disclosure practices, which include disclosure of all pension information in accordance with GASB standards,[538] disclosure of actuarial assumptions,[539] disclosure of the rules governing actuarial assumptions,[540] preparation of a supplemental alternative risk assessment study quantifying the likelihood and magnitude of future outcomes for the pension system,[541] and disclosure of an alternative pension liability measurement, discounted at a risk-free rate.[542] Another field hearing panelist emphasized that these elements are important and they help to establish a baseline for disclosure of pension funding obligations.[543] With respect to disclosure for particular issues of municipal securities, field hearing participants suggested that investors will be interested to know if an issuer's pension funding obligations result in a material adverse impact on an issuer's ability to pay principal and interest on an issue of bonds, impact their credit rating, or otherwise impair the security of the bonds.[544] Additional considerations for disclosure include whether the municipal issuer sponsors the plan or whether it is a participant in a multiple employer plan, in which case much of the information with respect to the plan would not be available to the issuer.[545]

e. Voluntary Disclosure Initiatives and GASB Standards Revisions

Voluntary efforts have focused on disclosure in this area. For example, NABL convened a "Municipal Market Task Force on Public Pension Disclosure" ("Task Force"),[546] whose mission was to develop a consensus approach to the appropriate disclosures related to an issuer's participation in a defined benefit public pension plan as well as to educate the NABL membership on how best to approach the preparation of primary offering disclosure on this topic.[547] NABL released its considerations for preparing disclosure in official statements regarding pension funding obligations on May 15, 2012.[548]

The GASB is currently working on a project related to post-employment benefit accounting and financial reporting with the objective of improving accountability and the transparency of financial reporting in regard to the financial effects of employers' commitments and actions related to pension benefits.[549] In June 2011, the GASB issued two Exposure Drafts proposing changes to financial reporting of pensions by state and local governments. The first primarily relates to reporting by governments that provide pensions to their employees.[550] The second addresses the reporting by the pension plans that administer those benefits.[551] The GASB has stated that this proposal is designed to reflect that, to the extent that the plan net assets will not be available to be invested for the long-term to make benefit payments, those future benefit payments would be made using the general resources of the government.[552]

Under the GASB's proposed pension guidance, unfunded pension liabilities would be required to be recognized in the financial statements rather than in the notes to the financial statements, as is currently the case.[553] Additionally, the proposal calls for robust information in notes to the financial statements and required supplementary information, including a schedule of changes in net pension liability over a ten year period.[554] The GASB expects that, if adopted, the new standards would put pension liabilities, on equal footing with other long-term obligations, lead to reporting of greater liabilities, provide greater clarity about changes in net pension liabilities and foster greater consistency and comparability across governments.[555]

3. Exposure to Derivatives

a. Overview

As noted above, some municipal issuers use derivative products in connection with their municipal securities offerings.[556] The most common derivative transaction that municipal issuers use is a fixed-for-floating swap, which allows municipal issuers to fix all or part of their exposure to variable interest rates.[557] The combined effect of issuing securities with variable interest rates and entering into a fixed interest rate-for-floating interest rate swap is a synthetic fixed rate obligation.[558] This type of derivative transaction exposes an issuer to a variety of risks, some of which may be significant.[559]

Since interest rate swaps are bilateral contracts entered into privately, there currently is no comprehensive data on how many municipal issuers are active in the $162 trillion U.S. dollar-denominated interest rate swap market,[560] although anecdotal evidence suggests a relatively wide use. For instance, a 2008 news article reported that a review of Pennsylvania Department of Community and Economic Development records reveals that 185 school districts, towns, and counties in Pennsylvania have entered into derivatives contracts since 2003, when the state's law was explicitly changed to allow for such contracts.[561] However, panel participants noted that the use of interest rate swaps has declined since the onset of the financial crisis in 2008.[562]

Although the use of derivatives can provide municipalities with benefits, such as the ability to reduce borrowing costs and/or manage interest rate risk, they also pose special risks to municipalities.[563] The special and significant risks posed by derivative instruments to municipal issuers has underscored the need to consider enhanced disclosure to provide investors a clear understanding of the terms of such instruments and the risks to the issuer.[564]

b. Municipal Issuer as "Purchaser" of a Derivative Product

i. Market Participant Observations and Other Commentary

Two of the field hearing panels focused on derivatives, addressing issues relating to the municipal issuer as the "purchaser" of a derivative product and disclosure issues related to derivative products entered into by municipal entities.[565]

Much of the discussion at the field hearings focused on conflicts of interest and other factors that may cause municipal issuers to enter into potentially disadvantageous derivatives transactions. First, panelists addressed the nature of the relationship between counterparties. Specifically, a panelist stated that although swap documents include an express denial of a fiduciary relationship between the two counterparties,[566] municipal entities typically rely upon and trust the financial institution with whom they are dealing.[567] Panelists also argued that swap advisors are inherently conflicted for a number of reasons, pointing out (1) that their compensation is contingent on completion of a transaction,[568] (2) that they rely on financial institutions for referrals,[569] and (3) that their relationships with the municipal entities are typically limited to the duration of the transaction, rather than lasting for the life of the swap (meaning that they would be unlikely to advise the municipal entity to pass up a particular transaction).[570]

One field hearing participant observed that legislative bodies may fail to consider the long-term economic cycle on the ability of the municipality to repay its financial obligations and pointed out that one legislative body may commit its future legislative bodies to pay financial obligations twenty or thirty years into the future.[571] Another participant suggested that political considerations often prevent municipal entities from hiring the most capable internal and external financial advisors.[572] Participants also stressed that many municipal entities have entered into derivative transactions that they did not understand.[573] Others, however, have noted that in their experience, the nature of credit risk, interest rate risk, and termination risk was carefully explained to issuers and understood by them.[574] Some market participants have suggested that swap dealers may offer up-front payments or reduced fees on other services (such as underwriting) to induce municipal entities to enter into derivative transactions.

Panelists suggested that these factors cause municipal entities to be comparatively disadvantaged in the terms that they receive and fees that they pay as parties to derivatives transactions.[575] One hearing participant used an interest rate swap transaction in connection with a taxable bond deal as an example of the excessive fees involved in municipal derivatives transactions.[576] In the panelist's example, the cost to taxpayers at the time of execution of the swap was $14 million and the average mark-up was 2%.[577] Another panelist noted that in 2009, the State of Tennessee supplemented its policies regarding the use of derivatives such as interest rate swap agreements. In addition to requiring that any interest rate swap agreement be related to a specific debt instrument and that government officials understand the complexity and risks of the financial transaction in question, the participant noted that the revised policies: (1) require that the CEO of the municipal entity and the governing body be jointly responsible for understanding the transaction, and that such parties be responsible for maintaining a competent staff to administer the transaction; and (2) encourage local governments that enter into such transactions to review and comply with the GFOA advisory on the use of debt-related products and derivatives checklist.[578]

Panelists urged the implementation of several regulatory mechanisms in order to protect issuers from entering into unsuitable transactions on unfavorable terms, including:

- limiting participation in the derivatives market to only the largest and most sophisticated issuers,[579] such as by prohibiting use of derivatives by a municipal issuer unless the issuer has at least $100 million in liabilities (as opposed to assets) and an outside financial advisor;[580]
- instituting derivatives policies,[581]

- better disclosure by swap dealers, counterparties, and swap advisors of conflicts of interest and profit margins;[582]
- use of independent and knowledgeable financial advisors subject to a fiduciary duty for swap transactions;[583]
- disclosure by swap dealers of the swap curve at the time of execution;[584]
- establishment of a Municipal Finance Protection Bureau to provide municipalities with information on the fair values of swaps, on request, prior to entry or exit;[585] and
- aggressive enforcement of expanded regulatory authority over the swap market.[586]

c. Enforcement Actions

The extent of the risks to municipal entities engaging in swaps and security-based swaps has been illustrated by several high-profile enforcement actions such as Orange County, California,[587] and the more recent cases involving Jefferson County, Alabama.[588] In addition to these cases, to date, the Commission has filed five settled enforcement actions against major financial institutions for their role in a series of complex, wide-ranging bid-rigging schemes involving derivatives utilized by municipalities and underlying obligors as reinvestment products.[589]

In addition, in August 2011 the Commission filed a civil injunctive action against Stifel Nicholas & Co. and a former Senior Vice President named David Noack for allegedly violating the federal securities laws in connection with the sale to trusts established by five Wisconsin school districts of $200 million of highly leveraged and unsuitably risky credit-linked notes involving synthetic collateralized debt obligations ("CDOs"). According to the complaint, Stifel and Noack misrepresented the risk of the investments and failed to disclose material facts to the school districts. In the end, the investments were a complete failure, but generated significant fees for Stifel and Noack. In particular, heavy use of leverage and the structure of the synthetic CDOs exposed the school districts to a heightened risk of catastrophic loss. Nevertheless, Stifel and Noack allegedly made sweeping assurances to the school districts, misrepresenting that it would take "15 Enrons," a catastrophic, overnight collapse for the investments to fail.[590]

In the enforcement actions involving Orange County, California, the Commission focused on the need to provide disclosure regarding risks relating to investment strategies, including risks to the municipal issuer arising from the use of derivative instruments, including swaps. Orange County had been heavily dependent on interest income from various County investment pools as a source of income to balance its current operating budget. Those pools implemented a risky investment strategy that ultimately resulted in the County filing for bankruptcy in December 1994.

In particular, the County Treasurer obtained additional funds through short-term reverse repurchase agreements and investing in securities with maturities of two to five years, many of which were volatile derivative securities known as inverse floaters that paid interest rates inversely related to the prevailing market interest rate. When market interest rates began to rise, the county pools' financial health declined.[591]

d. Business Conduct Standards of Swap Entities and Security-Based Swap Entities

Most of the problematic practices that market participants identified with respect to municipal issuers as "purchasers" of derivative products pre-dated passage of the Dodd-Frank Act. Title VII of the Dodd-Frank Act establishes a comprehensive framework for regulating the over-the-counter swaps markets. The Dodd-Frank Act generally provides the Commodity Futures Trading Commission ("CFTC") with authority to regulate "swaps,"[592] including the interest rate swaps that are the most common type of derivative product entered into by municipal entities.[593] The statute also provides the Commission with authority to regulate "security-based swaps," and both the CFTC and the Commission with authority to regulate "mixed swaps."[594]

The Dodd-Frank Act established new business conduct obligations for swap dealers and major swap participants (collectively, "Swap Entities"), and security-based swap dealers and major security-based swap participants (collectively, "SBS Entities"), in their dealings with counterparties.[595]

In addition, Congress imposed heightened business conduct requirements for dealings with "special entities," which included certain types of municipal entities.[596] The Commission has proposed[597] and the CFTC has recently adopted rules to implement these provisions.[598] Below is a summary of the requirements as adopted by the CFTC and proposed by the Commission.

Among other things, the rules would require Swap Entities and SBS Entities to verify whether a counterparty is a special entity, and disclose to the counterparty material information about the security-based swap or swap (collectively, "swap"), including material risks, characteristics, incentives, and conflicts of interest.

The rules also would define what it means to "act as an advisor" to a special entity, and would require that a swap dealer or security-based swap dealer who acts as an advisor to a special entity to:

- Act in the "best interests" of the special entity; and
- Make reasonable efforts to obtain information that it needs to determine that the recommendation is in the "best interests" of the special entity.

A Swap Entity or SBS Entity acting as counterparty to a special entity also would be required to reasonably believe that the counterparty has an independent representative who meets the following requirements:

- Has sufficient knowledge to evaluate the transaction and risks;
- Is not subject to a statutory disqualification;
- Is independent of the Swap Entity or SBS Entity;
- Undertakes a duty to act in the best interests of the special entity;
- Makes appropriate disclosures of material information concerning the swap; and
- Provides written representations to the special entity regarding fair pricing and appropriateness of the swap.

In addition, the swap dealer or security-based swap dealer, as well as the independent representative, would be subject to pay-to-play regulations.

One field hearing participant expressed concern regarding the possible adverse outcome arising from the proposed business conduct rules on swap dealers, particularly the additional restrictions related to swaps with "special entities," urging the SEC and CFTC to continue to coordinate efforts.[599]

e. Disclosure Issues

i. Market Participant Observations and Other Commentary

Participants in the field hearings also discussed issues relating to disclosure of derivatives exposure. For example, local government officials[600] discussed how disclosure of derivative obligations has changed since GASB Statement No. 53 was issued.[601] A panelist noted that prior to GASB Statement No. 53 these derivatives were reported as a footnote disclosure in financial statements or not at all.[602] Participants noted that GASB No. 53 could lead to consistent treatment of derivatives reporting but noted that without additional information (such as the effect of future interest rate changes) it could be misleading to investors.[603] Panelists suggested that the following types of practices would serve to better protect municipal securities investors:

- use of "plain English summaries" of the terms of the derivatives, the risks to the municipal issuer, the payment obligations (including any required termination payments), the name of the counterparty, and a brief description of the purpose of the derivative;[604]
- disclosure of scenario testing, to show how various interest rate scenarios would impact individual swap transactions, including termination payments and collateral posting requirements for lower-rated issuers;[605]
- disclosure of the credit quality of the swap counterparty;[606]
- reporting to the governing body the financial effectiveness of the swap and any potential risks in the current economic environment, on at least an annual basis;[607] and
- publication by municipal entities of financial effectiveness reports on websites on a regular basis and an opportunity for members of the public to ask questions about the continued financial effectiveness and cost of the transactions in a public meeting.[608]

The business conduct standards described above may facilitate improved disclosure by issuers. To the extent that issuers receive independent and more informed advice as a result of the Dodd-Frank Act business conduct standards and the related CFTC (and ultimately, SEC) regulations, they may be better equipped to provide effective disclosure to investors regarding the terms and risks of their exposure to derivatives.

4. Disclaimers of Responsibility for Information Included in Official Statements and Other Disclosures

Some municipal market participants attempt to disclaim responsibility for information included in official statements and other disclosure documents. Commission staff is also aware that legal counsel have encouraged the use of disclaimers in municipal offering documents in an attempt to protect against liability under Section 10(b) of the Exchange Act for portions of offering documents that have been prepared by "experts" and in part to avoid common law liability for implied warranties.[609]

The Commission has stated that "specific disclaimers of antifraud liability are contrary to the policies underpinning the federal securities laws."[610] As stated above, underwriters must have a reasonable basis for recommending any municipal securities and must review disclosure documents used in an offering for omissions and misstatements.[611] The

Commission has further stated that "disclaimers by underwriters of responsibility for the information provided by the issuer or other parties, without further clarification regarding the underwriter's belief as to accuracy, and the basis therefor, are misleading and should not be included in official statements."[612] One market participant has suggested that the Commission recognize additional limited circumstances where disclaimers may be appropriate in municipal securities official statements, and provided some examples of how the Commission could address these issues.[613]

Issues regarding appropriate uses of disclaimers also arise when disclosure documents include hyperlinks and website references. The Commission's interpretation on the use of electronic media which applies to all issuers including municipal securities issuers, addresses embedded hyperlinks and other references to websites and, in that context, discusses the issuer's responsibilities with respect to adoption of hyperlinked information.[614] In order to eliminate any confusion about whether the issuer has adopted information that is hyperlinked, the Commission stated that the issuer should ensure "that access to the information is preceded or accompanied by a clear and prominent statement from the issuer disclaiming responsibility for, or endorsement of, the information."[615]

5. Disclosure of Conflicts of Interest and Other Relationships or Practices

As highlighted in the 1994 Interpretive Release and Commission enforcement actions, information concerning financial and business relationships or practices, such as undisclosed payments, political contributions, and bid rigging, among offering participants or decision makers may be critical to investors.[616]

The role of advisors, such as swap and municipal advisors, to issuers also has raised questions regarding undisclosed conflicts of interest.[617] The MSRB recently issued interpretive guidance under MSRB Rule G-17 that includes a requirement that underwriters disclose certain conflicts of interest to municipal issuers.[618]

a. Pay-to-Play and Political Contributions

Among the types of relationships or practices that may affect municipal issuers are those involving pay-to-play[619] issues. The MSRB adopted Rule G-37 in 1994 to address pay-to-play issues relating to obtaining municipal securities underwriting and other financial engagements. Pay-to-play restrictions have also been adopted by the CFTC in the context of swap transactions and proposed by the Commission in the context of security-based swaps transactions with municipalities.[620] However, other forms of potentially problematic pay-to-play activities involving commodity trading advisors, municipal advisors, or other municipal securities market participants are not yet directly regulated but raise disclosure issues for investors and the market.

One form of political contribution that has been the subject of recent continued concern to market participants involves financial intermediaries funding bond ballot campaigns ("bond elections").[621] Bond elections often are required as a matter of state or local law to authorize the issuance of bonds, for example, to finance a particular project or group of projects. Independent ballot measure committees are typically formed to conduct campaigns in support of bond elections. Because governmental issuers are usually prohibited by state law from spending public funds to support bond elections, they are dependent on private third parties to support the campaign, either in the form of financial contributions or in-kind services (including the use of retained expert election consulting firms). Such private third parties can include municipal finance firms, law and accounting firms, construction firms, and architects.

Many state and local jurisdictions do not prohibit or otherwise restrict contributions by private parties to bond elections, although some do.[622] However, if the issuer pays back the contribution with bond proceeds, it may violate prohibitions on spending public funds to back a bond election. Depending on the state, public officials who violate the rules could be subject to criminal charges and the bond election could be invalidated.[623] Although this might not have a direct impact on the validity of bonds because bonds are generally not issued until after an election is "certified," municipal market participants reimbursed for political contributions from bond proceeds may be assisting issuer officials in violating criminal statutes. In addition, some have argued that pay-to-play activities for bond elections, whether direct or indirect, increase bond issuance fees and interest costs and undermine public trust.[624]

In addition, the MSRB recently amended Rule G-37 to require the mandatory public disclosure on amended Form G-37 of certain contributions to bond ballot campaigns made by municipal bond dealers and is continuing to study whether such contributions should be prohibited.[625]

b. Enforcement Actions

The Commission has taken a number of actions, including enforcement actions in the municipal securities arena, to address conflicts arising from political contributions.[626] The Commission has also brought a number of enforcement actions involving conflicts of interest and undisclosed payments. For example, in 2008 the Commission filed a litigated injunctive action against the then-President of Jefferson County Commission Larry Langford and others alleging they received material undisclosed payments in connection with municipal securities business and security-based swap agreements.[627] Mr. Langford was convicted in a subsequent criminal action involving substantially similar facts and is currently serving a 15-year prison sentence. The Commission also charged J.P. Morgan Securities for making undisclosed payments of $8.2 million in 2002 and 2003 at the direction of certain Jefferson County commissioners for little, if any, services in connection with $5 billion of County bond issues and swaps. The firm was censured, paid a $25 million penalty, and another $50 million in disgorgement and prejudgment interest, and forfeited more than $647 million in claimed termination fees under the swaps.[628] Moreover, the Commission filed a litigated injunctive action against two former J.P. Morgan investment bankers for allegedly directing the $8.2 million in undisclosed payments.[629]

The Commission has brought a series of enforcement actions against underwriters of municipal securities involving the payment of extravagant travel and entertainment expenses for friends and family members of public officials travelling to New York City, ostensibly for meetings with bond insurance and credit rating agencies, and then obtaining reimbursement for those expenses from the underlying municipal issuers.[630]

Public pension funds have also been subject to conflict of interest and undisclosed payment schemes that resulted in enforcement actions by the Commission. For example, in 2009 the Commission filed an injunctive action alleging that, from 2003 through late 2006, New York's former Deputy Comptroller, a top political advisor, and various placement agents participated in a fraudulent kickback scheme in order to win investment business from the New York State Common Retirement Fund.[631] Similarly, the Commission brought enforcement actions against the former treasurer of the State of Connecticut and others for awarding state pension fund investments to private equity fund managers in exchange for payments, including political contributions, funneled through the former treasurer's friends and political associates.[632]

Recently, the Commission filed an injunctive action charging a former Detroit mayor, a former Detroit treasurer, and an investment advisor to Detroit's public pension funds for their involvement in a secret exchange of lavish gifts to peddle influence over the funds' investment process.[633]

C. Other Identified Disclosure Issues

1. Access to Information

As noted above, retail and institutional investors alike have an interest in understanding and monitoring the financial health of the issuers of the municipal securities the investors own or may wish to acquire.[634] However, market participants have stated that access to current financial information about issuers or obligated persons may be limited, difficult to find, or unavailable.[635] While much financial information is available at the time of an offering, continuing disclosure is not necessarily available or available in a timely manner.[636]

As noted above, some investors expressed frustration that credit ratings may not be readily available to retail investors, although certain credit ratings are now available publicly on EMMA.[637] In addition, some market participants expressed concern that institutional investors may have access to more detailed information than retail investors.[638] One participant stated that institutional investors can contact issuers directly to request information and have access to electronic road shows, while such information and access may not be available to retail investors.[639] Another market participant noted that rating agencies have more access to information from issuers than investors.[640]

2. Use of Issuer Websites

In addition to the submission of annual financial information (including audited financial statements) on EMMA, many issuers now take advantage of the Internet[641] by providing disclosure to residents, investors, and other interested parties through issuer sponsored websites, a practice that has received the support of the GFOA.[642] Municipalities make use of websites to communicate large volumes of information to their residents, by for instance posting budget information, budget-to-actual comparisons, press releases, and minutes of meetings of governing bodies.[643] Municipalities that have issued municipal securities also use websites to communicate with and disclose information directly to a wide range of market participants, including underwriters, investors, and analysts. Disseminated information includes preliminary official statements, audited financial statements, CAFRs, press releases concerning important events, and notification of events for which disclosure is required to be submitted on EMMA under Rule 15c2-12.[644]

Although market participants generally viewed increased website disclosure as favorable, some expressed concern that information that is disclosed may not be presented in a manner that is useful to investors, may not be carefully prepared,[645] or may even be misleading.[646] Another market participant noted that website disclosure outside of the CAFR is often provided without any context.[647]

Additionally, the use of hyperlinks and website references in official statements affect what information might be considered to be part of the disclosure documents of a municipal securities issuer for purposes of compliance with Rule 15c2-12. The Commission has noted that "for purposes of satisfying its obligations under Rule 15c2-12, a municipal securities underwriter may rely on the municipal securities issuer to identify which of the documents on, or hyperlinked from, the issuer's [website] comprise the preliminary, deemed final and final official statements."[648] One market participant believes that this interpretation is too vague due to the increasing reference to issuer websites in offering documents[649] and suggested that the Commission revise its interpretation to state that the preliminary and final official statements are limited to the documents prepared for dissemination to investors together with any other materials expressly incorporated by reference into such documents.[650]

3. Presentation of Information and Comparability

The diversity and complexity of the municipal securities market appears to provide challenges for investors.[651] For example, some retail investors may have difficulty understanding lengthy disclosure documents[652] or the terms of complex municipal securities, and finding information about outstanding municipal securities. Many investors may not have a sufficient understanding of the terms and risks of municipal securities they own or might consider buying or selling. Participants at the field hearings also said that offering statements and ongoing disclosure documents often use complex, legalistic language that is opaque to all but financial or legal experts.[653]

Market participants have identified some areas in which they perceived a deficiency in the disclosures. According to the MSRB, investors have complained that the lack of standardized and detailed disclosure of the use of bond proceeds and other sources of funds is a factor that significantly impedes their ability to compare bond issues for possible investment.[654]

Some field hearing participants called for the use of a plain English executive summary, or "tear sheet," that describes in one or two pages, and in a clear and understandable format, the terms of an offering and the risks of purchasing a security,[655] (*i.e.,* the exposure that the issuer bears particularly for derivatives and other complex instruments), and one hearing participant suggested a simple rating scale as a means of providing greater clarity about risks to investors.[656]

4. Disclosure Controls and Procedures

As stated above, the issuer has ultimate responsibility for ensuring that its official statements meet the disclosure standards of the federal securities laws.[657] Additionally, any information released to the public by an issuer that is reasonably expected to reach investors and the trading markets is subject to the antifraud provisions.[658]

In preparing their official statements and other disclosures, some issuers look to written disclosure controls that they have in place while others do not have a formal disclosure control system.

Municipal issuers generally base their disclosure policies, procedures, and controls on state law requirements, other governmental mandates or their own customs and practices. However, issuers may also look to Commission enforcement actions or other Commission guidance.[659] Organizations of attorneys have suggested that basic elements of any such controls and procedures should "include (1) disclosure training for officials responsible for producing, reviewing, and approving disclosure, (2) establishing a procedure of accountability for review of relevant disclosure, and (3) ensuring that any procedures established are in fact followed."[660]

a. Enforcement Actions

In settling a number of enforcement actions, some issuers have agreed to improve their internal controls and disclosure policies and procedures in order to remedy disclosure and control deficiencies.[661] In one such case, the City of San Diego agreed to undertake a fundamental reorganization of the municipality's compliance structure.[662] The controls put in place as a result of the San Diego settlement have been cited by the attorneys in the municipal finance arena as a potential source of options that issuers should consider when determining what controls and procedures are appropriate for their circumstances.[663]

The San Diego restructuring included separating the city's audit function from financial management, and creating new positions, committees, and advisory groups to oversee the city's internal controls and disclosure.[664] One of the new advisory groups, the Disclosure Practices Working Group, was charged with developing, maintaining, and updating the city's disclosure protocols; the group was designed to be non-political and is tasked solely with ensuring that the city's disclosure is accurate and complete.[665]

Beyond these structural changes, San Diego hired new compliance staff, including employees with greater subject matter expertise,[666] and implemented a new computer system, with the input of outside consultants, designed to improve internal controls through better reporting.[667] Additional compliance enhancements included written documentation of processes, more robust training of personnel, and routine testing of internal systems.[668] The city has also implemented an anonymous whistleblower hotline to allow its employees to alert compliance personnel to problems.[669]

b. Market Participant Observations and Other Commentary

Participants at the Commission's field hearings also described the internal control and disclosure policies and procedures issuers have implemented.[670] One participant, for example, noted that a municipal entity has drafted written processes and policies to govern its work, including daily review of cash management and weekly or monthly review of debt.[671] Of note, he also stressed the fundamental utility of a broader governmental organization as a control device. For example, the participant indicated that the other boards, commissions, councils, and auditors comprising the political structure that includes the municipal entity act as a control *on* that entity because of the checks and balances that those other entities provide.[672] Similarly, he stated that the municipal entity's annual budget documents functioned as an additional disclosure mechanism because that process publicly discloses "legally controlling" information about the entity's financial condition.[673]

Other field hearing participants also recommended internal controls, specifically internal controls over financial reporting, and disclosure policies. These recommendations included the creation of an operational committee to help ensure that sound disclosure-related policies are observed, implementation of written policies and procedures governing controls, and the establishment of an independent internal audit function and employee compliance training programs that include internal and external advisors and participants.[674] Additionally, participants recommended Commission actions that would not involve additional rules or requirements for issuers:[675] specifically, one panelist recommended that the Commissioners or Staff use their "bully pulpit" in the form of speeches and roundtables to disseminate their views in this area.[676] The panelist also suggested that Commission enforcement actions provide meaningful, detailed descriptions of the deficiencies of issuer conduct.[677] These more detailed descriptions, it was suggested, would allow other municipalities to more clearly, determine which activities were deemed objectionable and which are being encouraged.

IV. MARKET STRUCTURE

A. Overview of Secondary Market for Municipal Securities

1. Municipal Securities

a. Overview

As discussed in Section I, the size of the municipal securities market is substantial and there is significant secondary market activity.[678] The municipal securities market also consists of many different types of securities, including general obligation bonds and various types of revenue bonds including conduit revenue bonds.[679] In addition, there is considerable variation in the specific terms of municipal securities due to, for example, the nature of the repayment source, credit enhancements, redemption features, and interest rate structure. Municipal securities are further differentiated by their tax implications, whether because of their state of issuance[680] or otherwise.[681]

b. Investors

Municipal securities, particularly tax-exempt municipal securities, are largely held by an individual or "retail" investor base.[682] Households as a group have represented the largest single category of owner of municipal debt outstanding for the past six consecutive years.[683] Individual investors today hold over 75% of the outstanding principal amount of municipal securities directly or indirectly (through mutual, money market, closed-end, and exchange-traded funds).[684]

c. Trading

Municipal securities trade in a decentralized over-the-counter dealer market.[685] Municipal bond dealers execute virtually all customer transactions in a principal capacity,[686] with a portion of these principal trades effected on a "riskless principal" basis.[687] Municipal bond trading is heavily concentrated, with the top ten municipal bond dealers accounting for approximately 75% of customer trades by par amount in 2011.[688]

The municipal securities market is characterized by relatively low liquidity and, following the initial distribution period, municipal securities trade only infrequently. For example, in 2011, about 99% of outstanding municipal securities did not trade on any given day.[689] For those bonds that do trade, the number of trades is very low, averaging only 14 customer trades during the first sixty days after issuance.[690] Newly issued municipal bonds are the most actively traded. While almost all municipal bonds trade in the first month after issuance, that figure drops to roughly 15% in the second month and declines substantially thereafter.[691] Once the bond finds its way into retail and institutional portfolios, the volume of trading tends to drop off dramatically.[692] An investor who wishes to buy municipal securities typically would request that its municipal bond dealer identify bonds with credit, payment, tax, maturity, and/or other characteristics that meet the customer's investment needs. The municipal bond dealer may recommend municipal securities that it holds in its own inventory or seek to obtain municipal securities from other municipal bond dealers in the over-the-counter market. If the municipal bond dealer wishes to contact another dealer, it may do so directly or use a "broker's broker": a municipal bond dealer that brokers transactions for other municipal bond dealers, typically through a combination of voice and electronic brokerage services.[693] The municipal bond dealer also may choose to access electronic platforms, including ATSs.[694] ATSs are designed to facilitate trading among municipal bond dealers by helping them locate other municipal bond dealers with municipal securities appropriate for their customers. While the municipal securities market is often described as a "buy-and-hold" market,[695] investors from time to time sell their bonds for a variety of reasons. An investor who wishes to sell municipal securities would typically contact a municipal bond dealer, who may offer to purchase the securities directly from the customer and take them into inventory.[696] If the municipal bond dealer does not wish to hold the customer's bond in inventory, it will assist its customer in finding a buyer, either by contacting other municipal bond dealers directly or by using a broker's broker or an ATS.[697] Once the customer's municipal bond dealer finds another municipal bond dealer willing to purchase the bonds, it typically will effect the transaction on a "riskless principal" basis by purchasing the securities from the customer and contemporaneously reselling them to the interested municipal bond dealer.[698]

The secondary market for municipal securities is relatively opaque.[699] As discussed below, while pricing information about completed trades (*i.e.*, post-trade information) has been available from the MSRB since 1995, information about the prices at which market participants may be willing to buy or sell a municipal security, and who might be interested, is not broadly available (*i.e.*, pre-trade information). In recent years, the necessity for market participants to undertake a more exacting analysis to value municipal securities has been made more apparent due to the declining use of bond insurance and other types of credit enhancement, as well as concerns about the reliability of credit ratings, both of which previously had been viewed as serving to "commoditize" assessments of the credit quality of disparate municipal securities and thereby often led market participants to make more simplified pricing judgments.[700]The relatively high overall levels of markups and other transaction costs in the municipal securities market generally are attributable to the illiquidity and opacity of the municipal securities market.[701] In addition, some studies have found that markups and transaction costs tend to be higher for smaller-sized "retail" trades than for larger institutional trades.[702] The lack of price transparency, as described below, also can make it difficult for customers – particularly retail customers – to assess the value of particular municipal securities, and the fairness of the prices that may be offered by municipal bond dealers.[703] Finally, the lack of price transparency undermines municipal bond dealers' ability to fulfill their fair pricing and best execution obligations, as well as regulators' ability to assess municipal bond dealers' compliance with those obligations.[704]

B. Specific Market Structure Topics

1. Price Transparency

a. Post-Trade Price Transparency

While the municipal securities market is relatively opaque, there have been significant improvements in recent years in the area of post-trade price transparency. The MSRB's Real-

Time Transaction Reporting System ("RTRS"), which, with limited exceptions, requires municipal bond dealers to submit transaction data to the MSRB within 15 minutes of trade execution, has been operational since 2005.[705] In addition, in early 2009, the MSRB implemented the Short-Term Obligation Rate Transparency ("SHORT") system to collect and disseminate current interest rates and related information for municipal auction rate securities and municipal variable rate demand obligations.[706]

Transaction data can be accessed by the public free-of-charge through the MSRB's EMMA website.[707] Data is searchable on EMMA and includes: trade date and time; security description and CUSIP number; maturity date; interest rate; price; yield;[708] trade amount;[709] trade type (i.e., customer bought, customer sold, or interdealer); and credit rating by S&P and Fitch, if available.[710]

Accordingly, current information about trades that have occurred in individual municipal securities is available today to those investors who seek it out,[711] as well as to data vendors who wish to incorporate it into their "value-added" products. This data also is available to regulators for surveillance and enforcement purposes.[712]

b. Pre-Trade Price Transparency

While the availability of post-trade transaction information has improved substantially in recent years, municipal securities investors have very limited access to pre-trade price information. Firm bid and ask quotations are generally not available for all municipal securities. Pre-trade price information is generally limited, as discussed below, to dealers providing indicative prices or submitting an RFQ through an electronic network operated by a broker's broker, an ATS, or otherwise.[713] This pre-trade price information, however, is not widely available to the public.

To the extent there is pre-trade price transparency in the municipal securities market, the Staff understands that it tends to be provided through electronic networks operated by broker's brokers, ATSs, or similar trading systems. Today, there are a number of ATSs and broker's brokers that provide municipal bond dealers with electronic access to other dealers who may be interested in trading municipal bonds.[714] While these trading platforms account for a substantial portion of municipal securities transactions, they represent only a small percentage of the dollar volume, which supports the premise that they are used primarily for smaller, retail-size orders.[715]

Larger institutional trades tend to be effected through more traditional means, such as direct voice negotiations with a municipal bond dealer or voice brokerage, and thus do not generate any pre-trade price transparency outside of the bilateral negotiation process.

ATSs and broker's brokers' systems tend to be "inventory-based," providing information only on the municipal securities their participating dealers would like to sell, and perhaps the prices sought (*i.e.*, offers).[716] Unlike a limit order book on an equities exchange or equity ATS, municipal securities ATSs typically provide no information on the participants who would like to buy or the prices at which they would be willing to do so (*i.e.*, bids). As an alternative to specifying a desired selling price, ATSs and broker's brokers may allow participants to disseminate an RFQ or bid-wanted message to initiate an ad hoc auction for the municipal securities they would like to sell.[717] While the RFQ alternative may be beneficial to selling municipal bond dealers in a variety of circumstances, it necessarily produces less in the way of publicly available pre-trade price transparency than an indicative quote, as responses to the RFQ generally are provided only to the selling municipal bond dealer.[718]

Although limited pre-trade price transparency for municipal securities is available through ATSs and broker's brokers, this information is not broadly accessible by the public for a number of reasons. First, the trading interest reflected on these systems is generally available only to their participating municipal bond dealers,[719] and is not directly accessible by or transparent to non-participants, such as retail investors.[720] While participating municipal bond dealers may at times share some of this information (*e.g.*, bonds offered from certain municipal bond dealer inventories) with particular customers (including retail investors) at their request or otherwise, this is done solely at the discretion of the municipal bond dealer. Second, the ATSs or broker's brokers may allow participants in their systems to limit the dissemination of their trading interest only to a subset of other municipal bond dealer participants in the system. For example, some ATSs permit a participant to apply filters so that their interest in a particular municipal security is conveyed only to its preferred trading partners. Thus, even the participants in an ATS or broker's broker's system may not have access to information about the trading interest of all other participants in that system.

c. Other Sources of Pricing Information

Because of the relative illiquidity and lack of transparency in the municipal securities market, market participants have developed alternative means to value municipal bonds.[721] For example, if there have been no recent trades reported to the MSRB, municipal bond dealers may look to see if recent trades have been reported in "comparable" bonds (*i.e.*, those with similar credit quality, maturity, and other key structural characteristics). Recent transactions in comparable securities provide insight into the price at which market participants may be willing to transact in a bond for which no recent trades have occurred.

In addition, market participants often rely on benchmark yield curves to assist in valuing a bond. A benchmark yield curve is a graph of the estimated current yield of bonds of similar credit quality across the range of possible maturities. Municipal Market Advisors ("MMA"), for example, publishes the "MMA AAA Median Municipal Benchmark," which represents an estimate of the mid-market price for a "natural" AAA-rated general obligation municipal bond (*i.e.*, has not been pre-refunded or insured) based on input MMA receives from a variety of municipal bond dealers and other institutions.[722] Similarly, Thomson Reuters' Municipal Market Data Group ("MMD") publishes the "MMD AAA-rated General Obligation Municipal Yield Curve."[723] The Staff understands that proprietary yield curves such as these are based both on objective facts – such as recent MSRB transaction reports – and subjective assessments of the opinions of market participants, news, economic conditions, and other factors. Market participants can use benchmark yield curves such as these to form judgments as to the value of a particular municipal bond by looking at the estimated yield for the comparable maturity and then making appropriate adjustments for differences in credit quality and other key characteristics.

Furthermore, because of the complexity of valuing illiquid municipal securities, market participants may rely on an independent professional pricing service to value their bonds.[724] These pricing services use available pre- and post-trade information to estimate the current market price of a particular municipal security, including the benchmark yield curves described above; relevant public information about the issuer, economic conditions, and other matters; and the pricing service evaluator's professional judgment.[725] Pricing services may be used, for example, by institutions to value their holdings, and by mutual funds to calculate daily net asset values.[726]

d. Access to Pricing Information

Municipal bond dealers generally have access to most or all of the sources of municipal securities pricing information described above, including transaction data reported to the MSRB; indicative quotes or RFQs disseminated by broker's brokers or ATSs; benchmark yield curves; and independent pricing services. Municipal bond dealers also may have access to other professional tools, such as Bloomberg terminals, that efficiently convey available pricing and other information (such as continuing disclosure filings) about a municipal issuer. Municipal bond dealers also may have the ability to do enhanced searches of transaction reports, enabling them to find efficiently last sale information of specific or comparable municipal securities.[727] Finally, municipal bond dealers maintain a variety of business relationships with competing dealers, customers, and other market participants that can informally provide them with insights into the supply and demand, valuation, market sentiment, and other key pricing determinants with respect to individual municipal securities.

Although institutional investors vary widely in size and sophistication, the larger ones tend to have access to a variety of sources of municipal securities pricing information.[728] This pricing information can include indicative quotes provided by their municipal bond dealer networks and post-trade transaction information provided by vendors and others.[729] Institutional investors also may directly employ analysts, traders, and other professionals who are experienced in using the available informational tools and making independent pricing judgments.[730]

Retail investors, on the other hand, have access to relatively little pricing information about municipal securities.[731] If they own municipal bonds, their monthly account statements typically include a valuation of the bonds, generally based on information from an independent pricing service.[732] Retail investors also can access the post-trade transaction information made available by the MSRB on EMMA for free. As noted above, however, most individual municipal securities trade only occasionally, so current prices may not be available. And because EMMA provides users with limited search capabilities, it can be difficult for a retail investor to look for recent prices of comparable securities.[733] While additional municipal securities pricing information, such as benchmark yield curves[734] and estimated prices,[735] is available on publicly accessible websites, retail investors generally may not be aware of it, may not have the expertise to use it effectively, or may not want to pay the fees required to access it. Unlike institutional investors, retail investors typically do not have access to indicative municipal bond dealer quotes, vendor services (such as market data vendors or third-party pricing services), or in-house experts. In fact, retail investors generally depend on their municipal bond dealers for quotes on municipal securities they would like to buy or sell.[736]

2. Transaction Costs

It is more expensive for investors to trade municipal securities than to trade corporate bonds or equity securities. For example, one study estimates that effective spreads[737] on retail-size trades of $20,000 are 1.98% for municipal bonds, compared to 1.24% for corporate bonds and 0.4% for equities.[738] Similar disparities are found for institutional-size trades.[739] Studies of dealer markups[740] have produced municipal security transaction-cost estimates of similar magnitude.[741] These relatively higher transaction costs have been attributed to the lack of liquidity and price transparency in the municipal securities market.[742]

Further, in the municipal securities market, transaction costs are generally higher, as a percentage of the par amount of the transaction, for retail investors than for institutional investors.[743] Effective spreads and dealer markups are higher for retail-size trades than for institutional-size trades.[744] The opposite is seen in the current U.S. equities market, where larger institutional-size trades tend to incur higher transaction costs than smaller retail-size trades.[745]

Some believe that the lack of price transparency in the municipal securities market is the primary reason that smaller trades in municipal bonds are more expensive than larger trades, rather than a municipal bond dealer's fixed trading costs.[746] In other words, in the view of some, because retail investors have less access to scarce pricing information than institutional investors, they are less able to bargain with dealers for a good price than are institutional investors.[747] Studies of trading in newly issued municipal securities have supported the premise that the opacity of the market contributes to the relatively higher prices paid by retail investors.[748] Additionally, studies have shown that retail-size trades in newly issued municipal securities occur at widely variable prices.[749] This phenomenon does not occur with larger institutional-size trades, and could indicate that institutional investors have more consistent access to better pricing information than retail investors.[750] The link between price dispersion and transparency is further supported by evidence that recent improvements in post-trade price transparency[751] dramatically reduced price dispersion.[752]

Others have provided additional suggestions for disparities between pricing of larger institutional-size trades and smaller retail-size trades. In the decentralized municipal securities market, extensive intermediation by multiple dealers may be required to find a willing counterparty, with each intermediary extracting compensation for its efforts. Consistent with this conjecture, one study documents that regardless of trade size, as the number of counterparties involved in placing a bond increases, so do trading costs.[753] There also is some evidence suggesting that there is more extensive dealer participation in smaller-size trades than in larger-size trades.[754] One study of an equity dealer market suggests that larger orders receive price improvement because of the structure of dealer markets.[755]

As noted above, trading in the municipal securities market is heavily concentrated, with the top ten dealers accounting for more than 70% of customer trades by principal amount.[756] Some data indicate that trading costs increase for municipal securities with the market power of the intermediating municipal bond dealer.[757] Average markups tend to increase the greater the municipal bond dealer's market share.[758] In addition, the significance of market power as a contributor to transaction costs is greater for smaller retail-size trades than for larger institutional-size trades.[759]

Finally, one study has concluded that, unlike equities, actively-traded municipal bonds do not have lower transaction costs than infrequently-traded ones.[760] According to this study, this phenomenon could be due to the lack of price transparency, among other reasons.[761]

3. Dealer Pricing Obligations to Customers

In general, MSRB rules require a municipal bond dealer effecting a transaction with a customer, whether as principal or agent, to trade at a fair price, and to exercise diligence in establishing the market value of the municipal security and the reasonableness of the compensation it receives.[762] With certain limited exceptions discussed below, these duties extend to all customers, whether retail or institutional, but not to other dealers.[763]

a. Fair Prices

MSRB rules require, among other things, that municipal bond dealers acting in a principal capacity with their customers purchase or sell municipal securities at a "fair and reasonable" price.[764] Specifically, MSRB Rule G-30(a) prohibits a municipal bond dealer from purchasing municipal securities for its own account from a customer or selling municipal securities for its own account to a customer except at an aggregate price (including any markdown or mark-up) that is fair and reasonable. In determining the price, the dealer must take into consideration all relevant factors, including its best judgment as to the fair market value of the securities at the time of the transaction, the expense involved in effecting the transaction, the fact that the dealer is entitled to a profit, and the total dollar amount of the transaction.[765] In addition, municipal bond dealers that charge excessive markups have been found to violate MSRB Rule G-17 which, among other things, requires them to deal fairly with their customers.[766]

Similarly, MSRB Rule G-18 requires municipal bond dealers acting in an agency capacity to make a reasonable effort to obtain a price for the customer that is fair and reasonable in relation to prevailing market conditions.[767] A dealer is expected to exercise the same level of care as it would if acting for its own account, including diligence in ascertaining prevailing market conditions.[768] Although these agency duties do not generally apply to dealers acting in a principal capacity, the MSRB has explicitly extended this obligation to a broker's broker acting on behalf of another dealer.[769] In addition, MSRB Rule G-30(b) prohibits municipal bond dealers from purchasing or selling municipal securities as agent for their customers for a commission or service charge in excess of a fair and reasonable amount, taking into consideration all relevant factors, including the availability of the securities involved in the transaction; the expense of executing or filling the customer's order; the value of the services rendered by the dealer; and the amount of any other compensation received by the dealer in connection with the transaction.[770]

The MSRB has interpreted a "fair and reasonable" price to be one that bears a reasonable relationship to the prevailing market price of the security.[771] The MSRB has noted that the most important factor is the yield, which should be comparable to the yield on other securities of comparable quality, maturity, coupon rate, and size then available in the market.[772] The MSRB has recognized that for some municipal securities - particularly those that are small in size and infrequently traded - it may be difficult for a dealer to determine the market value with precision and may require an assessment of market value based on a wider range of values than with well-known, more-liquid issues. The specific degree of accuracy, as well as the specific actions that a dealer may need to take to assess market value, will vary with the facts and circumstances. This could include a review of recent transaction prices for the issue or for comparable issues (*i.e.*, those with similar credit quality and features), or having a broker's broker use a bid-wanted procedure.[773]

In 2010, the MSRB sought comment on draft interpretive guidance with respect to the establishment of "prevailing market price" by dealers.[774] In the draft guidance, the MSRB viewed the prevailing market price as the inter-dealer market value of the securities at the time of the customer transaction.[775] The draft interpretive guidance would create a presumption that the prevailing market price is the dealer's contemporaneous cost.[776] If the dealer's cost is no longer contemporaneous, then the dealer would have to consider, in the following order: (a) any prices of contemporaneous inter-dealer transactions in the municipal security; (b) any prices of contemporaneous dealer transactions in the municipal security with institutional accounts; and (c) for actively traded municipal securities, any contemporaneous bids or offers for the municipal security made through an inter-dealer mechanism through which transactions generally occur at the displayed quotations.[777] In the event none of this pricing information is available, then other factors could be considered, including contemporaneous inter-dealer or institutional transactions in "similar" municipal securities; yields calculated from prices of contemporaneous inter-dealer or institutional transactions in similar securities; and yields calculated from validated inter-dealer bids or offers in similar securities.[778] Finally, if none of this information is available, then the dealer could consider prices and yields derived from appropriate economic models.[779] The MSRB received a variety of comments on its draft interpretive guidance,[780] but it has not yet filed a proposal with the Commission to incorporate that guidance into its rules.

b. Best Execution

Unlike in the equities and corporate fixed income markets,[781] there is no explicit MSRB rule regarding best execution that applies to market participants in the municipal securities market.[782] Common law duties of best execution, however, apply to municipal bond dealers, whether acting in a principal or agency capacity.[783] In agreeing to execute a customer's order, the municipal bond dealer makes an implied representation that it will execute the order in a manner that maximizes the customer's economic gain in the transaction.[784] This duty requires that a municipal bond dealer seek to obtain for its customer orders the most favorable terms reasonably available under the circumstances.[785] Although specific best execution requirements will vary depending on the particular facts and circumstances, municipal bond dealers generally should execute customer orders at the best reasonably available prices.[786] This requires municipal bond dealers to exercise diligence in informing themselves of the market value of a particular security.[787]

c. Customer Disclosure

MSRB Rule G-15 requires municipal bond dealers, at or before the completion of a transaction in municipal securities, to provide the customer with a written confirmation containing specified information about the transaction.[788] This includes information about the dollar price of the transaction and the resulting yield of the securities, calculated in a specified manner.[789] In addition, if the dealer is acting as agent, it generally must disclose any remuneration to be received from the customer in connection with the transaction.[790] If the dealer is acting as principal, however, there is no requirement that it disclose its markup on the confirmation, even for riskless principal transactions.[791] Although SEC Rule 10b-10 similarly does not require markup disclosure for riskless principal transactions in corporate bonds, it does require such disclosure on customer confirmations for equity securities.[792] Although the Commission has, in the past, proposed requiring confirmation disclosure of markups in riskless principal transactions for debt securities, it has never adopted such a requirement.[793]

In the Field Hearings, several commenters expressed concern about the lack of transparency surrounding dealer markups. Some complained that investors do not know how much they are paying in markups,[794] and others suggested that all markups and fees be disclosed to customers.[795]

V. RECOMMENDATIONS

This Report reflects input received from market participants through the public field hearings, meetings with Staff, and submissions to the Commission, as well as Staff-developed information, on the current state of the municipal securities market. The recommendations discussed below should be considered in conjunction with the relevant discussions contained in the body of the Report. While we believe, based on our review of the market as described in this Report, that these recommendations could help improve the municipal securities market, we recognize that any such further action on specific recommendations will involve further study of relevant additional information, including information as applicable related to the costs and benefits of the recommendations and the consideration as applicable of public comment.

A. Disclosure

In the disclosure context, the Report identifies a number of areas relating to primary and secondary market or continuing disclosure practices that should be improved. As described in this Report, market participants have called for greater and timelier disclosure by municipal issuers, raising specific concerns about disclosure in both primary offerings and on a continuing basis.[796] According to many market participants, the major challenge in secondary market disclosure continues to be the timeliness and completeness of filings.[797] In addition, market participants have noted that some issuers fail to comply with continuing disclosure agreements.[798] Market participants have also noted the lack of effective enforcement mechanisms to address non-compliance by issuers with continuing disclosure agreements.[799] As a result of this important input together with other information we have learned, we believe there are needed improvements in disclosure practices in the primary and secondary municipal securities market.

We recommend that Congress, the Commission and others could consider several potential approaches to further improve the municipal securities market and, in particular, to improve disclosure practices. We believe that improvements in the municipal securities market could involve a combination of approaches, including legislative, regulatory and industry-based initiatives. To the extent the Commission determines to pursue rulemaking efforts to implement any of these recommendations, the economic analysis, including costs and benefits, of any approach would be considered as part of a rule proposal.

First, in light of the Commission's limited regulatory authority, we recommend a number of potential legislative changes for consideration, which, if implemented by Congress, would provide the Commission with additional authority to take steps that it determines to be appropriate to directly impact municipal securities disclosures.

Second, there are a number of regulatory approaches that the Commission could consider pursuing under its existing authority. Although such measures could effect improvements, they may not be sufficient, on their own, to fully address the concerns discussed in this Report.

Third, we recommend that market participants continue to strive for high quality disclosure practices, through development and enhancement of best practices guidelines. Industry initiatives benefit from thorough knowledge and understanding of current market practices and consensus-building approaches. Rapid and meaningful change can be achieved through collaborative and concerted efforts by industry participants.

1. Legislative

The following are possible legislative approaches that could provide the Commission authority to establish improved disclosures and practices in the municipal securities market.

- Authorize the Commission to require that municipal issuers prepare and disseminate official statements and disclosure during the outstanding term of the securities, including timeframes, frequency for such dissemination and minimum disclosure requirements, including financial statements and other financial and operating information, and provide tools to enforce such requirements.

This legislative approach would provide the Commission authority to establish disclosure requirements and principles, timeframes and frequency of dissemination of municipal securities offerings and continuing disclosures. This legislative approach would not entail any repeal or modification to the existing proscriptions on the SEC or the MSRB requiring any presale filing of disclosure documents, known as the "Tower Amendment." Nor would this approach involve elimination of the exemptions for municipal securities under Section 3(a)(2) of the Securities Act or the exemptions under the Exchange Act. This legislative approach, however, would meaningfully enhance disclosure practices by municipal issuers and could be accomplished in a short period of time.

The Commission currently has limited authority over municipal issuers directly and providing enhanced authority with respect to municipal issuers' disclosures in connection with their municipal securities offerings would enable the Commission to enhance municipal securities disclosures and practices for all market participants. This Report has identified a number of areas in which the limited Commission authority over municipal issuers has affected its ability to improve disclosures and practices in the municipal securities market.

Provision of this authority is not intended to replicate corporate registration or periodic reporting requirements or to mandate Commission review of municipal securities disclosure. It would allow the Commission to consider scaled or tiered disclosure content and frequency provisions based on, among other things, the size and nature of the municipal issuer, the frequency of issuance of securities, the type of municipal securities offered and the amount of outstanding securities. This recommendation is intended to enhance disclosure in a meaningful way. The legislative proposal does not envision detailed line item disclosure requirements such as those applicable to corporate issuers under Regulation S-K. Rather it is intended as a more principles-based approach. Further, it would allow the Commission to consider appropriate exemptions based on the type of purchaser. Under this approach, the Commission could determine the appropriate dissemination mechanism, whether through Internet posting, submission to the MSRB's EMMA system or other electronic submission system. The Commission also could consider the appropriate disclosure policies and procedures that municipal issuers should have to assure that they will satisfy their primary and ongoing disclosure obligations.

- Amend the municipal securities exemptions in the Securities Act and Exchange Act to eliminate the availability of such exemptions to conduit borrowers who are not municipal entities under Section 3(a)(2) of the Securities Act, without differentiation based on the size of the financing due to the continuing availability of other exemptions, including those available for small businesses, private offerings, and non-profit entities that take into account different types of offerings and issuers.

This legislative approach, which the Commission first recommended over 15 years ago, would subject companies and other entities that use municipal securities to finance their projects to the registration and disclosure provisions of the federal securities laws - the same registration and disclosure standards that would apply if they issued their securities directly (not using municipal issuers as conduits).

Currently conduit borrowers (those non-municipal entities receiving proceeds from municipal securities offerings) may be subject to the Securities Act or Exchange Act registration or disclosure requirements because they may not be considered to be offering their own securities at the time of the municipal securities offering. It is important that investors have information about the entities that are responsible for the monies necessary to make payments on municipal securities in order to be able to assess their investments. This is especially true in light of the relatively high default rate of conduit bonds. As discussed above, conduit bonds have represented approximately 70% of all municipal bond defaults despite representing a relatively small percentage of municipal bonds issued.[800] In addition, many types of conduit municipal financings historically have been identified as providing substantially less continuing information than municipal securities not involving conduit borrowers.[801] Moreover, as discussed in the Report, the significant reduction in the use of financial guarantee insurance (bond insurance) for municipal securities means that there is a greater need for more information on the underlying conduit borrower, so that investors have the ability to evaluate their investment and exposure to the conduit borrower.

This approach would not eliminate other available exemptions, such as those for non-profit entities under Section 3(a)(4) of the Securities Act and other exemptions that are available to corporate issuers, such as the private offering exemption under Section 4(a)(2) of the Securities Act, without differentiation based on the size of the financing due to the continuing availability of other exemptions, including those available for small businesses, private offerings, and non-profit entities that take into account different types of offerings and issuers.

- Authorize the Commission to establish the form and content of financial statements for municipal issuers who issue municipal securities, including the authority to recognize the standards of a designated private-sector body as generally accepted for purposes of the federal securities laws, and provide the Commission with attendant authority over such private-sector body.

This legislative approach would provide explicit authority to the Commission to establish the form and content of financial statements used in municipal securities offerings and establish standards and designate a private-sector body as the GAAP standard setter for municipal issuer financial statements. As the Report notes, the Commission currently does not have authority to establish the form and content of financial statements of municipal securities issuers that are used in connection with primary offerings of municipal securities or provided on an ongoing basis in connection with outstanding municipal securities. Moreover, the Commission does not have direct authority over the standard setter for those financial statements. This authorization could be for purposes of the federal securities laws only, thereby allowing municipal issuers to continue to comply with other state accounting principles as applicable in the preparation of their financial statements. Most states already prepare their financial statements in accordance with GAAP as set by the GASB. This approach recognizes the importance of having financial statements of different issuers that are prepared on the same basis, thereby allowing comparisons between municipal issuers and municipal securities.

This approach would further the interests of the Commission and market participants in improving the presentation of financial information. As noted above, many market participants believed that adherence to GASB standards promotes consistency and comparability of financial information between and among municipal issuers and differing types of municipal securities.[802] In addition, many of the Commission's enforcement actions regarding materially misleading statements or omissions in official statements involved deficient financial statements provided by issuers or underlying obligors.[803]

- Authorize the Commission, as it deems appropriate, to require municipal securities issuers to have their financial statements audited, whether by an independent auditor or a state auditor.

Improving the quality of financial reporting by municipal securities issuers would further the interests of the Commission and market participants. As the Commission stated in the 1994 Interpretive Release, an audit is a "reasonable expectation" for investors to have.[804]

Additionally, audited financial statements are referred to in Rule 15c2-12[805] and in GFOA's guidelines and the CAFR program.[806] This legislative proposal could be a scaled or tiered requirement, beginning with the largest issuers.

- Provide a safe harbor from private liability for forward-looking statements of repeat municipal issuers who are subject to and current in their ongoing disclosure obligations that satisfy certain conditions, including appropriate risk disclosure relating to such forward-looking statements, and if projections are provided, disclosure of significant assumptions underlying such projections.

As noted above, improved availability of forward-looking or trend information regarding a municipal issuer or an obligated person is of importance to market participants.[807] At the same time, some market participants are concerned about potential legal risk involved when municipal issuers provide such information on an ongoing basis.[808] Currently municipal issuers, as any other issuer of securities, can rely on the case-law established "bespeaks caution" doctrine when providing forward-looking information. Notwithstanding this, some have expressed continuing concerns with respect to the provision of forward-looking information in the municipal securities market. There are options for the Commission to consider in terms of encouraging the provision of forward-looking information while at the same time preserving the application of the antifraud provisions of the federal securities laws to disclosures.

This safe harbor would encourage municipal issuers to provide forward-looking information and would be available only to those municipal issuers that provide ongoing public disclosures and provide such information on a current and timely basis. This safe harbor would be similar to the Private Securities Litigation Reform Act safe harbor for reporting public companies[809] and would apply only to private rights of action for antifraud violations.

- Permit the Internal Revenue Service to share with the Commission information that it obtains from returns, audits, and examinations related to municipal securities offerings in appropriate instances and with the necessary associated safeguards, particularly in instances of suspected securities fraud.

As discussed above, Section 6103 of the Code does not permit the IRS to disclose return information to the Commission and Commission staff in connection with civil enforcement of the securities laws.[810] Were the IRS able to share with the Commission in appropriate instances information it obtains from returns, audits, and examinations, Commission enforcement actions relating to municipal securities would be more consistent, comprehensive, and timely. Furthermore, it would promote the efficient use of our limited resources and improve compliance by participants in the municipal securities market.

In the past, IRS Tax Exempt Bonds Division Directors have publicly acknowledged the value of such increased information sharing, should Congress choose to pass the necessary legislation.[811] Moreover, this change would be consistent with the recent guidelines prepared by GAO to assist Congress in evaluating proposed exceptions to Section 6103.[812]

- To provide a mechanism to enforce compliance with continuing disclosure agreements and other obligations of municipal issuers to protect municipal securities bondholders, authorize the Commission to require trustees or other entities to enforce the terms of continuing disclosure agreements.

The Commission does not have authority to enforce issuer compliance with continuing disclosure agreements that are provided as a condition to an underwriting of municipal securities subject to Rule 15c2-12, and no entity is required to enforce the terms of continuing disclosure agreements. Additionally, as noted above, market participants have suggested that noncompliance with continuing disclosure agreements is a problem among some issuers,[813] and some have highlighted the lack of effective enforcement mechanisms to address such non-compliance.[814] Providing the Commission authority to require an enforcement mechanism for continuing disclosure agreements would allow the Commission to provide important protections for bondholders.

2. Regulatory

There are a number of possible actions that the Commission could pursue under its existing regulatory authority to improve disclosures and practices in the municipal securities market.

- The Commission could host market participants, regulators, and academics at an annual conference on the municipal securities markets.

The Commission could organize and host an annual conference on the municipal securities markets in order to allow market participants to confer with one another and to share with the Commission important developments in the municipal securities market. Through such a conference, market participants and the Commission would be able to discuss important issues in the municipal securities market, allowing the Commission to stay informed about municipal securities market conditions and ongoing issues in the market. In our view, such a conference would benefit the Commission and other interested parties, by fostering regulatory and industry cooperation through open and continuous dialogue.

- The Commission could consider issuing updated interpretive guidance regarding disclosure obligations of municipal securities issuers and others.

The Commission could consider updating the interpretive guidance the Commission previously provided to municipal securities market participants in the 1994 Interpretive Release. This guidance could recognize the significant improvements in municipal securities disclosure since the 1994 Interpretive Release and the adoption of amendments to Exchange Act Rule 15c212 and identify areas where the Commission thinks that improvement is still needed, based in part on the number of significant disclosure-related enforcement cases involving municipal securities brought since 1994, including, among other matters, financial statements and financial information, terms and risks of securities (including derivatives), and conflicts of interest and other relationships and practices. Updating the interpretive release would allow the Commission to provide further guidance through a means other than enforcement actions.

- The Commission could consider amendments to Exchange Act Rule 15c2-12 to further improve the disclosures made regarding municipal securities.

The Commission could consider further amendments to Exchange Act Rule 15c2-12 to improve the disclosures made with respect to municipal securities, both in primary offerings and on an ongoing basis. The Commission and market participants have identified a number of areas in which there could be improvements in the disclosure practices regarding municipal securities and where amendments to Rule 15c2-12 may be helpful. These amendments would not be needed, however, if the Commission receives direct authority over municipal issuer disclosures as discussed in the legislative recommendations above. The Commission could consider amendments to Exchange Act Rule 15c2-12, including the following:

- amend the definition of final official statement to include required disclosure about the terms of the offering, including the plan of distribution, any retail order period, and the price to be paid for the municipal securities in the initial issuance;[815]
- mandate more specific types of disclosures in municipal securities official statements and ongoing disclosures, including event disclosures relating to issuance of new debt (whether or not subject to Rule 15c2-12 and whether or not arising as a result of a municipal securities issuance), primary offering disclosures relating to risks of the

municipal securities, and disclosures about underlying obligors (regardless of the existence of credit enhancement or insurance);[816]

- provide a method to address noncompliance issues regarding continuing disclosure undertakings, including possibly by adding conditions that would require that issuers have disclosure policies and procedures in place regarding their disclosure obligations, including those arising under continuing disclosure undertakings;[817]
- consider modifications regarding application of the rule to demand securities and underwritten municipal fund securities offerings;[818] and
- improve the accessibility of disclosures, including the use of shortened or summary official statements and increased use of websites.[819]

The Commission should continue to work with the MSRB to strengthen its rules and further enhance EMMA

The MSRB has broad authority, as expanded by the Dodd-Frank Act, to adopt rules to regulate broker-dealers, municipal securities dealers and municipal advisors. In furtherance of its mission to protect investors, state and local government issuers, other municipal entities and the public interest by promoting a fair and efficient municipal market, the MSRB regularly evaluates the effectiveness of its rules as market practices evolve. In carrying out the Commission's responsibilities for overseeing self-regulatory organizations, the Staff works closely with the MSRB staff, as well as FINRA staff, through regularly scheduled meetings and informal discussions to discuss emerging trends and potential regulatory solutions. Market participants have widely praised the MSRB for its development of EMMA and its continued improvements to the system. We note that EMMA has significantly improved access to issuer disclosures and other market information for investors. The Commission should continue the collaborative work with the MSRB, especially in identifying potential rule changes or new rules that could address some of the issues discussed in this Report. New rules or rule changes could include amending Rule G-19 (suitability) in a manner generally consistent with recent amendments by FINRA to its Rule 2111, including with respect to the scope of the term "strategy"[820] and otherwise harmonizing MSRB rules with similar FINRA rules.

The MSRB also serves as the central repository for continuing municipal securities disclosure, through EMMA. EMMA has significantly improved access to issuer disclosures and other market information for investors. The MSRB should promptly pursue enhancements to its EMMA website, including those referenced in its Long-Range Plan for Market Transparency Products, so that retail investors have better access to disclosure with respect to municipal securities as soon as practicable.[821]

The Commission and the MSRB should continue to analyze and discuss potential further enhancements to EMMA including making improvements so that disclosure data can be analyzed by specific types of municipal securities and by having the MSRB list issuers that are non-compliant with their continuing disclosure obligations on EMMA in order to assist broker-dealers, municipal securities dealers and investors in determining which issuers are noncompliant.

3. Municipal Market Initiatives

We also recommend that municipal issuers and other market participants continue to work together on initiatives to improve municipal securities market disclosures and other practices.

- Municipal market participants should follow and encourage others to follow existing industry best practices and expand and develop additional best practices guidelines in a number of areas to enhance disclosures and disclosure practices in the municipal securities market.

Best practice guidelines allow market participants to develop solutions to issues that arise in a time- and cost-efficient manner. Participants in the municipal securities market historically have worked together to develop best practice guidelines in the disclosure and other arenas. As discussed in this Report, many industry groups have established best practice guidelines to address various aspects of disclosure practices.[822] There remain a number of areas, however, where market participants could develop additional best practices or work together to enhance existing best practices or industry guidelines that may further improve disclosures and disclosure practices in the municipal securities market.

While we are encouraged by the existing guidelines and the willingness of industry groups to voluntarily discuss and generate a consistent way of measuring successful disclosure and accounting processes, we believe that industry participants should continue to refine these guidelines and explore new areas for guidance.

Voluntary industry initiatives would be useful in improving practices relating to the following areas:

- disclosure policies and procedures for primary offering and ongoing disclosures, including issuer disclosure committees and training programs;[823]
- improve timeliness of financial information in primary offerings and on an annual basis;[824]
- availability of quarterly or other interim financial information;[825]
- increased use of issuer websites;[826]
- presentation of and access to information in municipal securities offerings and on an ongoing basis;[827]
- use of derivatives in connection with municipal securities;[828] and
- education efforts for investors, issuer officials and financial intermediaries.

B. Market Structure

Price transparency is vital for assuring that markets are fair and efficient, and providing meaning to fair pricing and best execution obligations. As discussed above, the municipal securities market is relatively illiquid and opaque, with substantially less transparency than the equities markets, particularly on a pre-trade basis. This inhibits the efficiency of the municipal securities market, which has relatively high-transaction costs compared to the equities market, especially for retail-size trades. The lack of price transparency may also undermine the ability of municipal securities dealers to fulfill their fair pricing and best execution obligations,[829] as well as investors and regulators to assess their compliance therewith.

Meaningful steps to improve price transparency should both improve the efficiency of the municipal securities market and better protect investors.[830] The wider availability of more robust pricing information should facilitate the ability of market professionals and their customers to determine the best price for a security and where to obtain it. This should promote price competition among market participants, thereby reducing transaction costs and improving market efficiency. Better transparency also should facilitate compliance by municipal securities dealers with regulatory requirements, and provide investors with critical information to help assess whether they receive the best prices.

Accordingly, there are a variety of recommendations that could be explored to improve transparency in the municipal securities market, both on a pre-trade and post-trade basis, and make more meaningful existing fair pricing and best execution obligations. To the extent the Commission determines to pursue rulemaking efforts to implement any of these recommendations, the economic analysis, including costs and benefits, of any approach would be considered as part of a rule proposal. We note that, although we examined these issues in the context of our review of the municipal securities market, the Staff also could consider further study of relevant additional information to determine the extent to which these issues or similar issues could be relevant to the market for corporate fixed income securities.

1. Improve Pre-Trade Price Transparency

Because there is so little pre-trade transparency in the municipal securities market today, we believe consideration should be given to possible ways to provide more information about bids and offers, or other trading interest, widely to market participants. Two ideas that we believe warrant serious thought are set forth below. As these or other potential initiatives to improve pre-trade price transparency are examined in more detail, consideration should also be given to the associated costs and benefits, including the potential impact on liquidity and dealer participation in the market.

- The Commission could consider amendments to Regulation ATS to require an alternative trading system (ATS) with material transaction or dollar volume in municipal securities to publicly disseminate its best bid and offer prices and, on a delayed and non-attributable basis, responses to "bids wanted" auctions.

The order display and execution access provisions of Regulation ATS currently do not apply to ATSs that trade municipal securities. A potential regulatory approach to this issue is to amend Regulation ATS to require an ATS with significant trading volume (*e.g.*, 5% of average daily transaction or dollar volume in municipal securities) to provide to the MSRB, for public dissemination, its best priced bids and offers for municipal securities that the ATS displays to more than one person.[831] In accordance with Regulation ATS, these material ATSs also would be required to provide municipal bond dealers fair access to those prices. The Commission also should work with the MSRB to explore the feasibility of enhancing the MSRB's EMMA (or other) system to collect best bids and offers from material ATSs and make them publicly available on fair and reasonable terms. Finally, the Commission could consider amending Regulation ATS to require material ATSs to provide to the MSRB on a delayed (*e.g.*, end-ofday) and non-attributed basis, for public dissemination, the best-priced bids submitted in response to "bids wanted" auctions conducted on the ATS.

As discussed above, while ATSs today represent only a small percentage of overall dollar volume in municipal securities, they account for a substantial portion of the number of transactions (perhaps as high as 30-50%), and appear to be used primarily for smaller retail size orders. Accordingly, the prices displayed by dealers on ATSs – which today often are available only to ATS subscribers – represent a potentially valuable source of pricing information to retail investors and their broker-dealers. Enhancing the transparency of the best prices on these platforms, and assuring that market participants have fair access to them, could facilitate best execution, improve market efficiency, and promote price competition in municipal securities.

- The MSRB could consider rules requiring a brokers' broker with material transaction or dollar volume in municipal securities to publicly disseminate the best bid and offer prices on any electronic network it operates and, on a delayed and non-attributable basis, responses to "bids wanted" auctions.

For similar reasons, the MSRB could consider rules requiring municipal bond dealers that are brokers' brokers, and that have significant trading volume in municipal securities, to provide to the MSRB for public dissemination, on a delayed (*e.g.*, end-of-day) and non-attributed basis, the best-priced bids submitted in response to "bids wanted" auctions conducted by such brokers' broker. The Commission also should work with the MSRB to explore the feasibility of enhancing the MSRB's EMMA (or other) system to collect this pricing information from material brokers' brokers and make it publicly available on fair and reasonable terms.

2. Improve Post-Trade Price Transparency

- The MSRB could consider requiring municipal bond dealers to report "yield spread" information to its Real-Time Transaction Reporting System (RTRS) to supplement existing interest rate, price and yield data.

Although the MSRB has made great strides in recent years in improving post-trade transparency for municipal securities, investors may benefit from additional information regarding completed transactions. For example, dealers often quote municipal securities prices in terms of "yield spreads" (*i.e.*, the difference between the yield on the municipal security traded and the yield on an applicable benchmark security). Yields spreads can be expressed by reference to risk-free Treasury securities, or to benchmark municipal yield curves such as those produced by MMA or MMD. In either event, yield spreads offer a standardized way of expressing the risk premium paid for a municipal security and, given the wide variety of municipal securities and their illiquidity, may help investors assess the pricing of municipal securities and make relative value comparisons. They also could help municipal securities dealers, academics and regulators assess the quality of trade executions in the municipal securities market.

Accordingly, the MSRB could consider amendments to MSRB Rule G-14 that would require municipal bond dealers to report additional transaction data to RTRS, including yield spread information, and make that information publicly available on its EMMA website.

- The MSRB should promptly pursue enhancements to its EMMA website so that retail investors have better access to pricing and other municipal securities information.

The transaction and other municipal securities information now available to investors on the MSRB's EMMA website represents a substantial improvement over what was available to investors prior to EMMA. As noted above, however, retail investors continue to have access to substantially less pricing information than institutional investors and municipal bond dealers. As the MSRB indicated in its recently-issued *Long-Range Plan for Market Transparency Products*,[832] and as noted by participants in the Commission's Field Hearings, additional steps could be taken to enhance both the nature of the information made available by the MSRB on the EMMA website, and the ease with which it can be utilized by retail investors. These could include enhanced search functionality (*e.g.*, based on characteristics of the security or issuer), analytical tools and research, and additional pricing-related market data, such as available yield curves.

In addition to the recommendations above concerning disclosure-related enhancements to EMMA, the MSRB should promptly pursue other enhancements to its EMMA website, including those referenced in its *Long-Range Plan for Market Transparency Products*, so that retail investors have easier access to pricing information as soon as practicable.

3. Buttress Existing Dealer Pricing Obligations Alternative Execution Options

- The Commission and the MSRB should consider initiatives to improve the understanding of retail investors as to the various ways in which they might buy or sell a municipal bond, and the relative advantages and disadvantages of each.

As discussed above, if a customer wishes to buy a municipal security, its broker may obtain the security in a variety of ways. The broker may sell the customer securities from its own inventory if it is a municipal securities dealer, or it may obtain them directly from another municipal securities dealer. Alternatively, the broker may use a brokers' broker to find the municipal securities or see if the securities are being offered on an ATS. Similarly, if a customer wishes to sell a municipal security, its broker may purchase the customer securities and hold them in inventory if it is a municipal securities dealer, or it may seek out another dealer that is willing to purchase them directly. A brokers' broker also may be used to find another dealer that wants to buy the securities, or the broker could make a "request for quote" on an ATS. The method the broker uses to purchase or sell a municipal security for its customer can materially impact the price and timeliness of the transaction. For example, a dealer may be able to quickly sell (purchase) a municipal security from (into) its inventory, providing the customer certainty of execution, but this may come at the expense of a better price that might be obtained if the customer's order were exposed to competition.

Retail investors may not be aware of the variety of options that exists for buying or selling a municipal security, or their relative advantages and disadvantages. Accordingly, the

Commission and the MSRB should consider initiatives to improve the understanding of retail investors in this area. For example, initiatives that would require municipal bond dealers to disclose to retail customers, at account opening and annually thereafter, relevant information about their execution options could be considered. Consideration also could be given to enhancements to investor education programs in this area. Relevant information to be conveyed to retail investors might include:

1) the customer may purchase the security from the municipal bond dealer's inventory, or sell to the dealer to hold in inventory, if the municipal bond dealer is in a position to do that;
2) the customer may have its dealer contact its network of other municipal bond dealers for potential interest;
3) the customer may have its dealer seek trading interest by using the services of a brokers' broker or an ATS to which it has access; and
4) the potential benefits, risks and costs of each of these execution options.

- The Commission and the MSRB could consider ways to encourage the use of ATSs or similar electronic networks that widely disseminate quotes and provide fair access.

Today, there is very limited pre-trade price transparency in the municipal securities market and, to the extent it exists, such transparency is provided through electronic networks such as ATSs. Pre-trade price transparency is beneficial to the markets, in that it facilitates best execution, improves market efficiency, and promotes price competition. These benefits are maximized if pre-trade pricing information is made widely available to market participants, and fair access is provided to the trading interest represented thereby. Fostering the development of ATSs or similar electronic networks that widely disseminate quotes and provide fair access could improve the market structure for municipal securities, and provide better prices for investors.

Accordingly, the Commission and the MSRB could explore ways to encourage the use of transparent execution venues such as these. For example, consideration could be given to a rule requiring municipal bond dealers to affirmatively offer retail customers the option of exposing their orders on one or more ATSs that widely disseminate quotes and provide fair access. These ATSs could include the "material" ATSs that may become subject to the order display and execution access provisions of Regulation ATS, if the review recommended above results in Regulation ATS amendments, as well as smaller ATSs that have elected to voluntarily meet these requirements. Such a rule could, as a practical matter, require dealers effecting municipal securities transactions for retail customers to become subscribers to these ATSs or arrange for indirect access to them. Customers that elect to expose their orders on such ATSs could obtain better prices, as well as contribute more broadly to the price discovery process in the municipal securities market. Another alternative that could be considered is requiring a municipal bond dealer to expose a retail customer order on one or more of these ATSs before it executes as principal, unless the customer affirmatively opts out of this process.

Disclosure of Pricing Information

- The MSRB should consider encouraging or requiring municipal bond dealers to provide retail customers relevant pricing reference information in connection with any municipal securities transaction a municipal bond dealer effects for such customer.

Retail investors today have access to substantially less pricing information than institutional investors and municipal bond dealers. Although the MSRB has enhanced the pricing and other information available to the public on its EMMA website, and we recommend further improvements as discussed above, retail investors may benefit from having relevant pricing reference information provided to them by their municipal bond dealers in connection with a municipal securities transaction. Among other things, ready access to such pricing reference information could allow retail customers to better assess whether they have received best execution and could discipline municipal bond dealer fair pricing obligations.

Accordingly, the MSRB should consider encouraging or requiring municipal bond dealers, in connection with any transaction effected for a retail customer, to provide such customer relevant pricing information. This information might include:

1) Recent transactions in the municipal security bought or sold by the customer, with an indicator as to whether they are interdealer or customer transactions, as reported to the MSRB's EMMA database; and if there are no recent transactions in such security, similar transaction information for comparable securities;
2) Current quotation information for the municipal security bought or sold by the customer, including those reflected on ATSs or similar electronic networks, as well as the bids received from any bids-wanted or RFQ process pursued by the dealer in connection with the customer's transaction; and
3) The "yield spread" of the customer's transaction to applicable benchmarks, such as to Treasury securities or municipal yield curves.

Enhanced Fair Pricing Guidance and Markup Disclosure

- The MSRB should consider issuing more detailed interpretive guidance to assist dealers in establishing the "prevailing market price" for a municipal security, for purposes of determining whether the price offered a customer (including any markup or markdown) is fair and reasonable.

As discussed above, determining the prevailing market price for municipal securities, particularly those that are illiquid, can be a complex task. If there have been no recent transactions in the particular security to be bought or sold, other sources of pricing information must be considered, such as the prices of "comparable" securities, benchmark yield curves or other economic models. In 2007, the Commission approved detailed interpretive guidance proposed by FINRA that establishes a framework for how a dealer should determine the prevailing market price for non-municipal debt securities in a variety of scenarios.[833] Although the MSRB, in 2010, sought comment on similar draft interpretive guidance that would apply to municipal securities, the MSRB has not yet filed a proposal with the Commission to incorporate that guidance into its rules. Providing municipal securities dealers a clear and consistent framework as to how they should approach the complex task of establishing the prevailing market price of municipal securities – particularly those that are illiquid – should enhance their ability to comply with fair pricing obligations, facilitate regulators' ability to enforce those obligations, and better protect customers.

Accordingly, the MSRB should consider possible rule changes that would set forth more detailed guidance as to how dealers should establish the "prevailing market price" for municipal securities, and that is consistent with that provided by FINRA for non-municipal debt securities.

- The MSRB should consider requiring municipal bond dealers to disclose to customers, on confirmations for riskless principal transactions, the amount of any markup or markdown.

While MSRB Rule G-15 generally requires municipal bond dealers to disclose to customers on the transaction confirmation the amount of any remuneration to be received from the customer, if they are acting as agent, there is no comparable requirement if the dealer is acting as principal. As discussed above, however, municipal bond dealers execute virtually all customer transactions in a principal capacity, including on a "riskless principal" basis. As a result, customers today receive very little in the way of confirmation disclosure of their dealer's compensation. Because riskless principal transactions are very similar, as a practical matter, to agency transactions, and the amount of the markup or markdown is readily determinable, confirmation disclosure of a municipal bond dealer's compensation in these circumstances should allow customers to more effectively assess the fairness of the prices provided by dealers.

This type of disclosure would be comparable to the Rule 10b-10 disclosures required when transacting in equity securities on a riskless principal basis.[834]

Accordingly, the MSRB should consider possible rule changes that would require municipal bond dealers acting as riskless principal to disclose on the customer confirmation the amount of any markup or markdown. The Commission should also consider whether a comparable change should be made to Rule 10b-10 with respect to confirmation disclosure of markups and markdown in riskless principal transactions for corporate bonds.

- The MSRB should consider a rule that would require municipal bond dealers to seek "best execution" of customer orders for municipal securities.

As discussed above, MSRB rules generally require municipal bond dealers to trade with customers at "fair and reasonable" prices and to exercise diligence in establishing the market value of municipal securities and the reasonableness of their compensation.[835] The MSRB, however, has not expressly imposed on municipal bond dealers an obligation to seek "best execution" for customer orders by evaluating where, among the variety of venues at which municipal securities may be executed, the most favorable price for the customer might be obtained.[836] We note that FINRA does impose such an obligation on corporate bond dealers by requiring them, among other things, to use reasonable diligence to ascertain the best market for the security, and buy or sell in such market so that the resultant price to the customer is as favorable as possible under prevailing market conditions.[837]

The municipal securities market offers a variety of options for executing a transaction, including the dealer buying or selling from its own inventory, seeking prices from other dealers, or using the services of a brokers' broker or ATSs. Which of these various options offers the most favorable terms reasonably available may vary substantially depending on the security in question, the needs of the customer, and the other particular facts and circumstances. Incorporating a best execution obligation into MSRB rules and providing related guidance, similar to FINRA's approach to corporate fixed income securities, could buttress dealer fair pricing obligations and improve execution quality for municipal securities investors.

Accordingly, the MSRB should consider possible rule changes that would require municipal bond dealers to seek "best execution" of customer orders in connection with municipal securities transactions and provide more detailed guidance to municipal bond dealers on how "best execution" concepts would be applied in connection with transactions in municipal securities.

End Notes

[1] In 1975 there were $235.4 billion of municipal securities outstanding after an issuance of $58 billion in that year. *See* The Bond Buyer's Municipal Finance Statistics, 1975 (June 1976).

[2] Staff generated statistics. Data source: Mergent's Municipal Bond Securities Database ("Mergent's MBSD"). This data is current through December 31, 2011. The number of issuers is inferred by the number of unique six-digit CUSIPs. The amount outstanding is consistent with data from the Federal Reserve Board, which points to $3.74 trillion of municipal securities outstanding at the end of the fourth quarter of 2011. *See also* Federal Reserve Board, "Flow of Funds Accounts of the U.S.," Table L.211 (Fourth Quarter 2011), *available at* http://www.federalreserve.gov/releases/z1/Current/z1.pdf ("Fourth Quarter Flow of Funds Data").

[3] *See* Securities Industry and Financial Markets Association ("SIFMA"), "US Bond Market Issuance, quarterly data," *available at* http://www.sifma.org/WorkArea/linkit.aspx?Link Identifier=id&ItemID=25100&lib ID=9266.

[4] *See* Fourth Quarter Flow of Funds Data, *supra* note 2. *See infra* § II.A.3 (Investors in Municipal Securities).

[5] *See, e.g.*, SIFMA, "U.S. Bond Markets Average Daily Trading Volume," *available at* http://www.sifma.org/uploadedFiles/Research/Statistics/StatisticsFiles/CM-US-Bond-Market-TradingVolume-SIFMA.xls (Mar. 14, 2012), accessed Apr. 18, 2012. *See infra* § II.A.5 (The Secondary Market for Municipal Securities).

[6] Municipal Securities Rulemaking Board ("MSRB"), "2011 Factbook (2011)" at 8-9, *available at* http://www.msrb.org/msrb1/pdfs/MSRB2011FactBook.pdf ("MSRB 2011 Factbook").

[7] If the retail-size cutoff was $100,000 instead of $25,000, the amount of principal traded in 2011 in "retail sized" trades was less than $183 billion in more than 5.9 million transactions. Staff generated statistics. Data source: MSRB 2011 Factbook at 44-45.

[8] *See* Chairman Mary L. Schapiro, "Remarks at Investment Company Institute 2010 General Membership Meeting" (as delivered by Andrew J. Donohue), Washington, DC (May 7, 2010), *available at* http://www.sec.gov/news/speech/2010/spch050710mls.htm.

[9] *See* SEC Release No. 2010-164 "SEC Sets Field Hearings on State of Municipal Securities Markets: First Hearing Scheduled for San Francisco September 21" (Sep. 7, 2010), *available at* http://www.sec.gov/news/press/2010/2010-164.htm.

[10] *See* SEC Release No. 2010-233 "SEC Announces Agenda and Panelists for Second Field Hearing on State of Municipal Securities Markets: Hearing Scheduled for December 7 in Washington, DC" (Nov. 23, 2010), *available at* http://www.sec.gov/news/press/2010/2010-233.htm.

[11] *See* SEC Release No. 2011-148 "SEC Announces July 29 Field Hearing on the State of the Municipal Securities Market" (July 15, 2011), *available at* http://www.sec.gov/news/press/ 2011/2011-148.htm. Budgetary constraints caused the Commission to reduce the number of hearings from six, as originally planned, to three.

[12] Agendas for each of the hearings, listing panel topics and panelist names and affiliations, are available at http://www.sec.gov/spotlight/municipalsecurities.shtml.

[13] These transcripts and videos, as well as a number of other documents, are available for reference at http://www.sec.gov/spotlight/municipalsecurities.shtml. The transcript of the San Francisco Field Hearing is hereinafter referred to as the "San Francisco Hearing Transcript." The transcript of the Washington, DC Field

Hearing is hereinafter referred to as the "Washington, DC Hearing Transcript." The transcript of the Birmingham Field Hearing is hereinafter referred to as the "Birmingham Hearing Transcript."

[14] *See* Exchange Act Release No. 62853, "State of the Municipal Securities Market Field Hearings" (Sept. 10, 2010), 75 FR 53392 (Sept. 10, 2010), *available at* http://www.sec.gov/rules/other/2010/34-62853.pdf. Memoranda documenting these meetings and conference calls, as well as comments from the public, are available at http://www.sec.gov/comments/4-610/4-610.shtml.

[15] The comment submission form is available at the website reference above. *See supra* note 13.

[16] At least fifty submissions from market participants, investors and others were made.

[17] The Internal Revenue Code ("IRC") delineates the purposes for which tax-exempt municipal bonds may be issued for the benefit of organizations other than states and local governments, *i.e.*, conduit borrowers. *See* IRC § 141.

[18] *See generally* American Bar Association Section of State and Local Government Law, American Bar Association Section of Business Law Committee on Federal Regulation of Securities, & National Association of Bond Lawyers, *Disclosure Roles of Counsel In State and Local Government Securities Offerings* (3d ed. 2009) ("Disclosure Roles of Counsel").

[19] *Id.* at 2.

[20] *Id.* at 78.

[21] Staff generated statistic. Data source: Mergent's MBSD, *supra* note 2.

[22] Staff generated statistic. Data source: Mergent's Fixed Income Securities Database ("Mergent's FISD") (data available as of June 2011).

[23] Fourth Quarter Flow of Funds Data, *supra* note 2, at Tables L.

[24] *See infra* note 58 and accompanying text.

[25] Staff generated statistics. Data Source: SDC Platinum. Long-term issuances – those with maturity of 13 months or longer – represented 78.5% of issuances and a corresponding 83.0% of principal in 2011. Issuance of long-term securities has experienced a general upward trend over the past 10 years, whereas the amount of short-term securities has fluctuated within a narrow band of $41-72 billion over the same period. The significant drop in municipal-bond issuance in 2011 was reflected in lower issuances of both long-term and short-term securities.

[26] *See, e.g.*, Ben Levisohn, "Five Reasons to Rethink the Muni Rally," Wall Street Journal, May 21, 2011, *available at* http://online.wsj.com/article/SB10001424052748 70428 1504576329791701338436.html; Morgan Stanley SmithBarney, Municipal Bond Monthly, Feb. 10, 2012 ("MSSB February Report") (discussing issuance patterns that were prevalent in 2011).

[27] *See, e.g.*, Rafael Costas, "2011 Year-End Municipal Bond Market Review," Franklin Templeton Investments Commentary, Dec. 8, 2011, *available at* https://www.franklin templeton.com/retail/app/commentary/views/ commentary_detailedpage.jsf?category= FUNDMGRCOM&commentaryURL=%2Ftemplatedata%2FCommentary%2F Commentary%2Fdata%2FUS_Market_Perspectives%2FCostas_2011_YearEndMuni Review.xml; MSSB February Report, *supra* note 26.

[28] *See, e.g.*, Lyle J. Fitterer and Robert J. Miller, "Low levels of municipal bond issuance may provide technical pricing support during the low-yield environment," Wells Fargo Advantage Funds, Municipal Fixed Income, Sept. 2011, *available at* http://www.wellsfargoadvantagefunds.com/wfweb/wf/funds/ perspectives/ ip_2011 0926.jsp?sel=%2fDTF% 2fFunds%2fCommentaries&pf=1.

[29] For a description of the types of municipal securities issued, *see generally* Robert A. Fippinger, *The Securities Law of Public Finance*, §1:6 (3d. ed. 2011) ("Fippinger"). *See also* Robert Doty, *Bloomberg Visual Guide to Municipal Bonds* (2012) at 43-78, for suggestions of municipal securities categories.

[30] In the last four years, conduit bonds represented roughly 10% of municipal principal issued. Staff generated statistic. Data source: Mergent's MBSD (based on corporate-backed bond data). For an alternative estimate see Nathaniel Popper, "Conduit Muni Bond Defaults Draw Scrutiny," Los Angeles Times, June 14, 2011, *available at* http://articles.latimes.com/ 2011/jun/14/business/la-fi-risky-municipals20110614 (suggesting that conduit bonds represent 20% of all municipal bonds based on data from Income Securities Advisors).

[31] Definition of "Conduit Financing" in Glossary of Municipal Securities Terms, Municipal Securities Rulemaking Board ("MSRB") (2d ed. 2004), *available at* http://www.msrb.org/msrb1/glossary/default.asp ("MSRB Glossary"); Exchange Act Release No. 33741, "Statement of the Commission Regarding Disclosure Obligations of Municipal Securities Issuers and Others" (Mar. 9, 1994), 59 FR 12748 (Mar. 9, 1994) ("1994 Interpretive Release").

[32] *See infra* notes 124 - 126 and accompanying text.

[33] *See* Neil O'Hara, SIFMA, *The Fundamentals of Municipal Bonds, 6th Edition* (2012) at 247 ("Fundamentals of Municipal Bonds 2012").

[34] *See* David L. Taub, *Understanding Municipal Derivatives*, Aug. 2005, Government Finance Review 21. One hearing participant noted that municipal entities in one state did not use derivatives prior to 1999 when the investment banking community lobbied government officials to sponsor legislation specifically authorizing interest rate swaps. Birmingham Hearing Transcript at 219-20 (Collier). A similar process occurred in many states. *See, e.g.*, Martin Z. Braun and William Selway, "Hidden Swap Fees by JP Morgan, Morgan Stanley Hit School Boards," Bloomberg, Feb. 1, 2008 (noting that financial firms pushed for changes to Pennsylvania law allowing derivative transactions in 2003), *available at* http://www.bloomberg.com/apps/news?pid=news archive&sid=ay5LDbjbjy6c ("Braun and Selway").

[35] W. Bartley Hildreth, and C. Kurt Zorn, *The Evolution of the State and Local Government Municipal Debt Market over the Past Quarter Century*, Public Budgeting & Finance, 25: 127–153 (2005). *See also* Birmingham Hearing Transcript at 241 (Collier) (indicating that interest rate swap agreements are essentially the only kind of municipal derivatives that she sees); 243-244 (Turner) (noting that some municipal entities have turned to interest rate caps to manage their exposure to interest rate risk). An interest rate cap is an option purchased by the issuer that pays the issuer if its interest costs exceed a specified rate. A collar is a pair of options that establish a cap and a floor. The issuer pays if its interest costs go below a specified rate and the counter-party pays if the interest costs exceed the specified rate. A collar reduces out-of-pocket, up-front costs of the option premium paid by the issuer but requires it to pay the counter-party if interest costs go below the floor established by the collar.

[36] *See* Fundamentals of Municipal Bonds 2012, *supra* note 33, at 247.

[37] Definition of "Zero Coupon Bond" in MSRB Glossary, *supra* note 31.

[38] Definition of "Variable Rate Demand Obligation" in MSRB Glossary, *supra* note 31. *See also* MSRB, "Municipal Auction Rate Securities and Variable Rate Demand Obligations: Interest Rates and Trading Trends," Sept. 2010, *available at* http://www.msrb.org/Publications/~/ media/Files/SpecialPublications/ MSRBARSandVRDOReportSeptember2010.ashx ("MSRB ARS and VRDO Publication").

[39] *See* MSRB ARS and VRDO Publication, *supra* note 38 ("Through the put or tender feature, holders seeking to liquidate a position can put the securities to a tender agent. A specified amount of notice is required to be provided to the tender agent and during that notification period, the remarketing agent seeks to find a purchaser for the securities that have been tendered. If the remarketing agent is unable to find a purchaser for the tendered securities, the tender agent will draw on a liquidity facility, such as a letter of credit or standby bond purchase agreement, to fund the purchase price of the tendered VRDO if the remarketing agent does not otherwise purchase the tendered VRDO.").

[40] *See, e.g.,* Fundamentals of Municipal Bonds 2012, *supra* note 33, at 38-39.

[41] Staff generated statistics. Data source: SDC Platinum. *See also* Fundamentals of Municipal Bonds 2012, *supra* note 33, at 39-40 ("VRDO issuance plummeted after the 2008 financial crisis, when banks came under pressure to boost their regulatory capital and became less willing or able to provide low margin standby liquidity facilities").

[42] Staff generated statistics. Data source: SDC Platinum. For purposes of generating these statistics, VRDOs were defined as long-term putable securities with variable rate coupons and put frequency of a year or less.

[43] Definition of "Auction Rate Securities" in MSRB Glossary, *supra* note 31.

[44] *See* Gary Gray and Patrick Cusatis, *Municipal Derivative Securities: Uses and Valuation* (1995) at 41("Gray and Cusatis").

[45] *See* MSRB ARS and VRDO Publication, *supra* note 38 (citing Jeffrey Rosenberg, *et al.*, *Debt Research –Cross Product*, Bank of America Report, (Feb. 13, 2008)).

[46] In testimony before the House of Representatives Committee on Financial Services in September 2008, then Director of the Division of Enforcement, Linda Chatman Thomsen, identified several factors that contributed to the freezing of the ARS market. ("One factor is the significant increase in the size of the ARS market, which had grown to $330 billion by the time of the freeze. This larger market required the firms to find more and more customers to bid in the auctions. An additional reason for the market seizure is the rating agencies' downgrades of the monoline insurers (*e.g.*, Ambac Financial Group Inc, and MBIA Inc.), which provided insurance for many ARS to ensure that holders would receive repayment of their principal if the issuer defaulted. These downgrades resulted in the loss of customers willing to invest in ARS. Another factor that contributed to the freeze is the sub-prime mortgage and credit crisis that unfolded throughout the second half of 2007, which limited the firms' ability to support the auctions with their own capital. In fact, firms stopped supporting the auctions in mid-February 2008, and the entire market froze in a matter of days. The securities

became illiquid, leaving tens of thousands of customers unable to sell their ARS holdings."). *See* "Testimony Concerning The SEC's Recent Actions With Respect to Auction Rate Securities" by Linda Chatman Thomsen, Director, Division of Enforcement, U.S. Securities and Exchange Commission, Before the Committee on Financial Services, Sept. 18, 2008, *available at* http://www.sec.gov/news/ testimony/2008/ts091808lct.htm. On March 14, 2008, the Commission staff issued a no-action letter setting forth its views that issuers and conduit borrowers of municipal ARS could – within the bounds of applicable laws and regulation – participate in auctions for their own securities. *See* Letter to Leslie M. Norwood and Anne Phillips Ogilby (Mar. 14, 2008), *available at* http://www.sec.gov/divisions/corpfin/cf-noaction/2008/mars031408.pdf.

[47] Since 2008, state and local governments have converted many of their ARS to other types of municipal securities and have redeemed more than half of the municipal ARS. *See* Michael McDonald, "Auction Supply 'Tsunami' Portends Municipal Losses," Bloomberg (Mar. 3, 2008), *available at* http://www.bloomberg.com/apps/news?pid=newsarchive&sid= aJpRkYBhnffQ. The Commission has settled enforcement actions with a number of large investment firms for alleged improper activity in the marketing and sales of ARS, including municipal ARS. Under the Commission settlements, the firms agreed to repurchase a significant amount, although not all, of the outstanding ARS that were sold improperly. *See, e.g.*, SEC Litigation Release No. 20166, "SEC Finalizes ARS Settlements With Bank of America, RBC and Deutsche Bank, Providing Over $6 Billion in Liquidity to Investors" (June 3, 2009), *available at* http://www.sec.gov/litigation/litreleases/2009/lr21066.htm; SEC Litigation Release No. 20824, "SEC Finalizes Auction Rate Securities Settlements With Citigroup and UBS Providing Nearly $30 Billion in Liquidity to Investors" (Dec. 11, 2008), *available at* http://www.sec.gov/litigation/litreleases/2008/lr20824.htm. Similarly, the Financial Industry Regulatory Authority ("FINRA") has announced settlement agreements with a number of firms relating to violations incurred in connection with the sale of ARS. *See, e.g.*, "FINRA Announces Agreements with Four Additional Firms to Settle Auction Rate Securities Violations" (May 7, 2009), *available at* http://www.finra.org/ Newsroom/NewsReleases/2009/P118646.

[48] Staff generated statistics. Data source: SDC Platinum. *See also* Gretchen Morgenson, "A Way Out of the Deep Freeze," New York Times, Nov. 8, 2009, at BU1, *available at* http://www.nytimes.com/2009/11/08/business/ economy/08gret.html; Jeremy R. Cooke, "Student Lenders Stifled by Auction Rate Bond Failures," Bloomberg (Apr. 4, 2008), *available at* http://www.bloomberg.com/apps/news?pid=newsarchive &sid=a8p51DTC.Pzk.

[49] *See infra* § II.C.6 (Credit Enhancers).

[50] "Letter of credit" in a municipal financing has been defined as a commitment, usually made by a commercial bank, to pay principal of and interest on the securities in the event the issuer cannot do so, subject to certain conditions and/or the occurrences of certain events. MSRB Glossary, *supra* note 31.

[51] *See* Gray and Cusatis, *supra* note 44, at 29-32.

[52] *See infra* § II.C.6 (Credit Enhancers) (noting that the major bond insurers suffered ratings downgrades).

[53] A "standby purchase agreement" is "an agreement with a third party, typically a bank, in which the third party agrees to purchase tender option bonds (typically variable rate demand obligations) tendered for purchase in the event that they cannot be remarketed. Unlike a letter of credit, a standby bond purchase agreement does not guarantee the payment of principal and interest by the issuer and is not an unconditional obligation to purchase the tender option bonds." MSRB Glossary, *supra* note 31.

[54] Staff generated statistics. Data source: SDC Platinum. However, governmental guarantee programs have grown since 2008. *See infra* note 284 and accompanying text.

[55] SEC Office of Economic Analysis & SEC Office of Municipal Securities, "Report on Transactions in Municipal Securities" (Jul. 1, 2004), at 30, *available at* http://www.sec.gov/ news/studies/munireport2004.pdf ("2004 Municipal Securities Report").

[56] IRC § 103. *See also* Treas. Reg. 1.103-1(a) under the Internal Revenue Code.

[57] Staff generated statistics. Data source: SDC Platinum.

[58] BABs allowed municipalities to issue an unlimited amount of taxable debt through the end of 2010, and entitled issuers to elect to either (1) receive an amount from the Treasury Department equal to 35% of the interest paid on the issued bonds or (2) provide bondholders with a tax credit equal to 35% of the stated interest on the bond that can be applied towards their income tax liability. *See generally* MSRB, "Build America Bonds," *available at* http://www.msrb.org/Market-Topics/Build-America-Bonds.aspx.

[59] In addition to BABs, the ARRA introduced two additional categories of taxable bonds, Qualified School Construction Bonds (IRC § 54F) and Recovery Zone Economic Development Bonds (IRC §§ 1400U-2), and expanded the authority to issue taxable New Clean Renewable Energy Bonds (IRC § 54C), Qualified Energy Conservation Bonds (IRC § 54D) and Qualified Zone Academy Bonds (IRC § 54E). Exchange Act Release

No. 62184A, "Amendment to Municipal Securities Disclosure" (May 26, 2010), 75 FR 33100, n.251 (June 10, 2010), *available at* http://www.sec.gov/rules/final/2010/34-62184afr.pdf. BABs emerged as the most popular of the three ARRA-created taxable bonds.

[60] Staff generated statistics. Data source: SDC Platinum.

[61] *See* United States Government Accountability Office ("GAO"), "Report to Congressional Committees, Municipal Securities: Overview of Market Structure, Pricing, and Regulation," GAO-12-265 (January 2012), at 5, *available at* http://www.gao.gov/assets/590/587714.pdf ("GAO Market Structure Report") (noting that retail investors tend to hold municipal securities to maturity).

[62] *See, e.g.,* Peter Fortune, *The Municipal Bond Market, Part I: Politics, Taxes, and Yields,* New England Economic Review, Sept./Oct. 1991, *available at* http://www.bos.frb.org/economic/ neer/neer1991/ neer591b.pdf.

[63] The Tax Reform Act of 1986 denied banks and other financial institutions a deduction for that portion of the taxpayer's otherwise allowable interest expense that is allocable to tax-exempt obligations acquired by the taxpayer after August 7, 1986. The Act provided an exception to the 100-percent disallowance rule for qualified tax-exempt obligations acquired by a financial institution. Under the Act, qualified tax-exempt obligations included any obligation which (1) is not a private activity bond as defined by the Act, and (2) is issued by an issuer which reasonably anticipates to issue not more than $10 million of tax-exempt obligations (other than private activity bonds) during the calendar year. Interest allocable to such obligations remained subject to the 20-percent disallowance contained in prior law. *See* Staff of the Joint Committee on Taxation, "General Explanation of the Tax Reform Act of 1986," May 4, 1987, at 558-566, *available at* http://www.jct.gov/jcs-10-87.pdf. The American Recovery and Reinvestment Act of 2009 (ARRA) temporarily increased the $10 million limit to $30 million and provided other incentives for banks to purchase tax-exempt bonds during 2009 and 2010.

[64] Staff generated statistic. Data source: "Federal Reserve Board, Flow of Funds Accounts of the United States, Annual Flows and Outstandings (1965 to 1974)" (June 8, 2001), *available at* http://www.federalreserve.gov/ releases/z1/20010608/annuals/a1965-1974.pdf.

[65] Staff generated statistic. Data Source: Fourth Quarter Flow of Funds Data, *supra* note 2.

[66] *See id.*

[67] *See id.*

[68] *See* Sara Lepro, "Banks Urged to Reassess Holdings of Muni Bonds," The Bond Buyer, Feb. 23, 2011, *available at* http://www.bondbuyer.com/issues/120 36/banks-municipal-bond-holdings-1023552-1.html.

[69] *See, e.g.*, Ianthe Jean Dugan, "Banks Turn to Public Borrowers," Wall Street Journal, Feb. 16, 2011, *available at* http://online.wsj.com/article/SB2000142405274870 331290457 6146511419336334.html; *See, e.g.,* James Ramage, "Direct Bank Purchases of Muni Debt Raise Issues," The Bond Buyer, Oct. 26, 2011, *available at* http://www.bondbuyer.com /issues/120_206/direct-bank-purchase-muni-debt-10324491.html?partner=sifma. The MSRB has published a notice to alert municipal market participants that, under existing legal principles described below, certain financings that are called "bank loans" may, in fact, be municipal securities. *See* MSRB Notice 2011-52, "Potential Applicability of MSRB Rules to Certain "Direct Purchases" and "Bank Loans" (Sept. 12, 2011), *available at* http://www.msrb.org/Rules-andInterpretations/Regulatory-Notices/2011/2011-52.aspx.

[70] *See, e.g.,* Banks Turn to Public Borrowers, *supra* note 69 (attributing the increase to: banks seeking alternatives to loans for mortgages and other "risky" areas; compliance with international rules that require banks to put aside more capital to buffer against losses (*see* description of Basel III *infra* notes 282-283); and banks seeking a means of restoring strained relationships with clients); Christine Albano, "Banks Bulked Up Their Muni Bond Portfolios in 2011," The Bond Buyer, March 27, 2012, *available at http://www.bondbuyer.com/issues/121_59/banks-holders-municipal-debt-1037847-1.html* (citing a market participant who noted that banks are able to avoid Basel III capital requirements and earn a tax-exempt spread rather than a taxable letter of credit fee); "Banks Urged to Reassess Holdings of Muni Bonds," *supra* note 68 (suggesting that bank relationships through deposit services, direct loans and other traditional banking products are critical at a time when banks are not lending heavily).

[71] *See* Definition of "Syndicate," MSRB Glossary, *supra* note 31.

[72] *See* Fundamentals of Municipal Bonds 2012, *supra* note 33, at 97 and Sylvan Feldstein and Frank Fabozzi, *The Handbook of Municipal Bonds* (1st ed. 2008), at 54 ("Feldstein and Fabozzi").

[73] Historically, road shows were conducted in person but market participants are increasingly conducting these presentations through the use of internet webcasting or similar technologies – so-called "electronic road shows." *See* Fundamentals of Municipal Bonds *2012*, *supra* note 33, at 104.

[74] *See id. See also* Fippinger, *supra* note 29, § 6:9.

[75] Staff generated statistics. Data source: SDC Platinum. In terms of principal amount issued in 2011, negotiated sales comprised 69.5% and competitive sales comprised 26.3%.

[76] Staff generated statistics. Data source: SDC Platinum. The relatively low percentage of competitively-bid transactions is consistent with the trend over the past 10 years. Some types of municipal securities, including general obligation bonds, may be required by state law to be offered under competitive bidding. *See* Fundamentals of Municipal Bonds 2012, *supra* note 33, at 70 and Feldstein and Fabozzi, *supra* note 72, at 52.

[77] Staff generated statistics. Data source: SDC Platinum.

[78] *See* Caitlin Devitt, "Private Placements Take Off Thanks to Expiring LOCs," The Bond Buyer, Feb. 13, 2012, *available at* http://www.bondbuyer.com/pdfs/2012_bb_stats_supp.pdf. *See also*, Michael McDonald, "Banks Cash in on Whitney's Muni Default Scare," Bloomberg, Dec. 14, 2011, *available at* http://www.bloomberg.com/news/2011-12-14/default-defying-muni-rally-shows-dimon-departs-fromwhitney-as-banks-buy.html.

[79] *See* Fundamentals of Municipal Bonds 2012, *supra* note 33, at 97, 102; *see also* Feldstein and Fabozzi, *supra* note 72, at 54.

[80] *See* Fundamentals of Municipal Bonds 2012, *supra* note 33, at 102.

[81] *Id.* at 97; *see also* Feldstein and Fabozzi, *supra* note 72, at 54-55. The Government Finance Officers Association ("GFOA") recommends that municipal entities select underwriters using a competitive RFP or request for qualifications ("RFQ"). *See* GFOA, *GFOA Best Practice: Selecting Underwriters for Negotiated Bond Sales* (2008), *available at* http://www.gfoa.org/downloads/SELECTINGUNDERWRITERS%20.pdf. A large number of municipal entities, however, use other practices. *See, e.g.*, State of Florida Report No. 2011-196, "Local Government Financial Reporting System Performance Audit" (June 2011), at 13, *available at* http://www.myflorida.com/audgen/pages/pdf_files/2011-196.pdf (finding that in 42% of its sample, the municipal entity did not use a competitive RFP or RFQ to select an underwriter for a negotiated bond sale).

[82] *See* Fundamentals of Municipal Bonds 2012, *supra* note 33, at 102.

[83] *See id.* at 102.

[84] *See id.*

[85] *See id.* at 102-103.

[86] *See id.* at 99, 101. *See also, e.g.,* Glenn L. Stevens, "Evaluation of Underwriter Proposals for Negotiated Municipal Bond Offerings, Public Administration and Management: An Interactive Journal," 4, 4, 1999, at 435-468, *available at* http://www.spaef.com/file.php? id=328.

[87] Kenneth N. Daniels and Jayaraman Vijayakumar, *Does Underwriter Reputation Matter in the Municipal Bond Market?*, JOURNAL OF ECONOMICS AND BUSINESS (2007), at 500-519; Alexander W. Butler, Larry Fauver, and Sandra Mortal, *Corruption, Political Connections, and Municipal Finance*, THE REVIEW OF FINANCIAL STUDIES (2009), at 2673-2705; Arthur C. Allen and Donna Dudney, *Does the Quality of Financial Advice Affect Prices?*, THE FINANCIAL REVIEW (2010), at 387-414.

[88] Mark D. Robbins, *Testing the Effects of Sale Method Restrictions in Municipal Bond Issuance: The Case of New Jersey*, PUBLIC BUDGETING & FINANCE (2002), at 40–56.

[89] Craig O. Brown, *Self-Dealing in Securities Issuance: Evidence from State Government Bond Pricing*, 2009, *available at* http://ssrn.com/abstract=1885301.

[90] *See id.* at 105; *see also* Feldstein and Fabozzi, *supra* note 72, at 52-53.

[91] *See* Fundamentals of Municipal Bonds 2012, *supra* note 33, at 97 and Feldstein and Fabozzi, *supra* note 72, at 53.

[92] *See* Fundamentals of Municipal Bonds 2012, *supra* note 33, at 99.

[93] MSRB Rule G-14(b). The MSRB's Real-Time Transaction Reporting System has been operational since 2005. *See* footnote 705 and related text. Prior to 2005, dealers were required to report transactions in municipal securities by midnight on the trade date. *See*, MSRB Notice 2004-29 "Approval by the SEC of Real-Time Transaction Reporting and Price Dissemination: Rules G-12(F) and G-14" *available at* http://www.msrb.org/Rules-and-Interpretations/Regulatory-Notices/2004/2004-29.aspx.

[94] MSRB Rule G-34(a)(ii)(C) requires underwriters to submit to a new issue information dissemination system a "Time of Formal Award" (as defined therein), a "Time of First Execution" (as defined therein) and certain other information.

[95] MSRB Rule G-14 RTRS Procedures § (a)(ii)(A) generally permits primary market sales transactions executed on the first day of trading to be reported by the end of the day on which the trade is executed instead of within 15 minutes of the time of trade as required for most trades.

[96] *See* Exchange Act Release No. 67344, "Notice of Filing of Proposed Rule Change to Amend Rule G-34, on CUSIP Numbers, New Issue, and Market Information Requirements" (SR-MSRB-2012-06) (Jul. 3, 2012), 77

FR 40668 (Jul. 10, 2012), *available at* http://www.sec.gov/rules/sro/msrb/2012/34-67344.pdf ("MSRB NRO Proposal").

[97] *Id. See also* Letter from Susan Gaffney, GFOA, to Elizabeth M. Murphy (Nov. 10, 2011), *available at* http://www.sec.gov/comments/4-610/4610-76.pdf ("GFOA NRO Letter") (indicating that real-time market reporting is provided to information vendors within minutes of a competitive sale bid opening or during a negotiated sale marketing period).

[98] *See* Definition of "NRO (Not Reoffered) Maturity" in MSRB Glossary, *supra* note 31.

[99] *See* MSRB NRO Proposal, *supra* note 96. A related issue is the practice of printing "NRO" in the final official statement.

[100] *See, e.g.*, GFOA NRO Letter, *supra* note 96; Letter from Thomas Doe, Municipal Market Advisors, to Alicia Goldin, Division of Trading and Markets (June 14, 2011), *available at* http://www.sec.gov/comments/4-610/4610-50.pdf.

[101] *See* GFOA NRO Letter, *supra* note 96. (Noting that the practice of "NRO" reporting may also assist in the "often discussed but never documented" practice of "parking" bonds with an investor at a special price during the underwriting period and then repurchasing or marking up those same securities after the end of the underwriting period).

[102] *See* MSRB NRO Proposal, *supra* note 96.

[103] *See, e.g.,* Lawrence E. Harris and Michael S. Piwowar, *Secondary Trading Costs in the Municipal Bond Market*, J.FIN. (June 2006) at 1361-1363 (analyzing municipal securities transactions using data through October 2000) ("Harris and Piwowar").

[104] A "principal trade" is "a securities transaction in which the broker-dealer effects the transaction for its proprietary account." Definition of "Principal Trade" in MSRB Glossary, *supra* note 31.

[105] *See* Harris and Piwowar, *supra* note 103, at 1363. Trading on a riskless principal basis is similar, conceptually, to a municipal bond dealer trading on an agency basis. In these transactions, the municipal bond dealer is not putting its capital at risk. For example, when it receives a customer order to buy, the municipal bond dealer will offset the sale to the customer by contemporaneously purchasing the security sold to the customer. *See e.g.*, Exchange Act Rule 3a5-1(b).

[106] "MSRB Registrants by Company Name," *available at* http://www.msrb.org/msrb1/pqweb/ registrants.asp (accessed Apr. 19, 2012).

[107] *See* GAO Market Structure Report, *supra* note 61.

[108] *See supra* notes 6-7 and accompanying text.

[109] *See supra* notes 5 (trading volume), 21 (municipal bonds outstanding) and 22 (corporate bonds outstanding). According to the MSRB, in 2011, the ADTV was $13 billion, with an average of 41,241 trades per day in 15,213 unique securities. *See* MSRB 2011 Factbook, *supra* note 6. If trading on the first day a security begins to trade is excluded (a rough proxy for excluding most primary distribution trades), approximately $10.3 billion in principal of municipal securities traded on a daily basis, with an average of 39,105 trades per day. This estimate was provided by MSRB staff based upon data collected for the MSRB 2011 Factbook. The Staff understands that the volume discrepancy between the SIFMA (11.3 billion ADTV in 2011) and MSRB ($13 billion of ADTV in 2011) is attributable in part to the inclusion by the MSRB of certain transactions not included by SIFMA. Specifically, the MSRB includes in its statistics special reporting transactions, such as repurchase agreements and commercial paper, which the Staff understands are not included in the SIFMA statistics.

[110] *See infra* notes 689 - 692 and accompanying text.

[111] *See supra* note 93. *See generally infra* § IV.B.1.a (Post-Trade Price Transparency).

[112] A monetary default occurs when an issuer fails to pay interest or principal due on its securities. A "technical" default occurs when an event of default occurs, such as when an issuer fails to comply with a specified term of the bond contract. In either case, the bond contract may provide for a cure period that allows the default to be remedied. Thus, a default may constitute only a brief interruption of payments, a payment from a reserve fund, or a period during which the issuer may remediate the violated covenant and does not necessarily indicate that there will be any interruption of payments on the underlying debt. Unless specified otherwise, references to default in this section refer to monetary default. A recent press article noted that default statistics can vary widely depending on the definition of default. *See* Robert Slavin, "Muni Defaults Up 111% and Down 38%, Depending on Data," The Bond Buyer, April 3, 2012, *available at* http://www.bondbuyer.com/ issues/121_64/muni-defaults-2012-up-and-down-1038128-1.html ("Slavin Article"). The article points to two different data sources: one that suggests that, in the first two months of 2012, municipal bond defaults decreased significantly compared to the same period in 2011 (S&P Capital IQ, based on a monetary default

definition); and another that suggests the opposite (Distressed Debt Securities Newsletter, based on a technical default definition).

[113] *See, e.g.*, Moody's Investors Service, "The U.S. Municipal Bond Rating Scale: Mapping to the Global Rating Scale And Assigning Global Scale Ratings to Municipal Obligations" (Mar. 2007), *available at* http://www.moodys.com/sites/products/DefaultResearch/ 102249_RM.pdf, ("Moody's Global Study"); Report to Accompany H.R. 6308, 110th Congress, Serial No. 110-835 (Feb. 14, 2008), § 205, *available at* http://frwebgate.access.gpo.gov/cgi-bin/getdoc.cgi?dbname=110_cong_reports&docid=f:hr835.110 (comparing the cumulative historical default rates of municipal and corporate bonds) ("Municipal Bond Fairness Act Report").

[114] "Obligations rated Baa are subject to moderate credit risk. They are considered medium grade and as such may possess certain speculative characteristics." *See* Moody's Investors Service, "Ratings Symbols and Definitions," Apr. 2012, *available at* http://www.moodys. com/researchdocumentcontentpage.aspx?docid= PBC_79004 ("Moody's Symbols and Definitions"). A "BBB" rating by S&P represents "[a]dequate capacity to meet financial commitments, but more subject to adverse economic conditions." *See* Standard & Poor's Ratings Services, Credit Ratings Definitions & FAQs, *available at* http://www.standardand poors.com/ratings/definitions-and-faqs/en/us (accessed on May 15, 2012) ("S&P Definitions").

[115] "Obligations rated Aaa are judged to be of the highest quality, with minimal credit risk." *See* Moody's Symbols and Definitions, *supra* note 114. A "AAA" rating by S&P represents "[e]xtremely strong capacity to meet financial commitments. Highest Rating." *See* S&P Definitions, *supra* note 114.

[116] *See* Moody's Global Study and Municipal Bond Fairness Act, *supra* note 113. More recently, Moody's Investors Service said in a study released in February 2010 that the 10-year average cumulative default rate in the municipal market was 0.09 percent from 1970 to 2009 for the municipal securities it rates, compared with 11.06 percent over the same time period for the corporate debt it rates. Most were concentrated among nonprofit health-care and housing projects. Moody's Investors Service, "U.S. Municipal Bond Defaults and Recoveries, 1970-2009" (Feb. 2010), *available at* http://www.naic.org/documents/ committees_e_capad_ vos_c1_factor_review_sg_related_docs_moodys_us _municipal_bonds.pdf. *See also* "Default Risk and Recovery Rates on U.S. Municipal Bonds, Fitch Ratings," 1 (Jan. 9, 2007), *available at* http://www.cdfa.net/cdfa/cdfaweb.nsf/ ordredirect.html?open&id=fitchdefaultreport.html ("Fitch Study") (finding that as of the end of 2002, regardless of rating, the 5-15 year cumulative default rate in the subsectors of state and local government general obligation, lease and tax-backed debt, single-family housing, public higher education, public power distribution and water and sewer revenue bonds averaged 0.24%, which was less than the 10-year cumulative default rate of 0.43% for "AAA" rated global corporate bonds).

[117] Fitch has observed that it is not aware of any state that permanently defaulted on its general obligation or tax-backed debt in the post-Civil War era. Additionally, in its study Fitch assumes a 100% recovery rate on several broad sectors of municipal bonds including state and local government tax-backed debt and appropriation-backed lease debt, and debt backed by a variety of public enterprises. Fitch Study, *supra* note 116, at 3. Moody's noted that "given the unique bankruptcy laws that govern municipalities and the anticipated near 100% recovery rate on any defaulted general obligation bond" they would expect that "general obligation bonds in default but with an anticipated recovery of 100 percent would likely be rated Ba1 on the corporate scale." "Special Comment: Moody's US Municipal Bond Rating Scale," Moody's Investor Service, 11 (Nov. 2002), *available at* http://www.moodys.com/ sites/products/DefaultResearch/2001700000407258.pdf. Historically, the amount of permanent losses on municipal debt is small when compared to the amount of municipal defaults. For example, permanent losses of principal and interest for the period 1945-1965 were less than .01% of the total municipal debt outstanding in 1965. Of the $13.5 billion of municipal bonds in default in 1932, only $200 million, or 1.48% of the bonds in default were permanent losses. *See* Ann Gellis, *Mandatory Disclosure for Municipal Securities: A Reevaluation*, 36 BUFFALO L. REV. 15, 26 n.30 (1987) (citing John Peterson, The Rating Game 110, 111 (1974)).

[118] *See generally* S&P, "A Complete Look at Monetary Defaults in the 1990s" (June 2000), *available at* http://www.kennyweb.com/kwnext/mip/paydefault.pdf ("S&P Report"). *See also* Moody's Global Study (regarding municipal defaults of Moody's rated municipal securities).

[119] Joe Mysak, "Subprime Finds New Victim as Muni Defaults Triple," Bloomberg (May 30, 2008), *available at* http://www.bloomberg.com/apps/news?pid=newsarchive &sid=aGP25 Nnw2JIY.

[120] Darrell Preston, "Municipal Defaults Continue at Triple the Typical Rate, Lehmann Says," Bloomberg (Jul. 16, 2010), *available at* http://www.bloomberg.com/news/2010-07-16/municipal-bond-defaults-continue-attriple-the-typical-rate-lehmann-says.html.

[121] *See* Nelson D. Schwartz, "A Seer on Banks Raises a Furor on Bonds," New York Times, Feb. 8, 2011, at B1, *available at* http://www.nytimes.com/2011/02/08/business/economy/ 08whitney.html; Ben Baden, "What Happened to the Muni Bond Blowup?" U.S. News and World Report, July 19, 2011, *available at* http://newsclips.sec.gov/?p=53983; Max Abelson and Michael McDonald, "Whitney Municipal-Bond Apocalypse Short on Specifics," Bloomberg (Feb. 1, 2011), *available at* http://www.bloomberg.com/news/ 2011-02-01/whitney-municipal-bond-apocalypse-is-short-on-defaultspecifics.html.

[122] In 2009, 194 issuers defaulted on $6.9 billion in municipal bonds. *See* Preston, *supra* note 120. S&P has reported that approximately 0.5% of all municipal bonds (by par value) are currently in monetary default and that 2011 saw $1.06 billion in defaults, down 60.8% from the same period in 2010. *See* Slavin Article, *supra* note 112. By contrast, the Slavin Article notes that Distressed Debt Securities Newsletter reported $25.36 billion of defaults in 2011, up 401.6% from 2010. As noted above in note 112, Distressed Debt Securities Newsletter uses the broader definition of "default" – technical default, which includes covenant violations.

[123] *See* S&P Report, *supra* note 118, at 5 (Non-rated bonds constituted 780 of the 917 defaults).

[124] *Id.*

[125] *See* Robert Doty, *Bloomberg Visual Guide to Municipal Bonds* (2012) at 8-20 (citing MMA data indicating that more than 90% of the municipal securities market from 1980 through 2002 occurred in market sectors dependent on private sector performance and citing Bloomberg data finding similar statistics for defaults from 2007 to 2010). *See also* Popper, *supra* note 30 (attributing statistics to Income Securities Advisors).

[126] Kroll Bond Ratings, "An Analysis of Historical Municipal Bond Defaults, Lessons Learned: The Past as Prologue," Nov. 14, 2011.

[127] Presentation: James E. Spiotto, "Unfunded Pension Obligations: Is Chapter 9 the Ultimate Remedy? Is there a Better Resolution Mechanism?" (June 2011), *available at* http://www.sec.gov/spotlight/municipalsecurities/ statements072911/spiotto-slides2.pdf.

[128] Henry C. Kevane, "Chapter 9 Municipal Bankruptcy: The New "New Thing"? Part I," Business Law Today, May 2011, *available at* http://www.pszjlaw.com/media/publication/ 416_Kevane%2C%20Chapter%209.pdf. Since the enactment of Chapter 9 in 1934, there have only been approximately 600 Chapter 9 filings.

[129] *See, e.g.*, Presentation: James E. Spiotto, "In Good Times and Bad Times, Financial Challenges Past, Present and Future," Nov. 2010, *available at* http://www.chapman.com/ events/20101116/SpiottoWebinar_111610.pdf. In contrast to Chapter 9, state refinancing authorities, receiverships and commissions do not deal with adjustment of debt but instead provide funds for continued provision of municipal services. *Id.* at 95.

[130] The bankruptcy suit for the City of Harrisburg was dismissed by a federal judge on November 23, 2011 and the City is in a state proceeding for distressed communities. *See* Sabrina Tavernise, "Judge Rejects Harrisburg's Bankruptcy," The New York Times, Nov. 23, 2011, *available at* http://www.nytimes.com/2011/11/24/us/ harrisburgs-bankruptcy-filing-is-rejected-by-judge.html; Steven Church and Romy Varghese, "Harrisburg May Get Receiver Even if Bankruptcy Judge Tosses City Petition," Bloomberg, Nov. 23, 2011, *available at* http://www.bloomberg.com/news/2011-1123/harrisburg-may-get-receiver-even-if-bankruptcy-judge-tosses-city-petition.html.

[131] Kelly Nolan, "Largest Municipal Bankruptcy Filed," The Wall Street Journal, Nov. 10, 2011; Katy Stech, "Judge: Jefferson County Chapter 9 Case Can Continue," The Wall Street Journal, Mar. 5, 2012.

[132] Randall Jensen, "Stockton Files for Bankruptcy," The Bond Buyer, June 29, 2012, *available at* http://www.bondbuyer.com/issues/121_125/stockton-california-slash-debt-budget-declare-bankruptcy-1041382-1.html.

[133] Steven Church and James Nash, "Mammoth Lakes, California, Seeks Bankruptcy Protection," Bloomberg, July 4, 2012, *available at* http://www.bloomberg.com/news/2012-07-03/mammoth-lakes-california-filesfor-bankruptcy.html. Additionally, in 1983, the Washington Public Power Supply System defaulted on $2.25 billion in bonds, though it did not file for bankruptcy. *See* Division of Enforcement, Securities and Exchange Commission, Staff Report on the Investigation in The Matter of Transactions in Washington Public Power Supply System Securities (Sept. 1988).

[134] Mike Clary, "As Debts Mount, Some See Doom Over Miami," Los Angeles Times, Dec. 3, 1996, at A1, *available at* http://articles.latimes.com/1996-12-03/news/mn-5280_1_dade-county.

[135] *Cf.* Mike "Mish" Shedlock, Detroit is Halting Garbage Pickup, Police Patrols in 20% of City: Expect Bankruptcy in 2011, Business Insider, Dec. 13, 2010, *available at* http://articles.businessinsider.com/201012-13/news/30065559 1 mayor-dave-bing-police-patrols-street-lights.

[136] Ian Lovett, "Third City in California Votes to Seek Bankruptcy," The New York Times, July 11, 2012, *available at* http://www.nytimes.com/2012/07/12/us/san-bernardino-council-votes-to-file-bankruptcy.html.

[137] The effect of a municipal bankruptcy on holders of municipal debt will typically differ according to the type of debt. For example, certain state statutes create a pledge ("statutory lien") often of taxes, in favor of bondholders. These statutes mandate that pledged tax revenues as collected be paid to the bondholders or the bond trustee without any bankruptcy court impairment or interference. *See* Remarks of James Spiotto, Birmingham, Alabama Field Hearing (Jul. 29, 2011), 1-2, *available at* http://www.sec.gov/spotlight/ municipalsecurities/statements072911/spiotto.pdf. This is also the case for bonds backed by special revenues. *Id.* Further, the bankruptcy court cannot impair the statutory lien or the lien on special revenue. *Id.* In the case of general obligation bonds, a municipality is generally not required to make payments of principal or interest during the continuation of the bankruptcy proceeding. *Id.* at 44-45.

[138] *See* Remarks of James Spiotto, Birmingham, Alabama Field Hearing (Jul. 29, 2011), 1-2, *available at* http://www.sec.gov/spotlight/municipalsecurities/statements072911/spiotto.pdf.

[139] *See, e.g.*, Birmingham Hearing Transcript at 32-42 (Clark) (noting also the difficulties municipalities face in dealing with financial disclosure during the midst of a financial crisis while also addressing other basic governmental functions).

[140] Birmingham Hearing Transcript at 41-42 (Clark).

[141] *See, e.g.*, Barnett Wright, "Jefferson County Commission Fails to Post Fiscal Documents Online," The Birmingham News, June 13, 2010, *available at* http://blog.al.com/spotnews/ 2010/06/jefferson county commission fa 1.html.

[142] The Securities Act has two basic objectives: require that investors receive financial and other significant information concerning securities being offered for public sale; and prohibit deceit, misrepresentations, and other fraud in the sale of securities.

[143] The Exchange Act empowers the Commission with broad authority over all aspects of the securities industry including the power to register, regulate, and oversee brokerage firms, transfer agents, and clearing agencies as well as the nation's securities self-regulatory organizations. The various stock exchanges, the MSRB, and FINRA are self-regulatory organizations. The Exchange Act also identifies and prohibits certain types of conduct in the markets and provides the Commission with disciplinary powers over regulated entities and persons associated with them. The Exchange Act also empowers the Commission to require periodic reporting of information by companies with publicly traded securities.

[144] *See* Securities Act § 3(a)(2); Securities Act § 12(a)(2); Exchange Act § 3(a)(12); Exchange Act § 3(a)(29).

[145] Securities Acts Amendments of 1975, Pub. L. No. 94-29, 89 Stat. 131 (1975).

[146] *See* Division of Market Regulation, Securities and Exchange Commission, "Staff Report on the Municipal Securities Market" (Sept. 1993), *available at* http://www.sec.gov/info/ municipal/mrmunimarketreport 1993.pdf ("1993 Staff Report").

[147] *See, e.g.*, Exchange Act §§ 15(c)(1), 15(c)(2); 17(a); 17(b), 15B(c)(1), and 21(a)(1). Enforcement activities regarding municipal securities dealers must be coordinated by the Commission, FINRA and the appropriate bank regulatory agency. Exchange Act §§ 15B(c)(6)(A), 15B(c)(6)(B), and 17(c).

[148] Exchange Act § 15B(b). The MSRB was not granted authority to enforce its rules. *See infra* § II.B.3.a (Municipal Securities Rulemaking Board).

[149] Exchange Act § 15B(d)(1). The Tower Amendment also prohibited the MSRB, either directly or indirectly, from requiring municipal issuers to furnish purchasers, prospective purchasers or the MSRB with any "application, report, document, or information" not generally available from a source other than the issuer. Exchange Act § 15B(d)(2). This section was intended to make clear that the legislation was not designed to subject states, cities, counties, or any other municipal authorities, to any disclosure requirements that might be devised by the MSRB. *See* 1993 Staff Report, *supra* note 146, Appx. A at 5 (citing to 94th Cong., 1st Sess., 121 Cong. Rec. 10727 (1975) (Remarks of Senator Tower)).

[150] *See* Exchange Act § 15B(d)(1). *See also* 1993 Staff Report, *supra* note 146, at 7-8.

[151] *See* 1993 Staff Report, *supra* note 146, at 8.

[152] The Dodd-Frank Wall Street Reform and Consumer Protection Act, Pub. L. No. 111-203, 124 Stat. 1376 (2010) ("Dodd-Frank Act") added references to municipal advisors in the 1975 Amendments. *See, e.g.*, Exchange Act § 15B(a)(1)(B).

[153] The Dodd-Frank Act § 976. *See* GAO, "Report to Congressional Committees, Municipal Securities: Options for Improving Continuing Disclosure," GAO-12-698 (July 2012), *available at* http://gao.gov/assets/600/ 592669.pdf. In addition, the Dodd-Frank Act requires the Comptroller General to submit (1) a report with an analysis of the mechanisms for trading, quality of trade executions, market transparency, trade reporting, price discovery, settlement clearing, and credit enhancements; the needs of the markets and investors and the impact of recent innovations; recommendations for how to improve the transparency, efficiency, fairness, and

liquidity of trading in the municipal securities markets; and potential uses of derivatives in the municipal securities markets and (2) a report concerning the role and importance of the Governmental Accounting Standards Board in the municipal securities market; and the manner and the level at which the Governmental Accounting Standards Board has been funded. Dodd-Frank Act, §§ 977-78. The former report was issued in January 2012. *See* GAO Market Structure Report, *supra* note 61. The GAO's study of the GASB was issued in January 2011 and is available at http://www.gao.gov/ new.items/d11267r.pdf.

[154] *See, e.g.*, Exchange Act Release No. 26100, "Municipal Securities Disclosure" (Sept. 22, 1988), 53 FR 37778 (Sept. 28, 1988) ("1988 Proposing Release"); Exchange Act Release No. 26985, "Municipal Securities Disclosure" (June 28, 1989), 54 FR 28799 (July 10, 1989) ("1989 Adopting Release"); 1994 Interpretive Release, *supra* note 31.

[155] *See infra* § II.B.1.b (Antifraud Authority).

[156] Exchange Act § 15B(b).

[157] *See* 1994 Interpretive Release, *supra* note 31 (also citing at note 83 earlier statements by SEC chairmen David S. Ruder (1987), John S.R. Shad (1985) and Harold M. Williams (1978)). *See also, e.g.,* Christopher Cox, Chairman, U.S. Securities and Exchange Commission, "Integrity in the Municipal Market," Los Angeles, (Jul. 18, 2007), *available at* http://sec.gov/news/speech/2007/spch071807cc.htm; U.S. Securities and Exchange Commission Staff White Paper to Congress, "Disclosure and Accounting Practices in the Municipal Securities Market" (Jul. 2, 2007), *available at* http://sec.gov/news/press/2007/ 2007-148wp.pdf. This historical legislative recommendation would subject companies and other entities that use municipal securities to finance their facilities to the registration and disclosure provisions of the federal securities laws - the same registration and disclosure standards that would apply if they issued their securities directly (not using municipal issuers as conduits).

[158] *See* 1994 Interpretive Release, *supra* note 31.

[159] *See id.*

[160] A "person" is defined in § 3(a)(9) of the Exchange Act as "a natural person, company, government, or political subdivision, agency, or instrumentality of a government."

[161] Exchange Act §10(b) and Securities Act § 17(a); Rule 10b-5 under the Exchange Act.

[162] *See* 1994 Interpretive Release, *supra* note 31 ("The adequacy of the disclosure provided in municipal security offering materials is tested against an objective standard: an omitted fact is material if there is a substantial likelihood that, under all the circumstances, the omitted fact would have assumed actual significance in the deliberations of the reasonable (investor.) Put another way, there must be a substantial likelihood that the disclosure of the omitted fact would have been viewed by the reasonable investor as having significantly altered the "total mix" of information made available" citing *TSC Industries, Inc. v. Northway, Inc.*, 426 U.S. 438, 449 (1976)).

[163] *See* 1994 Interpretive Release, *supra* note 31; Exchange Act §§ 15(c)(1) and (2).

[164] *See* 1994 Interpretive Release, *supra* note 31.

[165] *See* 1989 Adopting Release, *supra* note 154.

[166] *Id.* Exchange Act Rule 15c2-12 requires underwriters acting in a primary offering of municipal securities of $1,000,000 or more: (1) to obtain and review an official statement "deemed final" by an issuer of the securities, except for the omission of specified information, prior to making a bid, purchase, offer, or sale of municipal securities; (2) in negotiated sales, to send, upon request, a copy of the most recent preliminary official statement (if one exists) to potential customers; (3) to contract with the issuer to receive, within a specified time, sufficient copies of the final official statement to comply with the Rule's delivery requirement, and the requirements of the rules of the MSRB; and (4) to send, upon request, a copy of the final official statement to potential customers for a specified period of time.

[167] *See* Exchange Act Release No. 34961, "Municipal Securities Disclosure" (Nov 10, 1994), 59 FR 59590 (Nov. 17, 1994), *available at* http://www.sec.gov/rules/final/adpt6.txt ("1994 Amendment Release").

[168] Exchange Act Release No. 59062, "Amendment to Municipal Securities Disclosure" (Dec. 5, 2008), 73 FR 76104 (Dec. 15, 2008), *available at* http://www.sec.gov/rules/final/2008/34-59062fr.pdf. *See also* Exchange Act Release No. 59061, "Self-Regulatory Organizations: Municipal Securities Rulemaking Board; Notice of Filing of Amendment No. 1 and Order Granting Accelerated Approval of Proposed Rule Change, as Modified by Amendment No. 1 Thereto, Relating to the Establishment of a Continuing Disclosure Service of the Electronic Municipal Market Access System (EMMA)" (Dec. 5, 2008), 73 FR 75778 (Dec. 12, 2008), *available at* http://www.sec.gov/rules/sro/msrb/2008/34-59061.pdf.

[169] *See* Exchange Act Release No. 59966 (May 21, 2009), 74 FR 25790 (May 29, 2009), *available at* http://www.sec.gov/rules/sro/msrb/2009/34-59966.pdf. EMMA is *available at* http://emma.msrb.org. *See also*

Gretchen Morgenson, "Fresh Air in the Muni Market," New York Times, Aug. 30, 2009, at BU1, *available at* http://www.nytimes.com/2009/08/30/ business/30gret.html.

[170] Exchange Act Release No. 62184A "Amendment to Municipal Securities Disclosure" (May 26, 2010), 75 FR 33100 (June 10, 2010), *available at* http://www.sec.gov/rules/final/ 2010/34-62184a.pdf ("2010 Adopting Release"). As amended, Rule 15c2-12 requires disclosure of the following events in a timely manner not in excess of ten business days after the occurrence of the event: (1) principal and interest payment delinquencies; (2) non-payment related defaults, if material; (3) unscheduled draws on debt service reserves reflecting financial difficulties; (4) unscheduled draws on credit enhancements reflecting financial difficulties; (5) substitution of credit or liquidity providers, or their failure to perform; (6) adverse tax opinions, the issuance by the Internal Revenue Service of proposed or final determinations of taxability, Notices of Proposed Issue (IRS Form 5701-TEB) or other material notices or determinations with respect to the tax status of the security , or other material events affecting the tax status of the security; (7) modifications to rights of security holders, if material; (8) bond calls, if material, and tender offers; (9) defeasances; (10) release, substitution or sale of property securing repayment of the securities, if material; (11) rating changes; (12) bankruptcy, insolvency, receivership or similar event of the obligated person; (13) the consummation of a merger, consolidation, or acquisition involving an obligated person or the sale of all or substantially all the assets of the obligated person, other than in the ordinary course of business, the entry into a definitive agreement to undertake such an action or the termination of a definitive agreement relating to any such actions, other than pursuant to its terms, if material; and (14) appointment of a successor or additional trustee or the change of name of a trustee, if material. *See* Rule 15c2-12(b)(5)(C). Rule 15c212(b)(5)(D) also requires disclosure of a failure to provide required annual financial information on or before the date specified in the written agreement or contract.

[171] *Id.*

[172] *See infra* notes 353 - 362 and accompanying text.

[173] In addition to the matters described elsewhere in this report, the Commission has brought enforcement actions alleging tax or arbitrage-driven fraud that, at their core, involve material omissions about material risks that could affect the tax treatment of the municipal bonds being issued. *See, e.g.*, Securities Act Release No. 8412/Exchange Act Release No. 49596, "Commission Charges Ira Weiss and L. Andrew Shupe II with Violating the Anti-Fraud Provisions of the Federal Securities Laws in Connection with a $9.6 Million Offering of Municipal Securities" (Apr. 22, 2004; *Weiss v. SEC*, 468 F.3d 849 (D.C. Cir. 2006) (failure by bond lawyer to conduct a reasonable investigation into the facts underlying his opinion as to the tax-exempt status of the of the bonds)); Securities Act Release No. 8854, *In the Matter of CDR Financial Products, Inc., f/k/a Chambers, Dunhill, Rubin & Co.* (order) (Sep. 28, 2007), *available at* http://www.sec.gov/litigation/admin/2007/33-8854.pdf (failure of firm to disclose fee arrangement with a credit enhancement provider that created a risk to the tax-exempt status of the bonds); Securities Act Release No. 7663, *In the Matter of John E. Thorn, Jr. and Thorn Welch & Co., Inc., f/k/a Thorn, Alvis, Welch, Inc.* (order) (Mar. 31, 1999), *available at* http://www.sec.gov/litigation/admin/33-7663.txt (failure to disclose issuer's intentions regarding spending of offering proceeds, which would have jeopardized bonds tax-free status, found to violate antifraud rules).

[174] *See infra* § III.B.5.b (Enforcement Actions).

[175] *See infra* § III.B.2.a (Enforcement Actions).

[176] *See infra* § IV.B.3.a (Fair Prices).

[177] In particular, the Code prohibits the disclosure of "return information" (which includes taxpayer identity, information obtained through audits, and a broad scope of other information) in any manner except as specifically authorized by § 6103 of the Code. § 6103 precludes the IRS from disclosing not only the identity of the investors who may be taxed if the IRS determines that an issue of municipal bonds is taxable (which would generally be of no interest or benefit to the SEC), but also the identity of the issuer of such bonds or the offering. § 6103 exceptions enable law enforcement agencies to use relevant tax information to investigate and prosecute tax and nontax crimes and allow federal and state agencies to use it to verify eligibility for need-based programs and collect child support, among other uses. Although these § 6103 exceptions permit disclosure of return information in many situations, including disclosure to federal authorities for use in criminal investigations, disclosure to the Commission and Commission staff in connection with civil enforcement of the securities laws is not covered. For example, disclosure of return information is permitted to taxpayer designees, State tax officials and State local law enforcement agencies for the purpose of administration of State tax laws, persons with a material interest in the return, Committees of Congress, the President and designated White House officials, the Department of Justice, Department of Treasury and certain other Federal officers and employees for purposes of tax administration, criminal investigations and judicial proceedings. In addition, disclosure is permitted to a number of federal departments and agencies for

purposes other than tax administration, such as the Social Security Administration and Railroad Retirement Board, the Department of Labor and Pension Benefit Guaranty Corporation, federal agencies administering Federal loan programs, Federal, State and local child support enforcement agencies, the Department of Education in connection with the repayment of income contingent student loans, the U.S. Customs Service, and Secretary of Health and Human Services.

[178] 468 F.3d 849 (DC Cir. 2006).

[179] *See infra* note 589.

[180] Exchange Act § 15B(b)(2) as added by §975 of the Dodd-Frank Act provides that the term "municipal advisor" (A) means a person (who is not a municipal entity or an employee of a municipal entity) that— (i) provides advice to or on behalf of a municipal entity or obligated person with respect to municipal financial products or the issuance of municipal securities, including advice with respect to the structure, timing, terms, and other similar matters concerning such financial products or issues; or (ii) undertakes a solicitation of a municipal entity; (B) includes financial advisors, guaranteed investment contract brokers, third-party marketers, placement agents, solicitors, finders, and swap advisors, if such persons are described in any of clauses (i) through (iii) of subparagraph (A); and (C) does not include a broker, dealer, or municipal securities dealer serving as an underwriter (as defined in § 2(a)(11) of the Securities Act) any investment adviser registered under the Investment Advisers Act of 1940, or persons associated with such investment advisers who are providing investment advice, any commodity trading advisor registered under the Commodity Exchange Act or persons associated with a commodity trading advisor who are providing advice related to swaps, attorneys offering legal advice or providing services that are of a traditional legal nature, or engineers providing engineering advice. *See infra* notes 261- 263 (regarding the Commission's proposed temporary registration regime and proposed rules interpreting this provision).

[181] Exchange Act § 15B(b)(2) as added by § 975 of the Dodd-Frank Act defines the term "municipal financial products" to include municipal derivatives, guaranteed investment contracts, and investment strategies. The term "investment strategies" includes plans or programs for the investment of the proceeds of municipal securities that are not municipal derivatives, guaranteed investment contracts, and the recommendation of and brokerage of municipal escrow investments.

[182] Exchange Act § 15B(b)(2) as added by § 975 of the Dodd-Frank Act defines the term "solicitation of a municipal entity or obligated person" to mean a direct or indirect communication with a municipal entity or obligated person made by a person, for direct or indirect compensation, on behalf of a broker, dealer, municipal securities dealer, municipal advisor, or investment adviser (as defined in § 202 of the Investment Advisers Act of 1940) that does not control, is not controlled by, or is not under common control with the person undertaking such solicitation for the purpose of obtaining or retaining an engagement by a municipal entity or obligated person of a broker, dealer, municipal securities dealer, or municipal advisor for or in connection with municipal financial products, the issuance of municipal securities, or of an investment adviser to provide investment advisory services to or on behalf of a municipal entity.

[183] *See* Exchange Act § 15B(b)(2); Dodd-Frank Act, § 975.

[184] Dodd-Frank Act § 975(b). Prior to the passage of the Dodd-Frank Act, the MSRB Board was comprised of a majority of regulated entity members. The Dodd-Frank Act mandates that the MSRB Board be comprised of a majority of public members who are independent of regulated entities. The Commission approved amendments to MSRB Rule A-3 on the composition of the MSRB Board, Exchange Act Release No. 65424 (Sept. 28, 2011), 76 FR 61407 (Oct. 4, 2011); however, market participants have expressed their dissatisfaction with the transparency of the selection procedures for MSRB Board membership. *See, e.g.*, Letter from National Association of Independent Public Finance Advisors, September 12, 2011 re: SRMSRB-2011-11 ("NAIPFA 2011-11 Letter"), Letter from the Government Finance Officers Association, September 16, 2011 re: SR-MSRB-2011-11 ("GFOA 2011-11 Letter"). The MSRB has responded to this criticism by publishing, on its website, the names of all persons who applied for MSRB Board membership after the selection process has been completed.

[185] *See* MSRB Rules A-2 and A-3. Some market participants have expressed dissatisfaction with overall transparency of the MSRB's deliberative process and access to the MSRB Board. *See, e.g.*, NAIPFA 201111 Letter; GFOA 2011-11 Letter. Market participants have asked for open meetings and records noting that, unlike other self-regulatory organizations, the MSRB was created by Congress and regulated entities do not have a choice of whether to be bound by MSRB rules. *See* Letter from Robert W. Doty, Sep. 27, 2010 re: SR-MSRB-2010-08. The MSRB has indicated that it will continue to explore alternatives to promote transparency in MSRB Board processes. *See* Letter from the MSRB, Sept. 19, 2011 re: SRMSRB-2011-11. The MSRB

currently provides governance, financial, program, strategic objectives, long-range planning and additional information on its website at http://www.msrb.org/About-MSRB.aspx.

[186] Exchange Act § 15B(b)(2)(A). *See infra* § II.C.1 (Broker-Dealers, Municipal Securities Dealers, and Related Market Participants).

[187] Exchange Act § 15B(b)(2)(C).

[188] *See* Exchange Act § 15B(c)(5).

[189] *See* Dodd-Frank Act, §§ 301-26. Although the Office of Thrift Supervision ("OTS") formerly played a role, pursuant to Dodd-Frank Act §§ 301 through 326, OTS was ordered to be dismantled, and its responsibilities and functions reassigned to the FDIC, OCC and FRS.

[190] *See* Exchange Act § 15B(c)(7), which provides that the periodic examination of regulated entities shall be conducted by (a) a registered securities association in the case of dealers that are members of the registered securities association, (b) the appropriate regulatory agency ("bank regulators") in the case of dealers that are not members of a registered securities association, and (c) the SEC, or its designee, in the case of municipal advisors.

[191] *See* Exchange Act Release No. 59062, *supra* note 168.

[192] *See* Exchange Act Release No. 59966, *supra* note 169. EMMA was initially launched as a pilot in March 2008 and became fully operational in states throughout 2009. *See* Exchange Act Release Nos. 59212 (*infra* note 706), 59966 (*supra* note 169) and 59061 (*supra* note 168).

[193] *See* Andrew Ackerman, "For MSRB, From Many to One; EMMA Thriving as Sole NRMSIR," The Bond Buyer (July 7, 2010), *available at* http://www.bondbuyer.com/issues/ 119_377/msrb_repository-10144241.html. *See also* San Francisco Hearing Transcript at 41 (Colby), 83, 86, 106, 118 (Belsky), 238 (Kuhn), and 243 (Lehman).

[194] SEC Release 2008-286, "SEC, MSRB: New Measures to Provide More Transparency Than Ever Before for Municipal Bond Investors" (Dec. 8, 2008), *available at* http://www.sec.gov/news/press/2008/2008286.htm. The Staff understands that the MSRB's EMMA website has received over 20 million page views per year, and the MSRB is forecasting over 25 million page views in 2012.

[195] *See* Exchange Act Release No. 62183, "Notice of Filing of Amendment No. 2 and Order Granting Accelerated Approval of Proposed Rule Change, as Modified by Amendment Nos. 1 and 2 Thereto, Relating to Additional Voluntary Submissions by Issuers to the MSRB's Electronic Municipal Market Access System (EMMA)" (SR-MSRB-2009-10) (May 26, 2010), 75 FR 30876 (June 2, 2010), *available at* http://www.sec.gov/rules/sro/msrb/2009/34-62183.pdf. *See also* Exchange Act Release No. 60033, "Order Granting Approval of Proposed Rule Change Relating to the Voluntary Submission of Continuing Disclosure Documents to Its Upcoming Continuing Disclosure Service of the Electronic Municipal Market Access System (EMMA)" (SR-MSRB-2009-004) (June 3, 2009), 74 FR 27369 (June 9, 2009), *available at* http://www.sec.gov/rules/sro/msrb/2009/34-60033.pdf.

[196] *See* MSRB Press Release, "Municipal Securities Credit Ratings from Fitch Ratings and Standard & Poor's available on the MSRB's EMMA Website" (Nov. 21, 2011), *available at* http://www.msrb.org/News-and-Events/Press-Releases/2011/Municipal-Credit-Ratings-Available-on-EMMA.aspx. *See also,* Exchange Act Release No. 63086, "Order Approving Proposed Rule Change Relating to Amendments to the Continuing Disclosure Service of the MSRB's Electronic Municipal Market Access System (EMMA)" (SR-MSRB2010-03) (Oct. 13, 2010), 75 FR 63884 (Oct. 18, 2010), *available at* http://www.sec.gov/rules/sro/msrb/ 2010/34-63086.pdf. On November 21, 2011, the MSRB's EMMA website began providing investors and others with free public access to current municipal credit ratings from Fitch Ratings and Standard & Poor's Ratings Services.

[197] *See* MSRB Long-Range Plan for Market Transparency Products (Jan. 2012), *available at* http://www.msrb.org/msrb1/pdfs/Long-Range-Plan.pdf.

[198] *See* FINRA, "About the Financial Industry Regulatory Authority," *available at* http://www.finra.org/AboutFINRA (accessed on Apr. 19, 2012).

[199] *See* FINRA, FINRA 2010 Year in Review and Annual Financial Report (2011), *available at* http://www.finra.org/web/groups/corporate/@corp/@about/@ar/documents/corporate/p123836.pdf ("2010 FINRA Report").

[200] *See* FINRA Rule 0150 (Application of Rules to Exempted Securities Except Municipal Securities). Following the consolidation of the enforcement arm of the New York Stock Exchange, NYSE Regulation, Inc. ("NYSE"), the National Association of Securities Dealers ("NASD"), and FINRA in 2007, FINRA undertook a consolidation of the rules of the NASD and the NYSE. The reference herein to "FINRA's rules" means the rules included in the FINRA Manual, *available at* http://www.finra.org/Industry/Regulation/ FINRARules /index.htm.

[201] *See* MSRB Rule A-8. The MSRB and FINRA have agreed to harmonize MSRB rules and interpretations applicable to sales practices for 529 Plans and FINRA rules and interpretations applicable to sales practices for mutual funds. *See* MSRB Notice 2006-03 *available at* http://www.msrb.org/Rules-andInterpretations/Regulatory-Notices/2006/2006-03.aspx?n=1.

[202] *See* Exchange Act Release No. 65992, Notice of Filing of Amendment No. 1 and Order Granting Accelerated Approval to a Proposed Rule Change, as Modified by Amendment No. 1 Thereto, Consisting of Amendments to Rule G-16, on Periodic Compliance Examination, and Rule G-9, on Preservation of Records (SR-MSRB-2011-19) (Dec. 16, 2011), 76 FR 79738 (Dec. 22, 2011), *available at* http://www.sec.gov/rules/sro/msrb/2011/34-65992.pdf.

[203] *Id.*

[204] *See* 2010 FINRA Report, *supra* note 199.

[205] FINRA Regulatory Notice 10-41, "FINRA Reminds Firms of Their Sales Practice and Due Diligence Obligations When Selling Municipal Securities in the Secondary Market" (Sept. 2010), *available at* http://www.finra.org/web/groups/industry/@ip/@reg/@notice/ documents/notices/p122112.pdf.

[206] *See* Andrew Ackerman, "FINRA Looks at 'Flipping;' SEC Wants a More Independent MSRB," The Bond Buyer (Sept. 25, 2009), *available at* https://secure.bondbuyer.com/ issues/118_185/finra-msrb-10005531.html. According to the article, flipping occurs when dealers or institutional investors purchase municipal bonds and then immediately resell them to retail investors at a higher price. *See also* Lynn Hume, "FINRA Eyes Action Against Firms Selling Munis to Retail Without Disclosure," The Bond Buyer (May 7, 2010), *available at* http://www.bondbuyer.com/issues/119 336/finra enforcement firms muni-1011823-1.html.

[207] *See supra* note 190 and related text.

[208] *See* GAO Market Structure Report, *supra* note 61, at 9 ("FINRA oversees 98 percent of those MSRB- registered broker-dealers that are also registered members of FINRA, while federal banking regulators oversee the remaining 2 percent").

[209] *See* MSRB Rule G-16. *See also*, GAO Market Structure Report, *supra* note 61, at 9 ("During the period of our review, . . . the federal banking regulators conducted routine examinations of the firms under their jurisdiction once every two years for compliance with MSRB rules . . . .").

[210] For a brief overview of relevant types of state law and common law requirements governing issuers, *see* Fippinger, *supra* note 29,§ 1:6:5.

[211] *See, e.g.*, Ga. Const. art. IX § V, 1(a) ("The debt incurred by any county, municipality, or other political subdivision of this state, including debt incurred on behalf of any special district, shall never exceed 10 percent of the assessed value of all taxable property within such county, municipality, or political subdivision; and no such county, municipality, or other political subdivision shall incur any new debt without the assent of a majority of the qualified voters of such county, municipality, or political subdivision voting in an election held for that purpose as provided by law"); Cal. Const. art. 16 § 18(a) ("no county, city, township, board of education, or school district, shall incur any indebtedness or liability in any manner or for any purpose exceeding in any year the income and revenue provided for such year, without the assent of two-thirds of the voters of the public entity voting at an election to be held for that purpose. . .").

[212] Some states also require securities to be registered pursuant to state law before they may be offered to the public in that jurisdiction. However, since the adoption of the National Securities Markets Improvement Act of 1996, Pub. L. No. 104-290, 110 Stat. 3416 (1996), state laws requiring registration of municipal securities that are exempt securities under the Securities Act have been preempted by federal law – with the exception of the offer and sale of securities within the state in which the issuer is located. *See* Securities Act § 18(b)(4)(C).

[213] Municipal market participants are subject to the antifraud provisions of § 17(a) of the Securities Act and § 10(b) of the Exchange Act. *See supra* notes 158 - 164 and accompanying text. For a compilation of enforcement actions related to the municipal securities market organized by the relevant participants, *see* SEC Division of Trading and Markets, Office of Municipal Securities, "Cases and Materials," *available at* http://www.sec.gov/info/municipal.shtml.

[214] *See supra* § II.A.2 (Description of Municipal Securities).

[215] *See* Kenneth N. Daniels and Jayaraman Vijayakumar, *The Role and Impact of Financial Advisors in the Market for Municipal Bonds*, Journal of Financial Services Research, at 43-44 (Aug. 2006).

[216] *See generally infra* § IV.A.1.c (Trading) (discussing how secondary market trading occurs in the municipal securities market).

[217] Recently approved MSRB Rule G-43 defines a brokers' broker as: a dealer, or a separately operated and supervised division or unit of a dealer, that principally effects transactions for other dealers or that holds itself out as a broker's broker. A broker's broker may be a separate company or part of a larger company. An

alternative trading system, registered as such with the Commission, is not a broker's broker for purposes of this rule if, with respect to its municipal securities activities, it satisfies certain enumerated conditions specified in proposed MSRB Rule G-43(d)(iii). *See* Exchange Act Release No. 67238, "Order Granting Approval of a Proposed Rule Change, as Modified by Amendment No. 1, Relating to Proposed Rule G-43, on Broker's Brokers; Proposed Amendments to Rule G-8, on Books and Records, Rule G-9, on Record Retention, and Rule G-18, on Execution of Transactions; and a Proposed Interpretive Notice on the Duties of Dealers that Use the Services of Broker's Brokers" (effective six months after approval by the Commission), (SR-MSRB-2012-04) (June 22, 2012), 77 FR 38684 (June 28, 2012), *available at* http://www.sec.gov/rules/sro/msrb/ 2012/34-67238.pdf ("MSRB Broker's Broker Approval Order"). Brokers' brokers act as agents for broker-dealers and municipal securities dealers. *See* Harris and Piwowar, *supra* note 103, at 1363.

[218] *See* Harris and Piwowar, *supra* note 103, at 1363.

[219] *See supra* graph entitled "Distribution of Customer Trades Traded."

[220] *See* Harris and Piwowar, *supra* note 103, at 1363.

[221] *See* Exchange Act § 15(a).

[222] *See* Exchange Act § 3(a)(4).

[223] *See* Exchange Act § 3(a)(5).

[224] Banks are excepted from the definitions of "broker" and "dealer" with respect to transactions in municipal securities. *See* Exchange Act §§ 3(a)(4)(B) and 3(a)(5)(C).

[225] *See* Exchange Act § 3(a)(30).

[226] *See* MSRB Rule A-12.

[227] *See generally* Exchange Act §§ 15B and 17(b).

[228] Exchange Act §§ 15B(c) and 17(c).

[229] The National Examination Program ("NEP") in the Office of Compliance Inspections and Examinations recently published a National Examination Risk Alert describing its observations of municipal underwriters' compliance with their due diligence and supervisory obligations, as well as the specific provisions of Exchange Act Rule 15c2-12 and MSRB Rule G-27. In the Risk Alert, the NEP staff said that it had observed that some broker-dealers may not be engaging in the type or extent of due diligence activities discussed in previous Commission's guidance. The NEP also said that it had observed instances of municipal underwriters not maintaining, or requiring the creation and maintenance of, adequate written evidence that they complied with their due diligence obligations. OCIE, Strengthening Practices for the Underwriting of Municipal Securities, National Examination Risk Alert, Volume II, Issue 3 (Mar. 9, 2012) *available at* http://sec.gov/about/offices/ocie/riskalert-muniduediligence.pdf.

[230] Brokers, dealers and municipal securities dealers effecting transactions in municipal securities must comply with MSRB rules. *See* Exchange Act § 15B(c)(1). Exchange Act § 15A(f) prohibits FINRA from adopting rules applicable to transactions in municipal securities. *See generally* MSRB Interpretive Notice, "Guidance on Disclosure and Other Sales Practice Obligations to Individual and Other Retail Investors in Municipal Securities" (July 14, 2009), *available at* http://www.msrb.org/Rules-and-Interpretations/MSRB-Rules/General/Rule-G-17.aspx?tab=2#_DA15225F-907A-43CC-A319-26F55EFFDECE ("MSRB Guidance on Disclosure").

[231] Other significant regulations include those that address the duty of supervision (Exchange Act § 15(b)(4)(e); MSRB Rules G-19 and G-27), communications with the public (MSRB Rule G-21), and recordkeeping (Exchange Act Rules 17a-3(a)(17) and 17a-4; MSRB Rule G-8).

[232] *See* MSRB Guidance on Disclosure, *supra* note 230. As of December 22, 2010, MSRB Rule G-17 applies to municipal advisors as well. *See infra* note 235 and accompanying text.

[233] *See* MSRB Guidance on Disclosure, *supra* note 230.

[234] *Id.*

[235] MSRB Interpretive Notice, "Interpretative Notice Regarding Rule G-17, on Disclosure of Material Facts" (Mar. 20, 2002), *available at* http://www.msrb.org/Rules-and-Interpretations/MSRB-Rules/General/RuleG-17.aspx?tab=2#_E3855FB5-C65D-437E-AD6A-C564E0098D0A. *See also* MSRB Interpretive Notice, "MSRB Answers Frequently Asked Questions Regarding Dealer Disclosure Obligations Under MSRB Rule G-17" (Nov. 30, 2011), *available at* http://www.msrb.org/Rules-and-Interpretations/MSRBRules/General/ Rule-G-17.aspx?tab=2#_316FB763-1DC3-436E-9533-A8E1007050BD ("Dealer Disclosure Obligations Under Rule G-17"). Although MSRB Rule G-17 has been amended to apply to municipal advisors (*See supra* note 232), as of the date of this report, the MSRB interpretive guidance on Rule G-17 does not apply to municipal advisors. The MSRB filed with the Commission on August 24, 2011, a proposed interpretive notice concerning the application of MSRB Rule G-17 to municipal advisors, which was published for comment by

the Commission on September 8, 2011. *See* Exchange Act Release No. 65292, "Notice of Filing of Proposed Interpretive Notice Concerning the Application of Rule G-17 to Municipal Advisors" (SR-MSRB-2011-15) (Sept. 8, 2011), 76 FR 56826 (Sept. 14, 2011), *available at* http://www.sec.gov/rules/sro/ msrb/2011/34-65292.pdf. However, on September 9, 2011, the MSRB withdrew the proposal among other rule proposals relating to municipal advisors, pending the Commission's adoption of a permanent definition of the term "municipal advisor". *See* Exchange Act Release No. 65398, "Notice of Withdrawal of Proposed Interpretive Notice Concerning the Application of Rule G-17 to Municipal Advisors" (SR-MSRB-2011-15) (Sept. 26, 2011), 76 FR 60958 (Sept. 30, 2011), *available at* http://www.sec.gov/rules/sro/msrb/2011/34-65398.pdf.

[236] *See* Dealer Disclosure Obligations Under Rule G-17, *supra* note 235.

[237] MSRB Interpretive Notice, "Reminder of Customer Protection Obligations in Connection with Sales of Municipal Securities" (May 30, 2007), *available at* http://www.msrb.org/ Rules-and-Interpretations/MSRB-Rules/General/Rule-G-17.aspx?tab=2# C6E4C0D2-8338-4F8E-97BE-2D2071C2B133.

[238] *See* MSRB Rule G-22(a). Rule G-22 defines "a control relationship with respect to a municipal security [as a relationship where] a broker, dealer, or municipal securities dealer (or a bank or other person of which the broker, dealer, or municipal securities dealer is a department or division) controls, is controlled by, or is under common control with the issuer of the security or a person other than the issuer who is obligated, directly or indirectly, with respect to debt service on the security." *See also* MSRB Interpretive Letter, "Associated Person on Issuer Governing Body" (June 25, 1987), *available at* http://www.msrb.org/Rules-and-Interpretations/MSRB-Rules/General/Rule-G-22.aspx?tab=3#_761A9462-AE0E-4348-ADCB-1EE4469E3224 ("whether a control relationship exists in a particular case is a factual question").

[239] *See* MSRB Rule G-22(c).

[240] *Id.*

[241] *See Hanly v. SEC*, 415 F.2d 589, 596 (2d Cir. 1969). *See also* 1988 Proposing Release, *supra* note 154.

[242] *See, e.g.,* Securities Act Release No. 9262/Exchange Act Release No. 65404, *In the Matter of RBC Capital Markets, LLC* (Sept. 27, 2011) *available at* http://www.sec.gov/litigation/ admin/2011/33-9262.pdf (settled action finding violations of §§17(a)(2) and 17(a)(3) of the Securities Act where firm marketed and sold $200 million of unsuitable credit-linked notes tied to the performance of synthetic collateralized debt obligations to five Wisconsin school districts). *See also infra* note 590.

[243] A broker's suitability obligations are typically different for institutional customers than for non-institutional customers. *See, e.g.*, MSRB "Restated Interpretive Notice Regarding the Application of MSRB Rules to Transactions with Sophisticated Municipal Market Professionals" (effective July 9, 2012) Exchange Act Release No. 67064 (May 25, 2012), 77 FR 32704 (June 1, 2012) (SR-MSRB-2012-05) (providing guidance on how a dealer will fulfill its "customer-specific suitability obligations" under MSRB Rule G-19 with regard to Sophisticated Municipal Market Professionals ("SMMPs")), *available at* http://www.msrb.org/Rules-and-Interpretations/MSRB-Rules/General/Rule-G-17.aspx?tab=2#_D37D3EF9-F642-4A63-A40D-3A6B33B5260A. The GFOA has recently urged the SEC and MSRB to establish suitability standards under MSRB Rule G-17 to protect state and local governments from the sale of inappropriate financial products. *See* letter from Susan Gaffney, GFOA to Elizabeth M. Murphy, regarding SR-MSRB-2011-09, *available at* http://www.sec.gov/comments/sr-msrb-201109/msrb201 109-22.pdf.

[244] *Cf.* FINRA Rule 2111 (Suitability) (effective July 9, 2012, *see* FINRA Regulatory Notice 11-25, "New Implementation Date for and Additional Guidance on the Consolidated FINRA Rules Governing KnowYour-Customer and Suitability Obligations *available at* http://finra.complinet.com/net_file_store/new_rulebooks/f/i/ finra_11-25.pdf), which requires "a member or an associated person to have a reasonable basis to believe that a recommended transaction or investment strategy involving a security or securities is suitable for the customer." FINRA interprets "investment strategy" broadly. As noted above, FINRA's rules do not apply to transactions in or business activities related to municipal securities. *See supra* note 200.

[245] *See* MSRB Rule G-19(b). Under MSRB Rule G-19(b), a broker, dealer, or municipal securities dealer must, prior to recommending a transaction to a non-institutional customer, make reasonable efforts to obtain information concerning: (1) the customer's financial status; (2) the customer's tax status; (3) the customer's investment objectives; and (4) any other information considered reasonable and necessary in making a recommendation to the customer. *See also* MSRB Rule G-19(a). MSRB Rule G-19(a) also requires the collection of certain account information specified in MSRB Rule G-8(a)(xi).

[246] *See infra* note 771 (discussing the concept of "prevailing market price").

[247] See MSRB Guidance on Disclosure, *supra* note 230. *See also infra* note 790.

[248] *See* MSRB Interpretive Notice, "Review of Dealer Pricing Responsibilities" (Jan. 26, 2004), *available at* http://www.msrb.org/Rules-and-Interpretations/MSRB-Rules/General/Rule-G-30.aspx?tab=2#_A5756731-6EF3-45A9-BB32-0EACF2074FD8. Recent examples of FINRA enforcement actions in this area include: *Kuhns Brothers Securities Corporation*, AWC No. 2060053785-03 (Oct. 17, 2011)(firm fined for municipal securities pricing violations under MSRB Rules G-17 and G-30 in 15 transactions during the review period of May 2004 to August 2006); *Fifth Third Securities, Inc.*, AWC No. 20090181035-01 (Sept. 20, 2011) (firm fined $60,000 for municipal securities fair pricing violations under MSRB Rules G-17 and G-30 in 8 transactions during the review period of October 1, 2008 to January 13, 2009); *Morgan Stanley & Co., Inc.*, AWC No. 20060056031-01 (Oct. 28, 2011) (firm fined $500,000 for municipal securities fair pricing violations under MSRB Rules G-17 and G-30 in 193 transactions during the review period of 2007 to 2010, with markups ranging from 3.01 percent to 8.49 percent); *RBC Capital Markets*, AWC No. 20080136349-01, (Aug. 25, 2011) (firm fined $95,000 for municipal securities fair pricing violations under MSRB Rules G-17 and G-30 in 26 transactions during the first and fourth quarters of 2008); *Continental Investors Services, Inc.*, AWC No. 20090181045-01 (Aug. 14, 2011) (firm fined $35,000 for municipal securities fair pricing violations under MSRB Rules G-17 and G30 in 9 transactions during the review period of October 1, 2008 to December 31, 2008); *NEXT Financial Group, Inc.*, AWC No. 20090162729 (Aug. 20, 2010) (firm fined $400,000 for supervisory and fair pricing violations in 19 transactions during the review period of February 2008 to March 2009 with mark-ups and mark-downs ranging from 3.01% to 4.58%).

[249] *See* Reminder Notice on Fair Practice Duties to Issuers of Municipal Securities, MSRB Notice 2009-54 (Sept. 29, 2009); MSRB Rule G-17 Interpretive Letter- Purchase of new issue from issuer, MSRB interpretation of December 1, 1997, reprinted in MSRB Rule Book ("1997 Interpretation").

[250] *See* Exchange Act § 15B(b)(2)(A) as amended by Dodd-Frank Act § 975.

[251] MSRB Interpretive Notice Concerning the Application of MSRB Rule G-17 to Underwriters of Municipal Securities, effective August 2, 2012, *available at* http://www.msrb.org/Rules-and-Interpretations/MSRB-Rules/General/Rule-G-17.aspx?tab=2#_D54ECAF7-2CE6-4ED9-BB05-3C9B32FB7BF4 ("G-17 Interpretive Notice").

[252] *See* G-17 Interpretive Notice.

[253] See Rule 300(a) of Regulation ATS under the Exchange Act.

[254] See Rule 301(a) under Regulation ATS.

[255] The Staff understands from conversations with market participants that these ATSs represent very similar pools of liquidity (i.e., the same entities are providing the same liquidity across all of these ATSs).

[256] See infra note 715 (discussing trading volume on ATSs).

[257] Exchange Act § 15B(e)(4). See supra note 180.

[258] See Feldstein and Fabozzi, supra note 72, at 43.

[259] *See* Exchange Act Release No. 63576, "Proposed Rule for the Registration of Municipal Advisors," Dec. 20, 2010, *available at* http://www.sec.gov/rules/proposed/2010/34-63576.pdf; 76 FR 824 (Jan. 6, 2011) at 825.

[260] *See* Dodd-Frank Act, § 975(a)(1)(B).

[261] *See* Dodd-Frank Act, § 975(i). To enable municipal advisors to temporarily satisfy the registration requirement, and to make relevant information available to the public and municipal entities, the Commission adopted interim final temporary Rule 15Ba2-6T under the Exchange Act on September 1, 2010.

[262] *See* Exchange Act § 15B(b). As of December 31, 2010, municipal advisors were required to register with the MSRB and to pay initial and annual fees. *See* Exchange Act Release No. 63313, "Notice of Filing and Immediate Effectiveness of Amendments to Rule A-12, on Initial Fee, and Rule A-14, on Annual Fee" (SR-MSRB-2010-14) (Nov. 12, 2010), 75 FR 70759 (Nov. 18, 2010), *available at* http://www.sec.gov/rules/sro/msrb/2010/34-63313.pdf.

[263] *See* Exchange Act 15B(c). Specifically, Exchange Act § 15B(c)(1) provides that: "A municipal advisor and any person associated with such municipal advisor shall be deemed to have a fiduciary duty to any municipal entity for whom such municipal advisor acts as a municipal advisor, and no municipal advisor may engage in any act, practice, or course of business which is not consistent with a municipal advisor's fiduciary duty or that is in contravention of any rule of the Board." The Exchange Act does not impose a fiduciary duty with respect to advice to obligated persons.

[264] *See* Exchange Act Release No. 63599, "Order Granting Approval of Amendments to Rule G-5, on Disciplinary Actions by Appropriate Regulatory Agencies, Remedial Notices by Registered Securities Associations; and Rule G-17, on Conduct of Municipal Securities Activities" (SR-MSRB-2010-06) (Dec. 22, 2010), 75 FR 82119 (Dec. 29, 2010), *available at* http://sec.gov/rules/sro/msrb/2010/34-63599.pdf. *See also supra* § II.C.1.b.iv (Fair Dealing and Duty of Disclosure to Issuers).

[265] *See* MSRB Notice 2011-51, "MSRB Withdraws Pending Municipal Advisor Rule Proposals" (Sept. 12, 2011), *available at* http://www.msrb.org/Rules-and-Interpretations/Regulatory-Notices/2011/2011-51.aspx.

[266] *See* Fundamentals of Municipal Bonds 2012, *supra* note 33, at 17. Some of these functions may be carried out by a paying or fiscal agent. *Id.* Paying agents and fiscal agents are not trustees but perform certain functions that may also be performed by a trustee. *See* California Debt and Investment Advisory Commission, Overview of a Debt Financing, at 15 *available at* http://www.treasurer.ca.gov/cdiac/debtpubs/primer/chapter1a.pdf. An issuer may also collect and hold the revenues pledged to pay debt service on an issue of municipal securities and pay such debt service directly without the involvement of a private trustee. For example, the State of California generally acts as paying agent and registrar for all of its general obligation bonds and certain revenue bonds. *See* http://www.dof.ca.gov/accounting/. State statutes may require the treasurer of a city or county to act as registrar and fiscal agent for bonds issued by such city or county as well as other entities within such county (such as a school district). *See., e.g.,* Wash. Rev. Code §39.44.130 (1995). Although such provisions may allow a treasurer to appoint a private fiscal agent, it is not unusual for a county treasurer's office to serve as paying agent for all bonds issued by entities within the county. *See, e.g.,* Mojave County. Arizona Treasurer's Office *available at* http://www.co.mohave. az.us/contentpage.aspx?id=132.

[267] *See* Feldstein and Fabozzi, *supra* note 72, at 129.

[268] *See generally* Feldstein and Fabozzi, *supra* note 72, at 141. The trust indenture may require the bond trustee to provide certain continuing disclosure to bondholders (*e.g.*, periodic predefault notices). *See* Fippinger, *supra* note 29, § 9.9.

[269] In some instances, the trustee plays no role in connection with the continuing disclosure obligations of the issuer or obligated person.

[270] *See generally* NABL, "The Function and Professional Responsibilities of Bond Counsel," (3d. ed. 2011), *available at* http://www.nabl.org/uploads/cms/documents/ nabl_function_ and_professional_responsibilities_ of_bond_co unsel.pdf.

[271] *See* Disclosure Roles of Counsel, *supra* note 18, at 104.

[272] *Id.* at 105.

[273] See MSRB Rule G-12(e)(xi).

[274] *See* Disclosure Roles of Counsel, *supra* note 18.

[275] *See Weiss v. SEC*, 468 F.3d 849 (D.C. Cir. 2006).

[276] *See* Disclosure Roles of Counsel, *supra* note 18, at 89.

[277] *Id.* at 63. *See infra* § III.B.4 (Disclaimers of Responsibility for Information Included in Official Statements and Other Disclosures) for a discussion of disclaimers of responsibility for information included in disclosure documents.

[278] A 10b-5 opinion (or due diligence opinion) "addressed to an underwriter by underwriter's counsel customarily states that, based on certain specified inquiries, nothing has come to such counsel's attention indicating that the official statement contains any misstatements of material facts or any material omissions." MSRB Glossary, *supra* note 31 ("Due Diligence Opinion"). *See also infra* § III.B.4 (Disclaimers of Responsibility for Information Included in Official Statements and Other Disclosures) regarding disclaimers of liability.

[279] *See* Feldstein and Fabozzi, *supra* note 72, at 79-89.

[280] *See supra* notes 51 - 54 and II.A.2.b (Different Features of Municipal Securities).

[281] *See* Taylor Riggs, "S&P Issues New Bond Insurance Rating Criteria," The Bond Buyer (Aug. 25, 2011), *available at* http://www.bondbuyer.com/news/standard-and-poors-issues-bond-insurance-rating-1030444-1.html; Shannon D. Harrington, "S&P Bond Insurer Ratings Overhaul May Cause Downgrades," Bloomberg (Jan. 24, 2011), *available at* http://www.bloomberg.com/news/2011-01-24/s-p-may-be-forcedto-lower-bond-insurers-ratings-under-proposed-criteria.html. A new bond insurer was recently licensed by the State of New York. *See* Robert Slavin, "BAM Aims to Be New Insurer of Munis," The Bond Buyer (Jul. 23, 2012) *available at* http://www.bondbuyer.com/issues/121_141/new-bond-insurer-licensed1042133-1.html. *See also* Patrick McGee and Jeannette Neumann, "Start-Up Bond Insurer Promises Narrow Focus, Taxpayer Savings," The Wall Street Journal (Jul. 23, 2012) *available at* http://online.wsj.com/article/BT-CO-20120723-713037.html.

[282] Basel III is a comprehensive set of reform measures, developed by the Basel Committee on Banking Supervision, to "strengthen the regulation, supervision and risk management of the banking sector." *See* http://www.bis.org/bcbs/basel3.htm.

[283] *See* Dan Seymour, "Basel III May Curb Bank Debt," The Bond Buyer (Sept. 15, 2010), *available at* http://www.bondbuyer.com/issues/119_426/basel_iii_regulate_bank_debt-1017280-1.html. Banking regulators began measuring the liquidity coverage ratio in 2011 and will begin enforcing the 100%

minimum in 2015. Under Basel III, banks writing a letter of credit or standby bond purchase agreement for a municipal entity essentially would be required to buy and hold Treasury debt with principal equal to the size of the credit guarantee. Market participants say this additional cost to banks would likely be passed along to the municipal entity. *Id. See also* Washington, DC Hearing Transcript (Morning Session) at 5 (Collins).

[284] *See, e.g.,* Patrick McGee, "Assured All Alone On Top," The Bond Buyer (Apr. 16, 2010), *available at* http://www.bondbuyer.com/issues/119_321/assured_quarterly_rankings-1010938-1.html; The Bond Buyer's 2011 in Statistics, Feb. 13, 2012, *available at* http://www.bondbuyer.com/pdfs/2012_bb_stats_supp.pdf (reporting $19.5 billion long-term "guaranteed bonds" in 2011, and listing among the top guarantee providers a number of state-sponsored school district credit enhancement programs).

[285] *See* "The State of the Bond Insurance Industry," before the H. Subcomm. on Capital Markets, 110th Congress, Serial No. 110-91, at 87 (Feb. 14, 2008) (remarks of Chairman Kanjorski), *available at* http://archives.financialservices.house.gov/hearing 110/ht021408. shtml (noting that bond insurer downgrades have led to limited availability of bond insurance, which may cause municipal entities to pay higher interest on bonds or to delay much needed projects). *See also* Feldstein and Fabozzi, *supra* note72, at 270 (noting the importance of insurance in municipal bond context in reducing investor credit risk and expanding marketability of certain municipal bonds).

[286] *See, e.g.,* Birmingham Hearing Transcript at 297 (Lessley) (highlighting that municipal bond investing and understanding their underlying value has become even more complex, and is exacerbated by the decline of bond insurance); Jason Kephart, "Amid muni pall, Morningstar commences tax-exempt coverage," Investment News, July 16, 2012, *available at* http://www.investmentnews.com/article/20120716/FREE/120719945 (quoting the director of municipal analytics at Morningstar, "The importance of analyzing the credit risk of municipal bonds has taken on a new significance since the financial crisis.... Before, the credit quality of municipals was kind of taken for granted by investors."). The Commission will seek additional input from investors as we continue to evaluate investor disclosure needs in this area.

[287] *See, e.g.,* Joel Seligman, *The Municipal Disclosure Debate*, 9 DEL. J. CORP. L. 647, 660 (1985).

[288] *See, e.g.,* GAO Market Structure Report, *supra* note 61, at 14, n.29, and accompanying text; Birmingham Hearing Transcript at 297 (Lessley).

[289] *See, e.g.,* Washington, DC Hearing Transcript (Morning Session) at 23-24 (Deane) (noting that prior to 2008, credit risk was not considered to be a major differentiating factor among AAA insured bonds). The Commission has stated that in the context of municipal securities offerings, as well as other types of securities offerings, the existence of credit enhancement is not a substitute for information about the underlying obligor or other obligor entity. *See* 2010 Adopting Release, *supra* note 170.

[290] *See, e.g.*, Washington, DC Hearing Transcript (Morning Session) at 11 (McCarthy) (expressing the view that the bond insurers' credit underwriting and ratings, and the homogenization of the underlying credits, creates significant market liquidity and benefit to retail investors).

[291] Washington, DC Hearing Transcript (Morning Session) at 11 (McCarthy). *See also* Birmingham Hearing Transcript at 297 (Lessley) (noting that in the past municipal insurers provided comfort to investors through bond insurance, and that this enabled similar types of bonds to be priced similarly).

[292] Washington, DC Hearing Transcript (Morning Session) at 11 (McCarthy).

[293] *Id.*

[294] Washington, DC Hearing Transcript (Morning Session) at 7 (Doe).

[295] *See* Feldstein and Fabozzi, *supra* note 72, at 223. *See* Patrick McGee, "Kroll Bond Ratings Issues Its First Municipal-Bond Rating," Wall Street Journal, Mar. 29, 2012, *available at* http://online.wsj.com/article/BTCO-20120329-715631.html.

[296] *See* Securities and Exchange Commission, Annual Report on Nationally Recognized Statistical Ratings Organizations (Jan. 2011), at 6, *available at* http://www.sec.gov/ divisions/marketreg/ratingagency/ nrsroannrep0111.pdf ("2011 NRSRO Annual Report"). The Exchange Act definition of "nationally recognized statistical rating organization" identifies five classes of ratings: (1) financial institutions, brokers, or dealers (2) insurance companies, (3) corporate issuers, (4) issuers of asset-backed securities, (5) and issuers of government, municipal and sovereign securities (collectively "sovereign securities"). *See* Exchange Act § 3(a)(62). According to data compiled from NRSROs, the sovereign securities class, which includes municipal securities, represents the largest number of credit ratings by NRSROs at almost 77% of total ratings outstanding. *See* 2011 Annual NRSRO Report at 5.

[297] *See* Feldstein and Fabozzi, *supra* note 72, at 223.

[298] *Id.* at 223-224.

[299] *Id.* However, issuers of some insured municipal securities did not obtain underlying (unenhanced) ratings.

[300] *See* Feldstein and Fabozzi, *supra* note 72, at 223. Market participants have indicated that retail investors primarily focus on interest rate, maturity and credit rating.

[301] Washington, DC Hearing Transcript (Morning Session) at 23 (Collins).

[302] Washington, DC Hearing Transcript (Morning Session) at 23 (Doe), (noting that retail investors do rely on credit ratings and are dependent on the services of five entities, three credit rating agencies and two evaluation services).

[303] *See supra* note 196.

[304] One commenter argued that credit ratings, credit downgrades and other events and proprietary NRSRO reports should be available to anyone purchasing a bond. *See* Comments (email) from Nathan Saks (Mar. 28, 2010), *available at* http://www.sec.gov/comments/4-610/4610-30.pdf ("Saks Comments").

[305] *See* Exchange Act Release No. 55857, "Oversight of Credit Rating Agencies Registered as Nationally Recognized Statistical Rating Organizations" (June 5, 2007), 72 FR 33564 (June 18, 2007), *available at* http://www.sec.gov/rules/final/2007/34-55857fr.pdf. The implementing rules consisted of Form NRSRO and Rules 17g-1 through 17g-6 under the Exchange Act. The Commission has twice adopted amendments to some of these rules. *See* Exchange Act Release No. 59342, "Amendments to Rules for Nationally Recognized Statistical Rating Organizations" (Feb. 2, 2009), 74 FR 6456 (Feb. 9, 2009), *available at* http://www.sec.gov/rules/final/2009/34-59342fr.pdf; and Exchange Act Release No. 61050, "Amendments to Rules for Nationally Recognized Statistical Rating Organizations" (Nov. 23, 2009), 74 FR 63832 (Dec. 4, 2009), *available at* http://www.sec.gov/rules/final/ 2009/34-61050fr.pdf.

[306] *See* Exchange Act § 15E(c)(2)("Notwithstanding any other provision of law, neither the Commission nor any State (or political subdivision thereof) may regulate the substance of credit ratings or the procedures and methodologies by which any [NRSRO] determines ratings").

[307] *See* Dodd-Frank Act, §§ 932, 936, 938, 939A, 939B and 943. Pursuant to Dodd-Frank, the Commission has adopted changes to its rules that remove the credit rating agency exemption from Regulation FD and remove references to credit ratings in rules relating to securities offerings and issuer disclosure obligations. *See* Dodd-Frank Act, §939B (Removal from Regulation FD of the Exemption for Credit Rating Agencies). *See* Securities Act Release No. 9146/Exchange Act Release No. 63003, "Removal from Regulation FD of the Exemption for Credit Rating Agencies," (Sept. 29, 2010), 75 FR 61050 (Oct. 4,2010), *available at* http://www.sec.gov/rules/final/2010/33-9146fr.pdf,); §939A (Removing references to credit ratings in rules relating to securities offerings and in issuer disclosure obligations). *See* Securities Act Release No. 9245/Exchange Act Release No. 64975, "Security Ratings," (July 27, 2011), 76 FR 46603 (Aug. 3, 2011), *available at* http://www.sec.gov/rules/final/2011/33-9245fr.pdf.

[308] *See* Dodd-Frank Act, §943(Disclosure of Asset-Backed Securities Offerings). *See* Securities Act Release No. 9175/Exchange Act Release No. 63741, "Disclosure for Asset-Backed Securities Required by Section 943 of the Dodd-Frank Wall Street Reform and Consumer Protection Act," (Jan. 20, 2011), 76 FR 4489 (Jan. 26, 2011), *available at* http://www.sec.gov/rules/final/2011/33-9175fr.pdf.

[309] *See* Dodd-Frank Act, § 939A. Section 939A of the Dodd-Frank Act provides in part that each federal agency shall modify regulations identified in the required review to remove any reference to or requirement of reliance on credit ratings and substitute in such regulations such standard of credit-worthiness as each respective agency shall determine as appropriate for such regulations. *See* Securities Act Release No. 9193, "References to Credit Ratings in Certain Investment Company Act Rues and Forms," (Mar. 3, 2011), 76 FR 12896 (Mar. 9, 2011), *available at* http://www.sec.gov/rules/proposed/2011/33-9193fr.pdf; and Exchange Act Release No. 64352, "Removal of Certain References to Credit Ratings Under the Securities Exchange Act of 1934," (Apr. 27, 2011), 76 FR 26550 (May 6, 2011), *available at* http://www.sec.gov/rules/proposed/2011/34-64352fr.pdf.

[310] *See* Exchange Act Release No. 64514, "Nationally Recognized Statistical Rating Organizations" (May 18, 2011), 76 FR 33420 (June 8, 2011), *available at* http://www.sec.gov/rules/proposed/2011/34-64514fr.pdf.

[311] *See* San Francisco Hearing Transcript at 17 (Lockyer), 89 (Blake), 94 (Kiefer) and 132(McIntire).

[312] *See* San Francisco Hearing Transcript at 89 (Blake).

[313] *See* San Francisco Hearing Transcript at 17 (Lockyer).

[314] *See* San Francisco Hearing Transcript at 134 (McIntire) (noting that the average 10 year cumulative default rate for a AAA corporate bond is 0.5%, whereas the cumulative default rate for an A-rated municipal bond over the same time period is 0.03%).

[315] In 2008, a Congressional hearing addressed the concept of a "global" rating scale. *See* "Municipal Bond Turmoil: Impact on Cities, Towns, and States," Hearing Before the Committee on Financial Services, U.S.

House of Representatives, March 12, 2008, available at http://www.gpo.gov/fdsys/pkg/CHRG-110hhrg41730/pdf/CHRG-110hhrg41730.pdf. In 2010, Moody's announced and implemented a "recalibration" of outstanding municipal bonds to a global ratings scale that treats all issuers alike: private companies, sovereign governments, nonprofits and municipalities. *See* Lisa Lambert, "Moody's moves U.S. states to new 'global' rating scale," Reuters (Apr. 19, 2010), *available at* http://www.reuters.com/ article/2010/04/19/municipals-ratings-moodys-idUSN1920043720100419. Moody's had long held municipalities to a higher rating standard than sovereign governments, corporations and structured products. Fitch followed shortly thereafter and S&P maintained that its rating on municipal bonds had been on the global scale all along. The move to a global ratings scale resulted in the ratings of a large number of municipal securities being upgraded, despite there being no change in the underlying credit.

316 *See* San Francisco Hearing Transcript at 94 (Kiefer) (noting the Calpers Board's endorsement of a scale for municipal securities that is uniform, fair and consistent with other rated products), 17 (Lockyer) (suggested that international investors, who are increasingly subscribing to municipal bond issues but are less familiar with U.S. local governments than domestic investors, would also benefit from a global rating scale), and 132 (McIntire) (speaking in his capacity as a NAST Vice President).

317 *See, e.g.*, San Francisco Hearing Transcript at 98 (Belsky) (noting the confusion the move has caused because ratings in the corporate market measure default risk and recovery and municipals rarely default); San Francisco Hearing Transcript at 92 (Blake) (stating that governments should be rated on a completely different scale based upon the unique characteristics of governments); San Francisco Hearing Transcript at 132 (McIntire) (sharing his personal view that the recalibration and homogenization of ratings has made it increasingly difficult for investors to compare municipal credits relative to one another, and that municipal risk remains overstated relative to corporate risk because, despite recalibration, the scales are not the same with respect to measuring the ultimate risk of default or recovery); Washington, DC Hearing Transcript (Morning Session) at 26 (Kirkpatrick) (noting that the percentage of investment grade municipal securities went from 52% to 82% after the move to a global ratings scale).

318 *See, e.g.*, Washington, DC Hearing Transcript (Morning Session) at 33 (Wittman).

319 *See* San Francisco Hearing Transcript at 98-100 (Belsky), 92 (Blake), 18 (Lockyer), 133-134 (McIntire). *See also supra* note 317.

320 *See* San Francisco Hearing Transcript at 83-86 (Belsky).

321 *See* San Francisco Hearing Transcript at 92 (Blake).

322 One commenter also noted that investors should have access to information about whether a particular bond has been re-rated and how often. *See* Washington, DC Hearing Transcript (Morning Session) at 30 (Wittman).

323 *See, e.g.*, San Francisco Hearing Transcript at 18-19 (Lockyer), 90-91 (Blake), 95-96 (Kiefer), 135 (McIntire) (explicitly suggesting congressional action to bolster SEC oversight of rating agencies). *See also supra* note 306 and accompanying text (relating to the Commission's lack of authority to regulate rating methodologies).

324 San Francisco Hearing Transcript at 19 (Lockyer), 90-91 (Blake).

325 *See supra* § II.B.1.b (Antifraud Authority). *See also infra* § III.C.4.a (*Enforcement Actions*).

326 *See supra* § II.B.1.c (*Rule 15c2-12*).

327 *See* 1994 Interpretive Release, *supra* note 31.

328 *See supra* § III.B.3.a (Municipal Securities Rulemaking Board).

329 *See infra* § III.A.1 (Voluntary Disclosure Initiatives and Disclosure Guidelines).

330 *See, e.g.*, National Federation of Municipal Analysts, *Disclosure Handbook For Municipal Securities* (1990) ("NFMA Disclosure Handbook").

331 In 1994, the Commission recognized that there were extensive industry disclosure guidelines that market participants followed in preparing official statements for municipal securities offerings. *See* 1994 Interpretive Release, *supra* note 31.

332 Such guidelines are accessible at the websites maintained by the respective organizations: GFOA – www.gfoa.org; NABL – www.nabl.org; NFMA – www.nfma.org; and NASACT – www.nasact.org.

333 GFOA, GFOA Best Practice: Understanding Your Continuing Disclosure Responsibilities (2010), *available at* http://www.gfoa.org/downloads/GFOA_understanding continuingdis closureBP.pdf ("Understanding Your Continuing Disclosure Responsibilities"); GFOA, GFOA Best Practice: Governmental Accounting, Auditing and Financial Reporting Practices (1983, 1997 and 2006), *available at* http://www.gfoa.org/downloads/caafr practices.pdf; NFMA, Position Paper on Voluntary Interim Disclosure by State and Local Governments (2004), *available at* http://data.memberclicks.com/site/nfma/nfma position interim disclosure.pdf.

334 NABL, Considerations in Preparing Disclosure in Official Statements Regarding an Issuer's Pension Funding Obligations (Public Defined Benefit Pension Plans), May 15, 2012 ("NABL Considerations"), *available at*

http://www.nabl.org/uploads/cms/documents/ pension_funding_obligations_document_5-1812_b.pdf; NFMA, "White Paper on Disclosure for GASB 45" (Apr. 2009), *available at* http://data.memberclicks.com/site/nfma/DG.WP.gasb45_063009.pdf.

[335] *See infra* notes 339 - 341 and accompanying text.

[336] *See* Understanding Your Continuing Disclosure Responsibilities, *supra* note 333.

[337] *Id. See also* NFMA Position Paper on Voluntary Interim Disclosure by State and Local Governments, *supra* note 333.

[338] *See infra* note 436.

[339] *See* Disclosure Roles of Counsel *supra* note 18, at 240-241 (citing NASACT, A Proposal: Results of the Deliberation at the Meeting about Voluntary Interim Disclosures by State and Local Governments).

[340] These subdivisions are: general obligation and tax-supported debt, water/sewer debt, tax increment supported debt, public power debt, airports, toll roads, solid waste transactions, housing revenue bond issues, hospital debt, private college university transactions, land secured debt transactions, long-term care/senior living debt, variable rate and short-term securities and swaps. *See* NFMA, Recommended Best Practices in Disclosure (2004) ("Recommended Best Practices"). *See also* NFMA, Disclosure Guidelines, *available at* http://www.nfma.org/mc/page.do?sitePageId=91110&orgId=nfma (accessed May 23, 2012).

[341] *See* Recommended Best Practices, *supra* note 340, at 15.

[342] *See id.* at 16.

[343] *See supra* note 74.

[344] *See* Robert Dean Pope, *Making Good Disclosure – The Roles and Responsibilities of State and Local Officials Under the Federal Securities Laws* (2001).

[345] *See* Disclosure Roles of Counsel, *supra* note 18.

[346] *See id.* at 217-248

[347] *See e.g.,* San Francisco Hearing Transcript at 44 (Colby) ("frequent financial disclosure is generally limited to the healthcare sector and to many large frequent issuers"). *See also* 1994 Interpretive Release *supra* note 31, at 20 ("[W]hile large repeat general obligation issuers usually have comprehensive disclosure documents, small issuers and conduit issuers, particularly in the healthcare, housing and industrial development areas, do not always provide the same quality of disclosure.").

[348] *See infra* II.B.1.c (Rule 15c2-12).

[349] *See* 1988 Proposing Release and 1989 Adopting Release, *supra* note 154. The interpretation in the 1988 Proposing Release was modified slightly in the 1989 Adopting Release. The 1988 Proposing Release states that "in both negotiated and competitively bid municipal offerings, the Commission expects, at a minimum, that underwriters will review the issuer's disclosure documents in a professional manner for possible inaccuracies and omissions. In the 1989 Adopting Release, the Commission emphasized that "the presence of credit enhancement does not foreclose the need for a reasonable investigation of the accuracy and completeness of key representations concerning the primary obligor." *See also* 1994 Interpretive Release at, *supra* note 31, at §V.

[350] This information was intended to be the template as well for ongoing information provided to the market about the municipal securities being offered. *See infra* note 416. In 1994, the Commission highlighted certain aspects of primary offering disclosure as needing improvement: disclosure of potential conflicts of interest and material financial relationships among issuers, advisers and underwriters, including those arising from political contributions; disclosure regarding the terms and risks of securities being offered; disclosure of the issuer's or obligor's financial condition, results of operations, and cash flows; disclosure of the issuer's plans regarding the provision of information to the secondary market; and timely delivery of preliminary official statements to underwriters and potential investors. *See* 1994 Interpretive Release, *supra* note 31.

[351] *See* 1989 Adopting Release, *supra* note 154. The specific information about a governmental issuer can vary depending on its role in an offering: when the governmental issuer is the primary obligor, there generally is significant disclosure about the issuer in the official statement; however, in conduit offerings in which the governmental issuer may have limited or no ultimate payment obligations, disclosure about the governmental issuer may be limited, with the bulk of the disclosure about the conduit borrower. *See* Disclosure Roles of Counsel *supra* note 18, at 54.

[352] *See* Exchange Act § 10 and Rule 10b-5 thereunder. Issuers are primarily responsible for the content of their disclosure documents and may be held liable under the federal securities laws for misleading disclosure. *See* 1989 Adopting Release, *supra* note 154, n.84. As noted in the Staff's 1977 New York City Report, "[a]lthough municipalities have certain unique attributes by virtue of their political nature, insofar as they are issuers of

securities, they are subject to the proscription against false and misleading disclosure. *See* Staff Report on Transactions in Securities of the City of New York (Aug. 1977), Chapter III, at 1-2 ("NY City Report").

[353] Securities Act Release No. 7260/Exchange Act Release No. 36760, *In the Matter of County of Orange, California; Orange County Flood Control District and County of Orange, California Board of Supervisors* (order) (Jan. 24, 1996), *available at* http://www.sec.gov/ litigation/admin/337260.txt ("*In the Matter of County of Orange, California*").

[354] Securities Act Release No. 7354/Exchange Act Release No. 37748, *In the Matter of Maricopa County, Arizona* (order) (Oct. 3, 1996), *available at* http://www.sec.gov/ litigation/admin/337354.txt ("*In the Matter of Maricopa County*").

[355] Securities Act Release No. 7460/Exchange Act Release No. 39149, *In the Matter of City of Syracuse, New York, Warren D. Simpson and Edward D. Polgreen* (order) (Sep. 30, 1997), *available at* http://www.sec.gov/ litigation/admin/3-9452.txt ("*In the Matter of City of Syracuse*").

[356] Securities Act Release No. 8213/Exchange Act Release No. 47552, *In the Matter of the City of Miami, Florida* (order) (Mar. 21, 2003), *available at* http://www.sec.gov/litigation/ opinions/33-8213.htm ("*In the Matter of the City of Miami*").

[357] Securities Act Release No. 8260, *In the Matter of the Massachusetts Turnpike Authority and James J. Kerasiotes* (order) (July 31, 2003), *available at* http://www.sec.gov/litigation/ admin/33-8260.htm.

[358] Securities Act Release No. 8751/Exchange Act Release No.54745, *In the Matter of the City of San Diego, California* (order) (Nov. 14, 2006), *available at* http://www.sec.gov/ litigation/admin/2006/33-8751.pdf ("In the Matter of the City of San Diego").

[359] Securities Act Release No. 9135, *In the Matter of State of New Jersey* (order) (Aug. 18, 2010), *available at* http://www.sec.gov/litigation/admin/2010/33-9135.pdf.

[360] *See e.g.*, *In the Matter of City of San Diego*, *supra* note 358; SEC Litigation Release No. 20522, "SEC Charges Five Former San Diego City Officials With Fraud in Connection with City Municipal Securities Offerings" (Apr. 7, 2008), *available at* http://www.sec.gov/ litigation/litreleases/2008/lr20522.htm (Commission brought case against former San Diego city official for acting recklessly in failing to disclose material facts regarding the city's looming financial crisis and related underfunding of the city's pension and retiree health care obligations). *See infra* §II(C)(3) at Enforcement Actions regarding the settlement of this matter. *See also* Exchange Act Release No. 36761, "Report of Investigation in the Matter of County of Orange, California as it Relates to the Conduct of the Members of the Board of Supervisors" (Jan. 24, 1996), *available at* http://www.sec.gov/info/municipal/ mbonds/publicof.htm.

[361] *See, e.g.*, SEC Litigation Release No.20358, "SEC Obtains Final Judgment Against Robert A. Kasirer in Municipal Revenue Bond Offering Fraud" (Nov. 5, 2007), *available at* http://www.sec.gov/litigation/ litreleases/2007/lr20358.htm (Commission brought case against Heritage Housing Development Inc. and its president for the fraudulent offer and sale of over $131 million of municipal revenue bonds for various senior assisted living facilities in a type of Ponzi scheme from February, 1996 through August, 1999); SEC Litigation Release No. 19887, "Final Judgment Entered Against Defendant Bruce M. Perry" (Oct. 25, 2006), *available at* http://www.sec.gov/litigation/litreleases/2006/lr19887.htm (Commission brought case against Mount Sinai Medical Center and its CEO, Bruce Perry, for various false and misleading statements and omissions in disclosure documents issued by Mount Sinai in connection with a bond offering in May, 2001); Exchange Act Release No. 42992, *In the Matter of Allegheny Health, Education and Research Foundation* (June 30, 2000), *available at* http://www.sec.gov/litigation/admin/34-42992.htm ("*In the Matter of Allegheny*") (Commission brought case against the Allegheny Health, Education and Research Foundation – a major nonprofit health care organization – for grossly overstating the income of various hospitals and thereby masking the enterprise's deteriorating financial condition prior to its filing for bankruptcy).

[362] In 2000, the Commission brought an injunctive action against an underwriting firm and one of its principals in connection with a series of bond offerings to finance a residential development in southern California. After a trial, a federal district judge enjoined the firm for misrepresenting and omitting material facts in the offering documents concerning the value of the land used as security for the bonds, the status of the project, and the likelihood that the bonds would be repaid from the revenues of the project. *See* SEC Litigation Release No.17432, "Court Enjoins Municipal Underwriter in Real Estate Financing Fraud" (Mar. 22, 2002), *available at* http://www.sec.gov/litigation/litreleases/lr17432.htm. Similarly, the Commission filed suit against an underwriter and conduit bond issuer for failing to disclose the planned departure of a major tenant from an office building being financed with a municipal bond issue. *See Dolphin & Bradbury, Inc. v. SEC*, 512 F.3d 634 (DC Cir. 2008); Exchange Act Release No. 54143, "*In the Matter of Dolphin and Bradbury, Incorporated and Robert J. Bradbury*" (July 13, 2006), *available at* www.sec.gov/litigation/ opinions/2006/33-8721.pdf.

[363] A compendium of the Commission's enforcement cases involving municipal securities is available on the Commission's website at http://www.sec.gov/info/municipal.shtml.

[364] *See supra* § II.B.1.c (Rule 15c2-12).

[365] *See* 1994 Interpretive Release *supra* note 31.

[366] *See supra* § III.A.1 (Voluntary Disclosure Initiatives and Disclosure Guidelines).

[367] Annual disclosure obligations pursuant to continuing disclosure agreements include the dissemination of financial and operating information such as audited financial statements.

[368] *See supra* note 170 and accompanying text.

[369] *See* Understanding Your Continuing Disclosure Responsibilities, *available at* http://www.gfoa.org/index.php?option=com_content&task=view&id=1588; Maintaining an Investor Relations Program, *available at* http://www.gfoa.org/index.php?option=com_ content& task= view&id=1578; Using a Web Site for Disclosure, *available at* http://www.gfoa.org/index.php?option=com_content&task= view&id=1587; and Web Site Presentation of Official Financial Documents, *available at* http://www.gfoa.org/index.php? option=com content&task=view&id=1473.

[370] For example, many continuing disclosure delinquencies arise in offerings of 529 Plans. *See* MSRB Notice 2010-19, "Reminder on Submissions of Disclosure Documents to EMMA For 529 College Savings Plans" (June 28, 2010), *available at* http://www.msrb.org/Rules-and-Interpretations/RegulatoryNotices/2010/2010-19.aspx.

[371] NFMA, "NFMA Releases Results of Disclosure Survey" (May 23, 2002), *available at* http://data.memberclicks.com/site/nfma/disclosure_survey.pdf ("NFMA Survey"). In 2008, DPC/DATA published a study of obligors subject to disclosure requirements that issued bonds between 1996 and 2005. Peter J. Schmitt, "Estimating Municipal Securities Continuing Disclosure Compliance: A Litmus Test Approach," DPC DATA (2008), *available at* http://www.dpcdata.com/html/Estimating%20Municipal%20 Securities% 20Continuing%20Disclosure%20 Compliance.pdf ("DPC Study"). The DPC Study underscored the prevalence of delinquency, or the failure of obligors to comply at all or on a timely basis with their continuing disclosure covenants. The DPC Study was conducted prior to the establishment of EMMA as a central information repository, and at the time, data was submitted to one of four Nationally Recognized Municipal Securities Information Repositories (NRMSIRs), including DPC/DATA. As such, the DPC Study was limited to its internal records of filings received by it as a NRMSIR.

[372] *See* NFMA Survey, *supra* note 371.

[373] *Id.*

[374] *See, e.g.*, Birmingham Hearing Transcript at 94-95 (MacLennan) ("You've already heard from speakers in prior hearings that there have been improvements in the area of primary market disclosure, and these improvements, I believe, have been achieved in part through the combined and concerted efforts of many market organizations including the National Association of Bond Lawyers, National Federation of Municipal Analysts, the Government Finance Officers Association, as well as the Commission, the MSRB, SIFMA, among others. With respect to continuing disclosure and municipal secondary market generally, I believe that improvements can be achieved in the same manner, through the combined and concerted efforts of all participants in the municipal secondary market, and without necessarily additional regulations of issuers"), 99-100 (Presley) ("First, it is certainly true that disclosure practices in the municipal market can and should improve, but it is also true that significant advances have been made in disclosure practices in the municipal market in the last three decades as a result of various SEC enforcement actions, private anti-fraud actions and regulatory initiatives with respect to primary market official statements and continuing disclosure, the great majority of issuers have a very solid appreciation for their disclosure responsibilities"), 180 (Watkins) ("My opinion is that the current regulatory rime [sic] in the muni market has by and large worked and worked very well over the last 30 years").

[375] *See, e.g.*, San Francisco Hearing Transcript at 20 (Lockyer) ("There's a well-established framework for municipal disclosure. By and large, the existing system has served issuers and investors well. The size of the market and types of debt defined broadly as municipal obviously have grown and evolved. There's a need undoubtedly for regulatory improvement"), 191, 194 (Harrington) ("[W]e do not believe the SEC needs to have a larger role in municipal finance . . . . There are over 87,000 government entities in the United States. In California, over 800 separate government entities have issued debt this year alone. And with all this activity, I can count on one hand the number of investment grade government bonds that have failed to pay investors").

[376] *See, e.g.*, San Francisco Hearing Transcript at 20 (Lockyer) ("So I hope you'll please consider the need for disclosure standards that acknowledge the limited resources of small and infrequent municipal issuers, as well as the relevancy of standardized reports and uniform reporting timeframes"). *See also* Birmingham Hearing Transcript at 157 (Duggan) ("In our zeal to prevent unreasonable risks . . . we need not create elaborate

structures that cause all issuers to bear too large a burden"); San Francisco Hearing Transcript at 75 (McNally) ("[A] third category which is simply not feasible in this market, and that is an attempt to establish a standardized disclosure that would apply across the board by virtue of the diversity of the issuers and the nature of the security").

377 *See* Letter from Mary Colby, National Federation of Municipal Analysts, to Commissioner Elisse B. Walter (Oct. 6, 2010), *available at* http://www.sec.gov/comments/4-610/4610-9.pdf ("NFMA Comment Letter") ("We do not believe that the municipal market lends itself to a one size fits all approach to regulation but there should be a few basic requisites to participation in the public markets . . . Beyond these basic requirements, given the differences among issuers and debt instruments offered in the municipal market, it is difficult to prescribe specifics for either the contents of official statements or financial statements"). *See also* San Francisco Hearing Transcript at 20 (Lockyer) ("While it's desirable to have minimum disclosure standards, there may not be a single one size fits all solution. So I hope you'll please consider the need for disclosure standards that acknowledge the limited resources of small and infrequent municipal issuers, as well as the relevancy of standardized reports and uniform reporting timeframes"), 53 (McNally) ("Moreover, there cannot be a one size fits all approach to municipal disclosure given the wide range of purposes and structures of the over 50,000 municipal issuers"); Birmingham Hearing Transcript at 48 (Beardsley) (noting that lack of resources and infrequency of market access pose a particular problem for smaller issuers in establishing good disclosure practices), 122 (Presley), 180-81 (Watkins) ("The challenge . . . in regulating muni disclosure is basically, the composition of this market . . . and trying to write a uniform rule that would apply in a meaningful way to this disparate group of issuers and securities, I would submit to you is not challenging, but impossible").

378 *See, e.g.*, San Francisco Hearing Transcript at 21 (Lockyer) ("Disclosure standards, it seems to me, need to recognize the differences between issuers, the types of municipal debt issued [and] the relative security of the investment. For example, obviously there's a difference between a tax supported General Obligation Bond and the disclosure with respect to that are probably very different from what's needed with a utility revenue bond, which is not the same that you might have for land secured financing, largely because of different risks associated with the different issues"). *See also* San Francisco Hearing Transcript at 73 (Colby) (mandated level of disclosure should reflect the security of the bonds issued), 75-76 (McNally).

379 *See, e.g.*, San Francisco Hearing Transcript at 68 (Colby), 72 (Mayhew).

380 Birmingham Hearing Transcript at 90 (Scott) (noting that "additional requirements do not necessarily mean additional resources"). Another panelist argued that imposing new regulatory requirements on municipal issuers could have a devastating impact on state and local budgets at a time when it can be least afforded. *See* Birmingham Hearing Transcript at 180 (Watkins) ("I'm here to share my view and concerns that any additional SEC regulation of municipal disclosure could be intrusive, burdensome and unwarranted if not very, very carefully considered and crafted"); San Francisco Hearing Transcript at 135 (McIntire) ("I must emphasize that a repeal of the Tower Amendment and imposition of a set of uniform federal regulations on the issuance of municipal securities could have a devastating impact on state and local budgets, at a time when we can least afford it").

381 Birmingham Hearing Transcript at 122 (Presley).

382 Birmingham Hearing Transcript at 96 (MacLennan) ("[I]t would be a particularly inopportune time to restrict the use of [conduit structures] or otherwise increase the cost (thereby reducing the value) of this economic tool. For smaller communities especially, this may be the only financial incentive available to be offered for new commercial development").

383 *See, e.g.*, San Francisco Hearing Transcript at 63 (McNally) ("I think what you have to be very careful of, though, and speaking as counsel to issuers, is that we're mindful of the advice you gave us in the '94 interpretive release to the effect that anytime the information is reasonably likely, not even reasonably intended, reasonably likely to reach investors in the trading markets, it will be tested against 10(b)5 liability"), 216 (Keller) ("[L]iability concern, in other words, liability as an impediment. But there really is a focus on, okay, what is information that is designed for investors and therefore subject to, you know, potential liability").

384 *See, e.g.*, Birmingham Hearing Transcript at 142-43 (Borg) ("So with significant pressures on state and local government budgets, timely and complete disclosure in this market is now of greater concern. Now, given the historical levels of predominantly lax disclosure, there's certainly room for improvement. The decision that an investor will make on whether to invest in a municipal or governmental bond must be based on good, solid, reliable and timely information. Disclosure is the primary component of that information"), 163-65 (Johnston) ("I see the problems related to disclosure falling into three categories. First, timeliness. In my

sector it's very common to have to wait 2 hundred and 70 days for any kind of financial disclosure. This is just too long . . . . The second problem I would like to highlight is the frequency of disclosure. I fully understand it's impossible for all issuers to provide audited financial statements in 30 or 60 days following the end of a fiscal year, but does that mean it's impossible to get investors some type of recent information that can help me in making my investment decisions, and I'm afraid that some of obligors have fallen prey to I only need to provide audits, that's all I'm going to provide . . . . Third, I struggle with completeness, and this actually does affect the primary market as well as the secondary market. Many times compliance with continuing disclosure weakens over time . . . . And finally, I'll bring up road shows. I'd like to see road show presentations, whether done on-line or in person, made available for download"), 171-72 (Nolan) ("I think it needs to be stated up front-- consistent, timely and accurate information throughout the life of the bonds needs to be improved, especially in the secondary market, and particularly with regards to infrequent issuers. While disclosures from issuers has become [sic] over the years through 15c2-12 and the establishment of EMMA, as well as the amendments to 15c2-12, there is always room for improvement").

[385] *See supra* § II.C.6 (Credit Enhancers).

[386] *See supra* notes 374 - 375, and accompanying text.

[387] *See, e.g.*, San Francisco Hearing Transcript at 44 (Colby).

[388] *See* NFMA Letter, *infra* note 499.

[389] *See, e.g.*, John McDermott, "The Municipal Middle Man Misses Out Again," (July 14, 2011), *available at* http://ftalphaville.ft.com/blog/2011/07/14/622886/the-municipal-middle-man-misses-out-again.

[390] *See* San Francisco Hearing Transcript (Kuhn) at 260.

[391] *See, e.g.*, Letter from John M. McNally, NABL, to Commissioner Elisse B. Walter, (Sept. 2, 2011), (including attachment, in Appx. A, of Letter from Kathleen C. McKinney, NABL, to Commissioner Elisse B. Walter (May 14, 2010)), *available at http://www.sec.gov/ comments/4-610/4610-68.pdf* ("NABL Comment Letter").

[392] *See, e.g.*, NABL Comment Letter, *supra* note 391.

[393] *See* NABL Comment Letter, *supra* note 391.

[394] San Francisco Hearing Transcript at 41-43 (Colby) ("NFMA believes that disclosure in the muni market has made great strides in the last 16 years since the adoption of the 1994 amendments to 15c2-12 and in the last six years since the establishment of the Central Post Office . . . . With regard to secondary market disclosure, our comments are far less glowing. Secondary market disclosure continues to be spotty, particularly among infrequent issuers and those who have historically issued only with primary market bond insurance"). *See also* NFMA Comment Letter, *supra* note 377 ("disclosure in the municipal market continues to trail substantially that of other areas of the US financial markets, while the municipal market has become far more complex than it was in 1994"); Birmingham Hearing Transcript at 144 (Presley) ("[R]ecent SEC, state regulatory and FINRA actions clearly point to a growing concern regarding the lack of current official filings, the lack of transparency, and the lack of continuing financial records of some public borrowers. Look, this is almost a three trillion dollar market, and with weak disclosure this raises the anxiety levels of investors where current and continuing financial information is absolutely necessary for investors to do what we have always said in regulatory parlance, make informed investment decisions").

[395] *See, e.g.*, NFMA Comment Letter, *supra* note 377; Birmingham Hearing Transcript at 176 (Nolan) ("In our view, a uniform set standard on the exact type of information included in an OS is necessary, as well as what additional items will be disclosed over the life of the bonds on EMMA").

[396] Timeliness of financial information is discussed *infra* at § III.B.1.d (Timeliness of Financial Information); *see also* GASB Timeliness Study, *infra* note 429.

[397] Written Testimony of Mary Colby, Industry Practices Chairperson, National Federation of Municipal Analysts, San Francisco Field Hearing, Sep. 21, 2010, *available at* http://www.sec.gov/spotlight/municipalsecurities/statements092110/colby092110.pdf ("Colby Testimony").

[398] *See, e.g.*, Colby Testimony; Birmingham Hearing Transcript at 165 (Johnston).

[399] *See, e.g.*, Colby Testimony; Birmingham Hearing Transcript at 176 (Nolan).

[400] *Id.* Rule 15c2-12(b)(5)(i)(C)(6) requires notice within 10 business days of "[a]dverse tax opinions, the issuance by the Internal Revenue Service of proposed or final determinations of taxability, Notices of Proposed Issue (IRS Form 5701-TEB) or other material notices or determinations with respect to the tax status of the security, or other material events affecting the tax status of the security."

[401] *Id.*

[402] *See* Birmingham Hearing Transcript at 145 (Borg).

[403] Although the CAFR data is comprehensive and in many instances exceeds the requirements that issuers must file in accordance with their continuing disclosure agreements, (*See, e.g.*, Washington, DC Hearing Transcript

(Afternoon Session) at 20 (Firestine) it was suggested that some issuers: (1) fail to update CAFRs; (2) present the information in a different format from that used in the issuer's official statement, thus making comparability with the financial information and operating data contained in the official statement difficult; and that the comprehensive nature of the CAFR could make it difficult for investors to locate discrete but relevant information regarding a subsidiary credit.

404 *See, e.g.*, Birmingham Hearing Transcript at 179 (Nolan).

405 *See, e.g.*, Birmingham Hearing Transcript at 200 (Johnston).

406 *See infra* note 479 and accompanying text. A limited exception appears to exist in the health care sector, where the limited market for securities gives power to bond purchasers.

407 *See* Birmingham Hearing Transcript at 95 (MacLennan) ("With respect to continuing disclosure and municipal secondary market generally, I believe that improvements can be achieved in the same manner, through the combined and concerted efforts of all participants in the municipal secondary market, and without necessarily additional regulations of issuers"). *See also* Birmingham Hearing Transcript at 184 (Watkins) ("It's worked in the past, and I believe that it will work in the future, and I think that is really the better way to go is to let the stakeholders in the marketplace continue the evolutionary process of improving disclosure available to analysts and investors as we have in the past and resist the temptation of imposing a one- size-fits-all approach to improving information available in the market, and communication and education are the key").

408 *See, e.g.,* San Francisco Hearing Transcript at 44 (Colby). However, certain health care bond sectors (excluding hospitals) that are traditionally considered riskier are also evidencing disproportionately high levels of non-compliance with continuing disclosure obligations, including life care and nursing home financings according to the DPC Study.

409 San Francisco Hearing Transcript at 234 (Gill) ("Clients should be able to count on the same registration and disclosure standards to non-governmental conduit borrowers, as if they issued their securities directly, without using municipal issuers as conduits. These conduit-borrowing arrangements should be subject to the same level of disclosure as a corporate issuer directly obtaining financing in the public securities market"); Birmingham Hearing Transcript at 289 (Roberts) ("For sure it seems to me that conduit issuers should be treated like corporate borrowers, that governmental issuers should be subject to the same set of -required to satisfy the same set of accounting standard[s --270 days is] way too long to produce financial statements"). *But see* MacLennan *supra* note 382.

410 *See* 1994 Interpretive Release, *supra* note 31.

411 *See* Washington, DC Hearing Transcript (Afternoon Session) at 22 (Jones).

412 Examples of those differences from the point of view of the GASB are discussed in a GASB White Paper entitled "Why Governmental Accounting and Financial Reporting Is—and Should Be—Different," *available at* http://www.gasb.org/cs/ContentServer?c=Document_C &pagename=GASB%2FDocument_C%2FGASBDocumentPage&cid=1176156741340 ("GASB White Paper").

413 These include differing purposes of governments and for-profit enterprises, processes of generating revenues, stakeholders, budgetary obligations, and longevity, given the power to tax and hence to continue operating in perpetuity. *See generally* GASB White Paper, *supra* note 412. *See also* Washington, DC Hearing Transcript (Afternoon Session) at 21 (Jones).

414 GASB White Paper, *supra* note 412, at 1, 2.

415 *See* 1994 Amendment Release, *supra* note 167.

416 Pursuant to the continuing disclosure undertaking, annual financial information must be submitted for "each obligated person for whom financial information or operating data is presented in the final official statement . . . " Rule 15c2-12(b)(5)(i)(A). Annual financial information is defined as "financial information or operating data . . . of the type included in the final official statement with respect to an obligated person . . . ." Rule 15c2-12(f)(9). As the Commission previously stated, the definition of annual financial information specifies both the timing of the information—that is, once a year—and, by referring to the final official statement, the type of financial information and operating data that is to be provided. *See* Exchange Act Release No. 34961, "Municipal Securities Disclosure" (Nov. 10, 1994), 59 FR 59598 (Nov. 10, 1994). If financial information or operating data concerning an obligated person is included in the final official statement, then annual financial information would consist of the same type of financial information or operating data. *See* Rule 15c2-12(f)(3) for the definition of "final official statement."

417 *See* Rule 15c2-12(b)(5)(i)(B).

418 *In the Matter of Maricopa County, supra* note 354.

419 *See In the Matter of City of Syracuse, supra* note 355.

420 *See In the Matter of County of Orange, California, supra* note 353

[421] *In the Matter of the City of Miami, supra* note 356; *See also In the Matter of the City of San Diego, supra* note 358.

[422] *See In the Matter of City of Syracuse, supra* note 355; *In the Matter of Allegheny, supra* note 361; Exchange Act Release No. 51797, *In the Matter of Mount Sinai Medical Center of Florida, Inc., M. Brooks Turkel and Harvey W. Smith,* (June 7, 2005), *available at* http://www.sec.gov/litigation/admin/33-8580.pdf.

[423] Securities Act Release No. 7224/Exchange Act Release No. 36277, *In the Matter of Ronald Blaine,* (Sep. 26, 1995); Exchange Act Release No. 50134, *In the Matter of William F. Buettner, CPA,* (Aug. 2, 2004), *available at* http://www.sec.gov/litigation/admin/34-50134.htm; *SEC v. Thomas J. Saiz, and Calderon, Jaham & Osborn, An Accountancy Corporation,* Civil Action No. 07 CV 2308 L (JMA) (S.D. Cal.) (Filed Dec. 10, 2007), *available at* http://www.sec.gov/litigation/complaints/2007/comp20394.pdf.

[424] *See In re City of Syracuse, supra* note 355; Exchange Act Release No. 42743, *In the Matter of Albert Adamczak, C.P.A.,* (May 2, 2000), *available at* http://www.sec.gov/litigation/admin/ 34-42743.htm; Exchange Act Release No. 42742, *In the Matter of Stephen H. Spargo, C.P.A.,* (May 2, 2000), *available at* http://www.sec.gov/litigation/admin/34-42742.htm; Exchange Act Release No. 43910, *In the Matter of Charles P. Morrison, CPA,* (Jan. 31, 2001), *available at* http://www.sec.gov/litigation/admin/3443910.htm; *see also SEC v. Uberuaga, et al.* Civil Action No. 08 CV 0625 (S.D. Cal) (Filed Oct. 28, 2010), *available at* http://www.sec.gov/litigation/complaints/2008/comp20522.pdf ("*SEC v. Uberuaga*").

[425] With respect to companies with publicly-traded securities, federal securities laws authorize the Commission to set standards of accounting and financial reporting. The Commission historically has looked to private-sector standard-setting bodies to take the lead role in developing accounting standards. Pursuant to its authority under Section 19(b) of the Securities Act, the Commission has recognized the standards of the Financial Accounting Standards Board ("FASB") as "generally accepted" for purposes of the federal securities laws.

[426] The GASB is part of the not-for-profit Financial Accounting Foundation ("FAF") and was established by agreement of the FAF and ten national associations of state and local government officials in order to establish standards of financial accounting and reporting for state and local governmental entities. The FAF's trustees are responsible for selecting the members of the GASB and its Advisory Council, funding their activities and exercising general oversight-with the exception of the GASB's resolution of technical issues. The GASB historically was funded by voluntary payments and contributions from states and local governments and the financial community, and through sales of FAF's publications. The Dodd-Frank Act added § 19(g) to the Securities Act in order to create a permanent funding mechanism for GASB. On February 23, 2012, the Commission approved a proposed rule change by FINRA to establish a GASB annual accounting support fee, which will be allocated among FINRA members each quarter based on the members' municipal securities trading volume reported to the MSRB. As required by § 19(g) of the Securities Act, GASB accounting support fees collected by FINRA will be remitted to FAF. *See* Exchange Act Release No. 66454, "Order Granting Approval of Proposed Rule Change Relating to Establishing a Governmental Accounting Standards Board Accounting Support Fee" (SR-FINRA-2011-073) (Feb. 23, 2012), 77 FR 12340 (Feb. 29, 2012), *available at* http://www.sec.gov/rules/sro/finra/2012/34-66454.pdf.

[427] The stated mission of the GASB is to establish and improve standards of state and local governmental accounting and financial reporting that will result in useful information for users of financial reports and guide and educate the public, including issuers, auditors, and users of those financial reports. *See* GASB, Mission, Vision, and Core Value, *available at* http://www.gasb.org/jsp/GASB/Page/GASBSectionPage &cid= 1175804850352. Governments and the ethical requirements of the American Institute of Certified Public Accountants ("AICPA") have recognized the standards of the GASB as an official source of GAAP for state and local governments. *See* AICPA Ethics Rule 202.01 and Appendix A to that rule, *available at* http://www.aicpa.org/Research/Standards/CodeofConduct/Pages/et 202.aspx.

[428] Sometimes the use of other accounting principles is dictated by state law. For example, general purpose governments in New Jersey are required to use a statutory basis of accounting rather than GASB GAAP. *See* GASB Timeliness Study, *infra* note 429, at 9, fn 5.

[429] GASB Timeliness Study: The Timeliness of Financial Reporting by State and Local Governments Compared with the Needs of Users, Mar. 2011 at 8,9, *available at* http://www.gasb.org/cs/ContentServer?site= GASB&c=Document_C&pagename=GASB%2FDocument_C%2FGASBDocumentPage&cid=11761583 16214 ("GASB Timeliness Study").

[430] *Id.* at 9 ("These proportions may not be generalizable to smaller governments as a whole, because the AFRs that were not collected may be more likely to be non-GAAP, which would lower the proportions").

[431] Washington, DC Hearing Transcript (Afternoon Session) at 17 (Bean).

[432] In order to obtain the GFOA's Certificate of Achievement for Excellence in Financial Reporting ("CAFR Program"), for instance, the financial section of an issuer's comprehensive annual financial report, or CAFR, must include an independent auditor's report prepared in accordance with either generally accepted auditing standards (GAAS) or generally accepted government auditing standards (GAGAS) as set forth in the Government Accountability Office's Government Auditing Standards. *See* GFOA Certificate CAFR Program Eligibility Requirements, *available at* http://www.gfoa.org/downloads/CAFR Eligibility.pdf.

[433] For example, in 2007 the Texas legislature enacted a law, and the Connecticut General Assembly approved a bill (subsequently vetoed) to pull issuers out from under GASB standards and place them under systems of generally accepted accounting rules developed and administered by those respective states. The Texas law requires the State, and permits local governments in Texas, not to use GASB Statement 45, which requires governmental entities that provide health care, life insurance, and OPEBs to retirees to report the estimated accrued cost of the benefits. *See* Richard Williamson, "Texas Blinks in GASB Showdown: Bill Would Allow Option to Follow Rule 45," The Bond Buyer, Apr. 19, 2007, *available at*, http://www.bondbuyer.com/news/-268961-1.html. Connecticut's bill would have allowed the state comptroller to establish accounting standards for the State's budgetary purposes rather than follow GASB standards. *See* Mary Williams Walsh, "Connecticut Takes Up Fight Over Accounting Rules," The New York Times, June 2, 2007, *available at* http://www.nytimes.com/2007/06/02/business/02fiscal.html. *See* Jonna Stark, "Connecticut Weighs Bill Giving Comptroller Power over GAAP" The Bond Buyer, June 5, 2007, *available at* http://www.bondbuyer.com/news/-272255-1.html.

[434] *See* 1994 Interpretive Release, *supra* note 31.

[435] *See, e.g.*, Standard & Poor's Public Finance Criteria (2005) ("GAAP reporting is considered a credit strength . . . lack of an audited financial report prepared according to GAAP could have a negative impact on an issuer's rating, since questions about reporting will be raised").

[436] *See* GFOA Best Practice: Governmental Accounting, Auditing, and Financial Reporting Practices *(1983, 1997 and 2006), available at* http://www.gfoa.org/ downloads/caafr practices.pdf ("GFOA urges every state and local government to . . . issue timely financial statements for the entire financial reporting entity in conformity with GAAP as part of a CAFR . . .").

[437] *See* San Francisco Hearing Transcript at 32-33 (Mayhew) ("GAAP is nothing to be messed with . . . [m]y financial statements, which some people feel are inadequate, the footnotes are bigger than the entire financial -- annual financial statement of General Motors").

[438] *See* San Francisco Hearing Transcript at 40 (Mayhew) ("If you're going to issue in the public market and you're going to be rated, we want everybody to be on equal footing. We want GAAP financials rated against GAAP financials, reporting standards rated again reporting standards"). *See also* Washington, DC Hearing Transcript (Afternoon Session) at 24 (Firestine) (noting that when smaller issues use a basis of accounting other than GAAP, comparability is lost, and that GAAP prepared statements enable comparability); Washington, DC Hearing Transcript (Afternoon Session) at 25 (Jones) (consistent use of information is "very important" and hence the "use of GAAP financial statements is extremely important"). Stakeholders consulted in connection with a study undertaken by the GAO expressed the same view; *See also* GAO, "Dodd-Frank Wall Street Reform Act: Role of the Governmental Accounting Standards Board in the Municipal Securities Markets and Its Past Funding" at 15, *available at* http://www.gao.gov/assets/100/97254.pdf ("GAO GASB Study").

[439] This includes six allocation methods allowed under the current GASB standard for pension accounting. Washington, DC Hearing Transcript (Afternoon Session) at 25 (Bean).

[440] Washington, DC Hearing Transcript (Afternoon Session) at 21 (Firestine) ("Additionally, smaller governments, again, many of which do not issue debt, find it difficult and cost-prohibited [sic] to adhere to dozens of GASB standards. But it's wrong to assume or make a statement that when governments aren't following GAAP according to GASB that they aren't following any accounting or auditing standards. Not following GASB GAAP does not mean not following any accounting standards").

[441] *See* 1994 Interpretive Release, *supra* note 31.

[442] GASB identifies timeliness of financial reporting as one of the six characteristics financial information is expected to possess if it is to communicate effectively. *See* GASB, "Concept Statement No. 1, Objectives of Financial Reporting," *available at* http://www.gasb.org/ st/concepts/gconsum1.html.

[443] Bond ratings are only updated when a significant change is about to occur, and credit reports represent a costly alternative. *See* Jeff L. Payne and Kevin L. Jensen, *An Examination of Municipal Audit Delay,* J. ACC. & PUB. POL'Y, Vol. 21, Issue. 1, at 3 (2002).

[444] *See* GASB Timeliness Study, *supra* note 429, at 3.

[445] *See, e.g.*, San Francisco Hearing Transcript at 43 (Colby) ("The major challenge in secondary disclosure continues to be the timeliness and completeness of filings. While most issuers meet their promised deadlines for filing financial updates, the deadlines are typically 270 days, or nine months, after the end of the fiscal year, at which time the information is significantly out of date"); *See also* Birmingham Hearing Transcript at 163 (Johnston) (noting that it is common to wait 270 days for any type of financial disclosure).

[446] *See, e.g.*, San Francisco Hearing Transcript at 43 (Colby); *see supra* notes 396 - 399 and accompanying text (discussing timeliness of continuing disclosures); *see generally* Merritt Research Services, Just How Slowly Do Municipal Bond Audit Reports Waddle In After the Close of the Fiscal Year? (2010), *available at* http://www.bondbuyer.com/pdfs/ 1103DISC.pdf ("2010 Merritt Report") (analysis of audits performed on 4,600 municipal bond issuers during 2007-2009 showed audited annual report completed, on average, roughly five months after close of fiscal year, with final approval and release taking an additional month, and dramatic variation by sector and individual governmental body); *See also* GAO GASB Study, *supra* note 438, at 20 ("Untimely [government] financial statements may require analysts to rely on outdated information or to try to obtain additional, unaudited information from issuers").

[447] Exchange Act Rule 15c2-12, for instance, only requires that the municipal issuer or obligated person agree in the continuing disclosure undertaking to file *annual* financial information, not that it file such information within a specific timeframe, other than the timeframe set forth in the continuing disclosure agreement. Moreover, issuer and obligated persons are required to file audited financial statements only to the extent such audited financial statements are prepared and available. *See* Exchange Act Rule 15c212(b)(5)(i)(A).

[448] Disclosure timeframes vary substantially by size of the issuer, type of issuer, and accounting systems that are in place. *See* 2010 Merritt Report, *supra* note 446.

[449] *See, e.g.*, Birmingham Hearing Transcript at 163 (Johnston), *supra* note 385 and accompanying text (regarding Johnston's testimony at the Birmingham Hearing and discussion of timeliness of disclosure). This market participant noted further that there are a number of obligated persons who cannot even meet this deadline.

[450] *See* Exchange Act Release No. 62183, *supra* note 195. *See also* MSRB Notice 2010-15 (June 2, 2010), *available at* http://www.msrb.org/Rules-and-Interpretations/Regulatory-Notices/2010/2010-15.aspx?n=1. The Staff understands that, since the voluntary undertaking category was implemented in May 2011, five issuers have indicated that they will comply with the voluntary deadline.

[451] *See* Exchange Act Release No. 62183, *supra* note 195, at 5.

[452] *See* CAFR Program, *supra* note 432. An academic study published in 2000 found that municipalities that participate in the CAFR Program were associated with reduced audit delay. *See generally* Andrew J. McLelland and Gary Giroux, *An Empirical Analysis of Auditor Report Timing by Large Municipalities*, J. ACC. & PUB. POL'Y, Vol.19, Issue 3, at 263-281 (2000). The Staff understands that for calendar year 2010, roughly 3800 municipal issuers were awarded the GFOA's Certificate of Achievement for Excellence in Financial Reporting.

[453] *See* GASB Timeliness Study, *supra* note 429.

[454] *Id.* at 4-5.

[455] The GASB Timeliness Study focused on the timing to actual issuance of the audited annual financial report, or the time that elapses between the end of the fiscal year being reported on and the date that the financial report first becomes available to the public. This is generally later than the date of the audit report that coincides with the conclusion of an auditor's fieldwork. *See* GASB Timeliness Study, *supra* note 429, at 3-4.

[456] *See* 2010 Merritt Report, *supra* note 446.

[457] *Id.*

[458] *Id.* A 2011 follow-up indicated a similar correlation between slower reporting and weaker credit quality, although there was no complete analysis in order to make a conclusive determination. *See* Merritt Research Services, "Timing of Municipal Bond Financial Audits Leaves Room for Improvement" at 2 (2011), *available at* http://www.sec.gov/comments/4-610/4610-71.pdf ("2011 Merritt Report") (analysis of more than 25,500 audits performed during 2007-2010 showed average audit time across all credit sectors was 141.7 days after close of fiscal year).

[459] National Association of State Comptrollers, Time to Complete the State's CAFRs, Fiscal Years 2005, 2006, 2007, 2008, and 2009, *available at* https://www.nasact.org/nasc/ positions/downloads/CAFR_FY_05-09.pdf("NASACT Study").

[460] The ability to file in such shortened time frames has been attributed to the fact that the state's component agencies (*i.e.*, those subunits that report their results to the state government) operate on a fiscal year that ends on June 30, while the state's fiscal year ends 90 days later. *See* Andrew Ackerman, "Disclosure Guidance Irks

Issuers," The Bond Buyer, Jan. 29, 2010, *available at* http://www.bondbuyer.com/issues/119 269/disclosure-guidance-1006686-1.html?partner=sifma.

461 *See* NASACT Study, *supra* note 459.

462 *See, e.g.*, 2011 Meritt Report *supra* note 458; 2010 Merritt Report *supra* note 446; *See also* Peter J. Schmitt, "DPC Data Recent Trends in Continuing Disclosure Activities," DPC DATA, Feb. 3, 2011 ("DPC Report") (Issuers filing financial statements more than 180 days after the fiscal year end represented 63% of surveyed companies in 2009 and this trend seems to be increasing. For 2010 deals, the average covenant to file is 228 days). As noted above, DPC relies on its internal records of filings received by it as a NRMSIR. *See supra* note 371) *See also* California Debt and Investment Advisory Commission, Municipal Market Disclosure: CAFR Filings. A Test of Compliance Among California Issuers. (CDIAC No. 11-04) Nov. 2011, *available at* http://www.treasurer.ca.gov/cdiac/ publications/cafr.pdf.

463 *See* 2011 Merritt Report *supra* note 458, at 2.

464 *See generally* 2011 Merritt Report, *supra* note 458 (report goes through the differing timeframes for disclosing financial statements depending on various factors).

465 *Id.* at 4.

466 *See* GASB Timeliness Study, *supra* note 429; 2010 Merritt Report, *supra* note 446 ("By the time many annual governmental audits are received, many capital markets analysts and investors believe that they have lost significant value for assessing the current financial position of a municipal bond issuer.").

467 GASB Timeliness Study, *supra* note 429, at 17-18.

468 *Id.*

469 The study revealed that five of the 1,367 annual financial reports included in the research (1%) were issued within 45 days after the end of the fiscal year, the period when information is overwhelmingly considered most useful by respondents to the survey. Another 77 annual financial reports (14%) were issued within three months, a period during which information also is considered highly useful. The other annual financial reports were issued either between three and six months or over six months after the end of the fiscal year when the information became less useful. *See generally* GASB Timeliness Study, *supra* note 429.

470 The College of Urban Planning and Public Affairs (CUPPA) at the University of Illinois at Chicago and MuniNetGuide surveyed the seventy-five largest cities in the country to identify those with the best online investor information and noted that a few of these cities included monthly and even daily financial updates on their websites. *See* "Select Cities Lead the Pack in Providing Investor Relations Content" *available at* http://www.muninetguide.com/articles/select-cities-lead-the-pack-in-providing-investor-relations--416. This study also noted that even cities which were not among the 75 largest in the country, such as Akron, Ohio, provide monthly and quarterly revenue data. *Id. See also*, the website of the State Treasurer of the State of California which features monthly cash flow reports, monthly debt reports and a monthly bulletin from the Department of Finance which covers factors such as labor market conditions, building and real estate activity *available at* http://www.treasurer.ca.gov/bonds/recent.asp.

471 *See, e.g.*, Gretchen Morgenson, "Little Disclosure on U.S. Municipal Bonds," The New York Times, Aug. 31, 2008 (explaining that investors who hold municipal securities have limited means to detect when their investments could be negatively affected due to spotty financial reporting by municipal issuers).

472 *See, e.g.*, Ianthe Jeanne Dugan, "Bondholders Left in the Dark," The Wall Street Journal, Jan. 26, 2011 (explaining that "[m]any cities, states, hospitals and other public borrowers don't make general financial records accessible . . . and if they do, they are often so confusing or spotty that even professionals can't make sense of them").

473 *See* NABL Comment Letter, *supra* note 391.

474 *See* NASACT News (Jan. 2011), *available at* http://www.nasact.org/nasact/newscenter/ downloads/nasactnews/2011/Jan11.pdf.

475 *See* GFOA, "Best Practice, Maintaining an Investor Relations Program (1996, 2003 and 2010)," *available at* http://www.gfoa.org/index.php?option=com content&task=view&id= 1578.

476 *See* GAO Survey on Municipal Securities Disclosure, Market Participants (Phase 1), NASACT Response Dec. 15, 2011, *available at* http://www.nasact.org/downloads/CRC/ LOC/12_15_11GAO Survey Municipal Securities Disclosure.pdf.

477 *See, e.g.*, San Francisco Hearing Transcript, at 46 (Colby).

478 The Staff understands that, between July 1, 2009 and May 24, 2012, the health sector made 13,955 submissions of quarterly/monthly, interim and additional financial information on EMMA, out of a total of 30,236 such submissions (representing approximately 46% of such submissions). No other sector accounted for more than 10% of such submissions.

[479] Andrew Ackerman, "Opinions Divided Over Disclosure: Analysts Blast a Lack of Progress," The Bond Buyer, May 7, 2010, *available at* http://www.bondbuyer.com/issues/119_336/ disclosure_practices1011819-1.html (Quoting Ken Artis, Board Member of the National Association of Bond Lawyers).

[480] *See* MSRB Periodic Statistical Report, "Continuing Disclosure Statistical Summary, August 2011," *available at* http://www.msrb.org/msrb1/pdfs/MSRB-Continuing-Disclosure-Report-2011.pdf.

[481] *See id.*

[482] *See id.*

[483] Washington, DC Hearing Transcript (Afternoon Session) at 21 (Firestine).

[484] *See* Washington, DC Hearing Transcript (Afternoon Session) at 20 (Firestine).

[485] Birmingham Hearing Transcript, at 80-81 (Watkins).

[486] *See* MRSB, MSRB Notice 2011-20, Mar. 23, 2011, *available at* http://www.msrb.org/Rules-and-Interpretations/Regulatory -Notices/2011/2011-20.aspx.

[487] *See* GFOA Comment Letter to Exchange Act Release No. 61237, at 2 (Jan. 25, 2010), *available at* http://www.sec.gov/comments/sr-msrb-2009-10/msrb200910-26.pdf ("GFOA Jan. 2010 Comment Letter").

[488] *See* NAIPFA Comment Letter to Exchange Act Release No. 61237, at 2 (Feb. 5, 2010), *available at* http://www.sec.gov/comments/sr-msrb-2009-10/msrb200910-28.pdf.

[489] *See* City of Portland Comment Letter to Exchange Act. Release No. 61237, at 2 (Sept. 1, 2009), *available at* http://www.sec.gov/comments/sr-msrb-2009-10/msrb200910-18.pdf.

[490] *See, e.g.*, Washington, DC Hearing Transcript (Afternoon Session) at 30 (Firestine) (describing practical difficulties attributable to need to incorporate financial data from component issuers). *See also* GFOA Jan. 2010 Comment Letter, *supra* note 487.

[491] *See, e.g.*, Washington, DC Hearing Transcript (Afternoon Session) at 30 (Firestine) ("As I mentioned in my testimony, the fact that... you could probably do some of this faster if you're willing to accept the estimates, but then you create a less accurate, I think, financial statement versus trying to get... more actual information."); (Jones) (suggesting that letting go of the 'belief that everything has to be to the penny' could accelerate disclosure); at 20 (Firestine) ("... there is a lower level of tolerance for estimates in closing the books. The focus, instead, is on capturing actual expenditures and revenue accruals.")

[492] *See, e.g.*, Washington DC Hearing Transcript at 20 (Firestine) (noting the limited number of auditors, something exacerbated by the lower rates that local governments are willing to pay, which leads to delays in reporting financial results); GFOA Jan. 2010 Comment Letter in response to Exchange Act Release No. 61237, at 2 (noting lack of qualified auditors, and that acceleration of reporting deadlines would pressure governments to use audit firms not well qualified in governmental accounting and auditing standards). *See also,* City of Portland Comment Letter to Exchange Act. Release No. 61237 at 2 (Sept. 1, 2009), *available at* http://www.sec.gov/comments/sr-msrb-2009-10/msrb200910-18.pdf.

[493] *See* GFOA Jan. 2010 Comment Letter at 2; *See also* San Francisco Hearing Transcript at 163 (Lanzarotta); (speaking generally about the difficulties for smaller issuers to comply with GASB standards).

[494] *See, e.g.*, Washington, DC Hearing Transcript (Afternoon Session) at 20 (Firestine).

[495] *See generally* Andrew Ackerman, "Opinions Divided Over Disclosure; Analysts Blast a Lack of Progress," The Bond Buyer, May 7, 2010; *See also* San Francisco Hearing Transcript at 45 (Colby) ("As issuers are already preparing interim statements for internal use, we do not anticipate that the additional step of filing a limited financial update to the market will present an undue burden, particularly given the user friendly format provided by the EMMA System"); Birmingham Hearing Transcript at 184 (Watkins) (requesting that issuers look to interim information they provide to other stakeholders and make it available to all investors); San Francisco Hearing Transcript at 46-48 (Colby).

[496] One market participant notes that the budget, which is publically available and legally controlling, is the most important financial publication for governments, more so than overall financial statements. *See* San Francisco Hearing Transcript at 192 (Harrington). This participant further noted that the focus on timelier financial information ignores the fact that unlike the corporate market: (1) there is a great deal of information disclosed by governments in newspapers, public hearings, websites and various other media (2) there are few instances of dramatic economic changes and (3) issuers of government debt have an almost perfect record of paying back bondholders. *See* San Francisco Hearing Transcript at 193-196 (Harrington).

[497] *See* National Association of State Auditors, Comptrollers and Treasurers Position Paper, "A Proposal: Results of the Deliberations at the Meeting about Voluntary Interim Disclosure by State and Local Governments," Sept. 25, 2003 (Issued Dec. 17, 2003) available as Exhibit A in National Federation of Municipal Analysts, Position Paper on Voluntary Interim Disclosure by State and Local Governments, *available at* http://data.memberclicks.com/site/ nfma/nfma_position_interim_disclosure.pdf ("NASACT Proposal Paper").

[498] Birmingham Hearing Transcript at 164 (Johnston).

[499] *See* Letter from The National Federation of Municipal Analysts to Commissioner Elisse B. Walter, at 2 Oct. 6, 2010, *available at* http://www.sec.gov/comments/4-610/4610-9.pdf ("NFMA Letter").

[500] *See* San Francisco Hearing Transcript at 43-44 (Colby); *See also* NFMA Letter, *supra* note 499.

[501] *See* NASACT Proposal Paper, *supra* note 497.

[502] *Id.* at 1.

[503] Andrew Ackerman, "Opinions Divided Over Disclosure: Analysts Blast a Lack of Progress," The Bond Buyer, May 7, 2010, *available at* http://www.bondbuyer.com/issues/119_336/ disclosure_practices1011819-1.html.

[504] *See* NASACT Proposal Paper, *supra* note 497, at 1.

[505] Birmingham Hearing Transcript at 80-81 (Watkins).

[506] Birmingham Hearing Transcript at 105 (Presley).

[507] U.S. Census, 2009 Survey of State and Local Public-Employee Retirement Systems (Washington, D.C. 2011), *available at* http://www2.census.gov/govs/retire/2009summary report.pdf ("2009 Census Retirement Survey").

[508] *See* GAO, "State and Local Government Pension Plans: Economic Downturn Spurs Efforts to Address Costs and Sustainability," GAO-12-322, Mar. 2012, *available at* http://www.gao.gov/assets/590/589043.pdf ("GAO 2012 Pension Report") (citing 2009 Census Retirement Survey). Generally, state and local governments offer defined benefit pension plans, in which retirement benefits are determined by formula on the basis of factors such as the employee's recent salary and total years of service. By contrast, most pension plans in the private sector are defined contribution plans, in which employers commit to annual payments toward employees retirement savings but not to a particular amount of benefits. *See* Congressional Budget Office ("CBO"), CBO Economic and Budget Issue Brief: "The Underfunding of State and Local Pension Plans" at 2, May 2011, *available at* http://www.cbo.gov/ftpdocs/120xx/doc12084/05-04-Pensions.pdf ("CBO Brief").

[509] *See generally* CBO Brief, *supra* note 508, at 3-6; *See also* Washington, DC Hearing Transcript (Afternoon Session) at 19, 25 (Bean); GASB, Summary of Statement No. 25: Financial Reporting for Defined Benefit Pension Plans and Note Disclosures for Defined Contribution Plans, Nov. 1994, *available at* http://www.gasb.org/st/summary/gstsm25.html.

[510] At the time of these offerings, City officials knew that the City faced severe difficulty funding its future pension and health care obligations unless new revenues were obtained, pension and health care benefits were reduced, or City services were cut. *See In the Matter of the City of San Diego, supra* note 358.

[511] Four of those former officials, without admitting or denying the allegations, settled with the Commission. *See* SEC v. Uberuaga, *supra* note 424.

[512] Under the settlement terms, three of the former officials (Uberuaga, Ryan, and Frazier) each paid a penalty of $25,000 and the fourth (Vattimo) paid a penalty of $5,000. *Id.*

[513] The offering documents for these securities created the false impression that the two pension plans were being adequately funded. *See* Securities Act Release No. 9135, *In the Matter of the State of New Jersey.* (Aug. 18, 2010) (settled action).

[514] *See* Alicia H. Munnell, Jean-Pierre Aubry, Josh Hurwitz, Madeline Medenica and Laura Quinby, "The Funding of State and Local Pensions: 2011-2015," Center for Retirement Research at Boston College, May 2011, *available at* http://crr.bc.edu/wp-content/uploads/2012/05/slp_24-508.pdf ("Boston College Report") (The sample in this study includes 109 state-administered plans and 17 locally-administered plans, based on accounting methods issued by the GASB). *See also* Iris J. Lav and Elizabeth McNichol, "Misunderstandings Regarding State Debt, Pensions, and Retiree Health Costs Create Unnecessary Alarm: Misconceptions Also Divert Attention from Needed Structural Reforms," Center on Budget and Policy Priorities, at 2, Jan. 20, 2011, *available at* http://www.cbpp.org/files/1-20-11sfp.pdf ("CBPP Article") ("State and local shortfalls in funding pensions for future retirees have gradually emerged over the last decade principally because of the two most recent recessions, which reduced the value of those assets in those funds and made it difficult for some [governments] to find sufficient revenues to make required deposits into the trust fund. Before these two recessions, state and local pensions were in aggregate, funded at 100 percent of future liabilities"); GAO 2012 Pension Report, *supra* note 508, discussing state responses to underfunding ("[T]he majority of states have modified their existing defined benefit systems to reduce member benefits, lowering future liabilities. Half of states have increased required member (that is, employee) contributions, shifting costs to employees. Only a few states have adopted primary plans with defined contribution components, which reduce plan sponsors' investment risk by shifting it to employees. Some states and localities have also taken action to lower pension contributions in the short term by changing actuarial methods, and a few have issued pension bonds to finance their contributions or to lower their costs by reducing the gap between plan assets and liabilities").

[515] *See* United States Senate Committee on Finance, "State and Local Government Defined Benefit Pension Plans: The Pension Debt Crisis that Threatens America," at 1, Jan. 2012, *available at* http://hatch.senate.gov/public/_cache/files/ecfaf678-a3ec-45a4-a2bf-3bca4fe 9475d/Hatch%20Report%20-%20The%20Pension%20Debt%20Crisis%20that%20 Threatens%20America.pdf.

[516] Although market asset values in 2011 were significantly higher than in 2010, funding levels still declined slightly from 2010 to 2011. The study suggests that liabilities grew faster than asset value during this time due to actuaries' practice of smoothing market gains and losses over a five-year period, but that liabilities have been growing at a slower pace over recent years. *See* Boston College Report, at 2. A separate study notes that for the 99 state retirement systems that reported actuarial data for 2010, pension assets and liabilities were $1,671.4 billion and $2,538.4 billion, respectively, representing a funding ratio for these 99 state pension plans of 66%, up from 62% for the same plans in 2009. *See* Julia K. Bonafede, Steven J. Foresti, and Russell J. Walker, "2011 Wilshire Report on State Retirement Systems: Funding Levels and Asset Allocation," at 3, Feb. 28, 2011, *available at* http://www.nasra.org/resources/Wilshire_2010.pdf ("Wilshire Report").

[517] *See* CBO Brief, *supra* note 508. According to a 2011 study, the average underfunded plan has a ratio of assets-to-liabilities of 65%; *See* Wilshire Report, *supra* note 516, at 3.

[518] *See* GASB Statement No. 27, "Accounting for Pensions by State and Local Governmental Employers," at paragraph 9.

[519] *See* GASB, GASB Statement No. 27, "Accounting for Pensions by State and Local Governmental Employers," at paragraph 10c. *See also* CBO Brief, *supra* note 508; Letter from Patricia Macht, Director, External Affairs Branch, CalPERS to Commissioner Elisse B. Walter (Nov. 12, 2010) (attaching letters from CalPERS to the GASB dated July 29, 2009 and September 17, 2010), *available at* http://www.sec.gov/comments/4-610/4610-14.pdf ("CalPERS Letter") In its letters to the GASB, CalPERS states that it believes the estimated long-term yield for the pension plan is the appropriate rate for discounting projected benefits.

[520] *See* CBO Brief, *supra* note 508, at 3 ("Currently, the median of pension plans' assumptions for future returns on state and local pension assets is about 8.0 percent, or 4.5 percent after removing the effect of the median assumed rate of inflation").

[521] Seattle City Employees' Retirement System, "Actuarial Valuation as of January 1, 2010" at 2, *available at* http://www.seattle.gov/retirement/documents/sera0237.pdf (Letter from Milliman describing process used for valuations and summarizing report below).

[522] *See infra* notes 524 - 525. This approach more closely resembles how public companies value pension liabilities. *See* CBO Brief, *supra* note 508, at 4.

[523] *Id.*

[524] *Id.; See also* Robert Novy-Marx and Joshua Rauh, *Public Pension Promises: How Big Are They and What Are They Worth?* J. FIN., Vol. LXVI (Aug. 2011) ("Given the protections that state constitutions provide to accrued public pension promises, beneficiaries face a negligible probability of default on benefits they have already earned . . . . The approximation we employ for the default-free curve is the Treasury zero-coupon yield curve . . . [u]nder [which] . . . total liabilities are $4.43 trillion").

[525] *See, e.g.*, Robert Novy-Marx and Joshua Rauh, *The Liabilities and Risks of State-Sponsored Pension Plans,* J. ECON. PERSP. 23(4), at 191-210 (2009) (arguing that the requirement that states discount future pension payments at a rate equivalent to the expected return on pension assets, creates an incentive for states to invest their pension funds in risky assets with higher rates of return. Specifically, the study notes that "under the current accounting standards, state governments could ostensibly meet their obligations using futures contracts on the stock market to maintain a leverage ratio of 10 to 1"); *See also* San Francisco Hearing Panelist Statements (Crane) ("[S]tate and local government pension funds are perversely incentivized to assume the highest rates of return at those pension funds in order to minimize reported liabilities and then to "swing for the fences" in investing the capital of those funds in the hopes of actually achieving those returns, producing even more risk for the taxpayers who must make up for pension fund shortfalls."), *available at* http://www.sec.gov/spotlight/municipalsecurities/ statements092 110/craned092110.htm. *But see,* CBPP Article, *supra* note 514, at 3 ("While economists generally support use of a riskless rate in valuing state and local pension liabilities, they do not generally argue that the investment practices of state and local pension funds should change. State and local pension funds historically have invested in a market basket of private securities and have received rates of return much higher than the riskless rate . . . . The 8 percent discount rate that most funds now use reflects actual returns over the past 20 years."); CalPERS Letter *infra* note 519 (stating, in its letter to the GASB, that it believes the estimated long-term yield for the pension plan is the appropriate rate for discounting projected benefits).

[526] *See, e.g.*, Ronald Picur and Lance J. Weiss, *Addressing Media Misconceptions about Public-Sector Pensions and Bankruptcy,* Government Finance Review, at 7-8 (Feb. 2011); *See also* CBPP Article, *supra* note 514.

[527] GAO, "State and Local Government Pension Plans: Current Structure and Funded Status," GAO-08-983T at 2 (Jul. 2008), *available at* http://www.gao.gov/new.items/d08983t.pdf. *See also* San Francisco Hearing Transcript at 159 (McIntire). Based on post-recession data, thirty-four states had funding ratios lower than 80 percent as of 2010. *See* Pew Center on the States, The Widening Gap Update, at 2 (June 2012), *available at* http://www.pewstates.org/uploadedFiles/PCS_Assets/2012/Pew_Pensions_Update.pdf ("Pew Report").

[528] *See* Boston College Report, *supra* note 514, at 2-3.

[529] *See* GASB, Summary of Statement No. 45: Accounting and Financial Reporting by Employers for Postemployment Benefits Other than Pensions (Issued 6/04), *available at* http://www.gasb.org/st/summary/gstsm45.html.

[530] GASB Statement No. 45 became effective in three phases. For governments with total annual revenues of $100 million or more, it became effective for periods beginning after December 15, 2006; for governments with total annual revenues of $10 million or more but less than $100 million, it became effective for periods beginning after December 15, 2007; and for governments with total annual revenues of less than $10 million, it became effective for periods beginning after December 15, 2008. *Id.*

[531] Pew Report, *supra* note 527.

[532] *See* GFOA, "Need for Considerable Caution in Regard to OPEB Bonds," 2007, *available at* http://www.gfoa.org/downloads/corbaopebbonds.pdf.

[533] *Id.*

[534] Legislation entitled the "Public Employee Pension Transparency Act," has been introduced in the U.S. House of Representatives and the Senate, which would require states to report their pension finances according to both prevailing discounting methodologies. The legislation also contains measures tying financial reporting to the availability of tax-exempt status, and would provide an express ban on federal bailouts. *See* Sara Murray, "GOP Bill Takes Aim at Pension Disclosure," Wall Street Journal, Feb. 22, 2011, *available at* http://online.wsj.com/article/SB10001424052748703803904576152882725460082.html.

[535] The Commission recently formed a specialized group within its Division of Enforcement to focus on, among other items, public pension accounting and disclosure violations. *See* "SEC Names New Specialized Unit Chiefs and Head of New Office of Market Intelligence," Jan. 13, 2010, *available at* http://www.sec.gov/news/press/2010/2010-5.htm.

[536] *See, e.g.*, San Francisco Hearing Transcript, at 148-149 (Mayhew) ("this is an issue of disclosure . . . . Now whether somebody agrees or disagrees with the methodology PERS has used, it's not for my jurisdiction. My jurisdiction, my job is to report those things as accurately as the auditors tell me to report them, and we do").

[537] *See, e.g.*, Submission from Allen Davis, Investment Research Analyst, Invesco Unit Trusts, Mar. 21, 2011, *available at* http://www.sec.gov/comments/4-610/4610-21.htm (requesting quarterly pension disclosure); Submission from Mark W. Gee, Taxpayer and Town Councilor, Mar. 3, 2011, *available at* http://www.sec.gov/comments/4-610/4610-19.htm (stating that investors and the general public need a better understanding of the full impact of money which has already been obligated for future pension and OPEB payments). *See also* Birmingham Hearing Transcript at 45 (Fallon) ("there has been very little transparency in many cases around the pension and other post-employment benefits").

[538] San Francisco Hearing Transcript at 158 (McIntire).

[539] San Francisco Hearing Transcript at 158 (McIntire). *See also* San Francisco Hearing Transcript at 148 (Mayhew).

[540] San Francisco Hearing Transcript at 148 (Mayhew).

[541] *See generally* San Francisco Hearing Panelist Statements (McIntire), *available at* http://www.sec.gov/spotlight/municipalsecurities/statements092110/mcintirej092110.pdf.

[542] *See* San Francisco Hearing Transcript at 159 (Crane), citing New York City best practices.

[543] *See* San Francisco Hearing Transcript at 69-70 (McNally).

[544] For example, a field hearing participant suggested that disclosure counsel should work with issuers to provide information beyond that required by the GASB, by asking key questions such as: "What does it mean to [an investor] and what does it mean to the issuer's budget?" San Francisco Hearing Transcript at 69-70 (McNally).

[545] *See* NABL Considerations, *supra* note 334, at 2.

[546] The task force is advised by the GASB and certain consulting actuaries, and is composed of members of the following organizations: American Institute of Certified Public Accountants; Bond Dealers of America; GFOA; Investment Company Institute; NABL; National Association of Pension Plan Attorneys; National Association of State Auditors, Comptrollers and Treasurers; National Association of State Retirement

Administrators; National Association of State Treasurers; National Council on Teachers Retirement; National Federation of Municipal Analysts, and SIFMA. *See* letter from Kristin H.R. Franceschi and Kenneth R. Artin to Commissioner Elisse B. Walter, Feb. 9, 2012, *available at* http://www.sec.gov/comments/4-610/4610-84.pdf ("Task Force Letter"). *See also* NABL Considerations, *supra* note 334, at Appendix A.

547 *See* Task Force Letter, *supra* note 546.

548 *See supra* note 334.

549 GASB Project Pages: Postemployment Benefit Accounting and Financial Reporting, *available at* http://gasb.org/cs/ContentServer?c=GASBContent_C&pagename=GASB%2 FGASB Content_C%2FProject Page&cid=1176156645919.

550 Proposed Statement of the GASB, "Government Accounting Standards Series, Exposure Draft: Accounting and Financial Reporting for Pensions-an amendment of GASB Statement No. 27," June 27, 2011, *available at* http://gasb.org/cs/ContentServer?site=GASB&c= Document_C&pagename=GASB%2FDocument_C%2FG ASBDocumentPage&cid=117 6158723743 ("GASB Exposure Draft on Statement No. 27").

551 Proposed Statement of the GASB, "Government Accounting Standards Series, Exposure Draft: Financial Reporting for Pension Plans – an amendment of GASB Statement No. 25," June 27, 2011, *available at* http://gasb.org/cs/ContentServer?site=GASB&c=Document_ C& pagename=GASB%2FDocument_C%2FG ASBDocumentPage&cid=1176158723674 ("GASB Exposure Draft on Statement No. 25"). Under the proposed revisions, projected benefit payments would be discounted to their present value using the single rate that would reflect (a) the long-term expected rate of return on pension plan investments that are expected to be used to finance the payment of pensions to the extent that (1) plan net position is projected to be sufficient to make the benefit payments that are projected to occur in a period and (2) assets are expected to be invested using a long-term investment strategy and (b) an index rate for a 30-year, tax-exempt municipal bond rated AA/Aa or higher (or equivalent quality on another rating scale) to the extent that the conditions in (a) are not met. *See* GASB Exposure Draft on Statement No. 27, *supra* note 550.

552 *See* GASB, "The User's Perspective: GASB Proposes to Significantly Improve Pension Reporting," July 2011, *available at* http://www.gasb.org/cs/ContentServer?site=GASB&c= GASB Content_C&pagename=GASB%2 FGASBCo ntent C%2FUsersArticlePage&cid= 1176158721550.

553 *Id.*

554 *Id.*

555 *Id.*

556 *See supra* notes 33 - 35 and § II.A.2.a (Types of Municipal Securities).

557 *See* Craig Underwood, *et al.*, "Interest Rate Swaps: Application to Tax-Exempt Financing" Bond Logistix LLC & Orrick, Herrington & Sutcliffe LLP, 2004, *available at* http://www.orrick.com/fileupload/430.pdf.

558 *See id.*

559 *Id.*

560 Accurate as of December 2011. *See* Bank for International Settlements, Semiannual Over-The-Counter (OTC) Derivatives Market Statistics, *available at* http://www.bis.org/statistics/ otcder/dt21a21b.pdf.

561 *See* Martin Z. Braun, "Deutsche Bank Swap Lures County as Budgets Crumble," Bloomberg, Nov. 26, 2008, *available at* http://www.bloomberg.com/apps/news?pid=newsa rchive&sid= aBM8ziXQK1xw&refer=home.

562 *See, e.g.*, Birmingham Hearing Transcript at 239-240 (Turner); *See also* Birmingham Hearing Transcript, at 243 (McElroy) (noting that municipal entities are still engaging in hedging for natural gas and other fuels).

563 *See id.*

564 *See, e.g.,* 1994 Interpretive Release, *supra* note 31 (noting that investors need to be aware of the terms and particular risks arising from these products, including exposure to interest rate volatility under all possible scenarios). *See also In the Matter of County of Orange, California*, *supra* note 353.

565 Panel entitled "Disclosure of Certain Significant Liabilities," San Francisco Hearing Transcript at 124-187 and Panel entitled "Derivatives Use in Municipal Finance," Birmingham Hearing Transcript at 212-267.

566 *See* Birmingham Hearing Transcript at 216 (Brooks) ("In essence, [the ISDA confirmation letter states] that each counterparty has made their own independent judgment or is relying on its own advisors. Most importantly, there is an explicit denial of a fiduciary relationship between the two counterparties."); *See also* Andrew Ackerman, "Mixed Reactions on OK of OTC Swap Bills: Dealers Reps Predict Derivatives' Demise," The Bond Buyer, Apr. 22, 2010, *available at* http://www.bondbuyer.com/issues/119 325/otc swap bills-1011169-1.html.

567 *See, e.g.*, Birmingham Hearing Transcript at 215-216 (Brooks) ("the most significant problem related to derivatives use in municipal finance is that derivatives are sold and . . . not bought. Specifically, commission hungry and ethically questionable derivatives salespeople are not the best source of ideas for creative and

innovative solutions to complex municipal problem"); Birmingham Hearing Transcript at 256 (Turner) (noting that smaller entities may not have the money to hire outside advisors to assist them in swap transactions).

[568] *See e.g.*, Birmingham Hearing Transcript at 226 (Kalotay) ("The problem with swap advisors is not the lack of technical expertise, but how they are compensated. The incentives are skewed: The deal must go through in order for the swap advisors to get paid."); Birmingham Hearing Transcript at 246-247 (McElroy) ("the advisor cannot be a commission-based advisor if you're going to expect a good outcome. It should be on retainer for a fixed fee to provide services for a period of time").

[569] *See* Birmingham Hearing Transcript at 245 (Kalotay).

[570] *See* Birmingham Hearing Transcript at 250 (Collier).

[571] *See id.* at 222.

[572] *See e.g.*, Birmingham Hearing Transcript at 258-259 (Brooks).

[573] *See, e.g.*, San Francisco Hearing Transcript at 165 (Singer); *see also* Birmingham Hearing Transcript at 221, 253 (Collier), 248 (Kalotay).

[574] *See, e.g.*, Birmingham Hearing Transcript at 237-238 (Turner).

[575] *See, e.g.*, Birmingham Hearing Transcript at 215 (Brooks) ("It should be suspect that often the very idea promoted by the financial institution would never be done at that same institution."), at 224-225 (Kalotay) (referring to poorly structured bond and swap transactions as "Wall Street's multi-billion dollar hidden tax on 'Main Street'").

[576] *See* Birmingham Hearing Transcript at 226-227 (Kalotay) (discussing a 30 year, $750 million bond deal by Denver schools that was swapped for a fixed rate).

[577] *See* Birmingham Hearing Transcript at 226-230 (Kalotay) (noting that the 2% markup would not be tolerated by corporate issuers. Mr. Kalotay further stated that banks tend to defend their profit margin by claiming exposure to municipal credit risk but due to the low rate of municipal defaults and the high margin on unwinding derivatives, he was unconvinced by that claim.); *See also* Braun and Selway, *supra* note 34 (noting that in some Pennsylvania swap deals banks charged municipal entities up to 10 times the amount in fees than they would normally charge).

[578] *See* Birmingham Hearing Transcript at 219-221 (Collier).

[579] *See* San Francisco Hearing Transcript at 166 (Singer) (Taking issue with the provision in the Dodd-Frank Act which allows municipal entities with over $50 million of investable assets to be an "eligible contract participant"). One hearing participant noted that the standard in the State of Washington requires a municipal entity to have at least $100 million of bonds outstanding and a financial advisor. *See* San Francisco Hearing Transcript at 168 (McIntire).

[580] *See id.* at 169 (McIntire).

[581] *See, e.g.*, San Francisco Hearing Transcript at 170 (Singer). Another participant noted however, that based on the recent experience of municipal entities, merely having a swap policy and a debt policy was not enough. *See* Birmingham Hearing Transcript at 219-222 (Collier); *See also* "Auditor General Jack Wagner Asks Department of Community and Economic Development to Strengthen Oversight of Interest Rate Swaps," Pennsylvania Department of the Auditor General, May 10, 2010, *available at* http://www.auditorgen.state.pa.us/Department/Press/WagnerAsksDCEDStrengthenOversightInterestRateS waps.html.

[582] *See, e.g.*, Birmingham Hearing Transcript at 217 (Brooks), 230 (Kalotay) ("[A]t a minimum, the banks should be required to disclose the swap curve at the time of execution. Also, any side agreement with the swap advisor should be disclosed as a matter of course.")

[583] *See, e.g.*, Birmingham Hearing Transcript at 217 (Brooks), 223 (Collier). Ms. Collier further suggested that special entities that enter into agreements be required to maintain a competent staff or advisors to serve in a fiduciary role not only during the transaction but for the life of the swap. *See also* State of Tennessee Guidelines for Interest Rate and Forward Purchase Agreements, §§ IV (J) and V (H), *available at* http://www.tn.gov/ comptroller/lf/pdf/SFB%20Guidelines%2010-9%20Final.pdf (determines the skill and knowledge requirements for any entity proposing to enter into an interest rate or forward rate agreements).

[584] *See* Birmingham Hearing Transcript at 230 (Kalotay) (suggesting that experts can come to consensus on the "fair value" of a swap using the prevailing swap curve).

[585] *See id.*

[586] *See* San Francisco Hearing Transcript at 23 (Lockyer).

[587] *See* Exchange Act Release No. 36761, Report Under § 21(a) of the Exchange Act: "Report of Investigation in the Matter of County of Orange, California as it Relates to the Conduct of the Members of the Board of Supervisors," Jan. 24, 1996, *supra* note 360; *see also In the Matter of Orange County, California*, *supra* note 353. *See also* Public Policy Institute of California, "When Government Fails: The Orange County Bankruptcy

— A Policy Summary," The Second Annual California Issues Forum, After the Fall: Learning from the Orange County Bankruptcy, Mar. 18, 1998, *available at* http://www.ppic.org/content/pubs/ op/OP 398OP.pdf.

[588] *Securities and Exchange Commission v. Larry P. Langford, William B. Blount, Blount Parrish & Co., Inc., and Albert W. LaPierre*, Case No. cv-08-B-0761-S (N.D. Ala., filed Apr. 30, 2008), *available at* http://sec.gov/litigation/litreleases/2008/lr20545.htm; Securities and Exchange Commission v. Charles E. LeCroy, and Douglas W. MacFaddin, Case No. cv-09 U/B 2238-S (N.D. Ala., filed Nov. 4, 2009), *available at* http://sec.gov/litigation/ litreleases/2009/lr21280.htm.

[589] Collectively, the five financial institutions, Banc of America Securities LLC, UBS Financial Services Inc. and J.P. Morgan Securities LLC, Wachovia Bank, N.A., and GE Funding Capital Market Services, Inc., paid $205 million to settle the Commission actions, all of which was distributed to hundreds of harmed municipal entities or borrowers, located in 47 states, the District of Columbia, Guam, and Puerto Rico, as well as an additional $540 million to settle parallel proceedings by other federal and state authorities for their misconduct. Exchange Act Release No. 63451, *In the Matter of Banc of America Securities, now known as Merrill Lynch, Pierce, Fenner & Smith Incorporated, successor by merger*, (Dec. 7, 2010), *available at* http://www.sec.gov/litigation/admin/2010/34-63451.pdf; *Securities and Exchange Commission v. UBS Financial Services Inc.*, Civil Action No. 11-CV-2885 (D.N.J. May 4, 2011), *available at* http://www.sec.gov/litigation/litreleases/ 2011/lr21956.htm; and *Securities and Exchange Commission v. J.P. Morgan Securities LLC.*, Civil Action No. 11-CV-3877 (D.N.J. Jul. 7, 2011), *available at* http://www.sec.gov/litigation/litreleases/2011/lr22031.htm; *Securities and Exchange Commission v. Wachovia Bank, N.A., now known as Wells Fargo Bank, N.A., successor by merger,* Civil Action No. 2:11cv-07135-WJM-MF (D.N.J. Dec. 8, 2011), *available at* http://www.sec.gov/litigation/litreleases/2011/lr22183.htm; *Securities and Exchange Commission v. GE Funding Capital Market Services, Inc.*, Civil Action No. 2:11-cv-07465-WJM-MF (D.N.J. Dec. 23, 2011), *available at* http://www.sec.gov/litigation/litreleases/ 2011/lr22210.htm.

[590] *Securities and Exchange Commission v. Stifel, Nicolaus & Co., Inc. and David W. Noack,* Civil Action No. 2:11-cv-00755-AEG, (E.D. Wisc. Aug. 10, 2011), *available at* http://www.sec.gov/litigation/litreleases/ 2011/lr22064.htm. The Commission also charged, and settled with, RBC Capital Markets, LLC for their involvement in these sales. RBC negligently recommended and sold these investments, despite significant internal concerns about the suitability of the investments for municipalities like the school districts. Moreover, RBC's marketing materials failed to explain adequately the risks associated with the investments. *See In the Matter of RBC Capital Markets, LLC, supra* note 242.

[591] *See In the Matter of County of Orange, California, supra* note 353.

[592] Dodd-Frank Act § 712(a). *See, e.g.,* § 2(a)(1)(A) of the Commodity Exchange Act (jurisdiction of the CFTC) and Section 1a(47) (defining "swap" to include, among other things, an interest rate swap).

[593] *See, e.g.,* Birmingham Hearing Transcript at 241 (Collier) and 244 (Turner).

[594] Dodd-Frank Act § 712(a). *See also* "Further Definition of "Swap," "Security-Based Swap," and "Security-Based Swap Agreement"; Mixed Swaps; Security-Based Swap Agreement Recordkeeping, issued by the Commission and the CFTC, Exchange Act Release No. 64373 (Apr. 27, 2011), *available at* http://www.sec.gov/rules/proposed/2011/33-9204.pdf, 76 FR 29818 (May 23, 2011) (joint proposed rules and proposed interpretations regarding products definitions).

[595] *See* Dodd-Frank Act, §§ 724-733 (dealing with various disclosure requirements and counterparty requirements in swap transactions). *See also* Dodd-Frank Act, § 764 (directing SBS entities to conform with such business conduct standards as may be prescribed by the Commission).

[596] Commodity Exchange Act § 4s(h)(2)(C) and Exchange Act § 15F(h)(2)(C) define the term "special entity" to include a state, state agency, city, county, municipality, or other political subdivision of a state, as well as any governmental plan, as defined in § 3 of Employee Retirement Income Security Act of 1974 ("ERISA"). By comparison, the definition of "municipal entity" under Exchange Act § 15B(e)(8) is any state, political subdivision of a state, or municipal corporate instrumentality of a state, including – any agency, authority, or instrumentality of the State, political subdivision, or municipal corporate instrumentality; any plan, program, or pool of assets sponsored or established by the State, political subdivision, or municipal corporate instrumentality or any agency, authority, or instrumentality thereof; and any other issuer of municipal securities".

[597] Exchange Act Release No. 64766, "See Business Conduct Standards for Security-Based Swap Dealers and Major Security-Based Swap Participants" (June 29, 2011), 76 FR 42396 (Jul. 18, 2011) (business conduct standards for SBS Entities proposed by SEC), *available at* http://www.sec.gov/rules/proposed/2011/3464766.pdf ("SEC Business Conduct Proposal").

[598] Business Conduct Standards for Swap Dealers and Major Swap Participants with Counterparties, 77 FR 9734 (Feb. 17, 2012) (business conduct standards for Swap Entities adopted by CFTC) *available at* http://www.cftc.gov/LawRegulation/FederalRegister/ FinalRules/2012-1244 ("CFTC Business Conduct Final Rule").

[599] Birmingham Hearing Transcript at 233 (McElroy). The Commission and CFTC coordinated extensively with respect to these proposals and jointly held dozens of consultations with market participants. *See* http://www.sec.gov/comments/df-title-vii/swap/swap.shtml# meetings and http://www.sec.gov/comments/s7-25-11/s72511.shtml# meetings (for records of the meetings held jointly between the Commission and the CFTC).

[600] *See* San Francisco Hearing Transcript at 149 (Mayhew). *See also* Birmingham Hearing Transcript at 252, 262-263 (Collier), 263 (McElroy).

[601] GASB Statement No. 53 was issued on June 30, 2008 and effective for financial periods beginning after June 15, 2009. *See* GASB, Summary of Statement No. 53, Accounting and Financial Reporting for Derivative Instruments (Issued June, 2008), *available at* http://www.gasb.org/cs/ContentServer?c=Pronouncement_ C&pagename=GASB%2FPronouncement_C%2 FGASBSummaryPage&cid=1176156706600. Statement No. 53 requires that the "fair value" of derivatives or derivative instruments be reported in the financial statements of state and local governments. GASB, Derivative Instruments: A Plain-Language Summary of GASB Statement No. 53, at 1, June 30, 2008, *available at* http://www.aci-na.org/static/entransit/Derivative%20 Instruments.pdf ("Summary of GASB 53"). Notably, not all instruments are subject to Statement No. 53. *See id.* at 4.

[602] *See* San Francisco Hearing Transcript at 149 (Mayhew). *See also* Summary of GASB 53, *supra* note 601, at 6 ("Although prior standards required governments to disclose information about their derivatives in the notes to the financial statements, few derivatives were reported on the face of the financial statements.").

[603] *See* San Francisco Hearing Transcript at 152 (Singer).

[604] In particular, this panel participant noted that municipal issuers should include: the timing, size, and rationale of the trade; whether the derivative is tied to specific bonds; the identity of the counter-party; whether there are events that will cause the municipality to have to meet a significant capital call; how low the credit rating of the municipal entity will have to fall before the counter-party can force the entity to terminate the trade and make a payment; the use of floating rate debt, and the mark-to-market of each of the derivative products; and how the mark-to-market will change as interest rates change in the future. *See* San Francisco Hearing Transcript at 151-152 (Singer).

[605] *See id.* at 152-154.

[606] Birmingham Hearing Transcript at 265 (Collier).

[607] *See id.* at 223.

[608] *See id.* at 224.

[609] *See, e.g.*, NABL Comment Letter, *supra* note 391. This advice is based on analogies drawn from § 11 of the Securities Act in establishing defenses to liability under § 10(b) of the Exchange Act for expertised portions of registration statements. *See also* Disclosure Roles of Counsel, *supra* note 18, at 211-214 (discussing why disclaimers are prevalent in official statements).

[610] SEC Release No. 33-7856, SEC Interpretation: "Use of Electronic Media," Apr. 28, 2000 at n. 61, *available at* http://www.sec.gov/rules/interp/34-42728.htm ("Electronic Media 2000 Release") ("We do not view a disclaimer alone as sufficient to insulate an issuer from responsibility for information that it makes available to investors whether through a hyperlink or otherwise. To conclude otherwise would permit unscrupulous issuers to make false or misleading statements available to investors without fear of liability as long as the information is accompanied by a disclaimer. Further, we remind issuers that specific disclaimers of anti-fraud liability are contrary to the policies underpinning the federal securities laws.")

[611] *See supra* note 349.

[612] 1994 Interpretive Release, *supra* note 31, at n. 103.

[613] *See, e.g.*, NABL Comment Letter, *supra* note 391; *see also*, Disclosure Roles of Counsel, *supra* note 18.

[614] Electronic Media 2000 Release, *supra* note 610, at n. 54 and accompanying text (noting that liability for third party hyperlinked information under the "adoption" theory would depend upon whether, after its publication, an issuer, explicitly or implicitly, endorses or approves the hyperlinked information and laying out factors that are relevant in deciding whether an issuer has adopted information on a third-party web site to which it has established a hyperlink).

[615] *Id.* This Commission viewpoint was reiterated in its 2008 release, Commission Guidance on the Use of Company Websites, in which it paraphrased footnote 61 from the 2000 Electronic Media Release: "With

regard to the use of disclaimers generally, as we noted in the 2000 Electronics Release, we do not view a disclaimer alone as sufficient to insulate an issuer from responsibility for information that it makes available to investors whether through a hyperlink or otherwise. Accordingly, a company would not be shielded from antifraud liability for hyperlinking to information it knows, or is reckless in not knowing, is materially false or misleading. This would be the case even where the company uses a disclaimer and/or other features designed to indicate that it has not adopted the false or misleading information to which it has provided the hyperlink. Our concern is that an alternative approach could result in unscrupulous companies using disclaimers as shields from liability for making false or misleading statements. We again remind issuers that specific disclaimers of anti-fraud liability are contrary to the policies underpinning the federal securities laws." *See* Exchange Act Release No. 58228, "Commission Guidance on the Use of Company Websites," at text accompanying n. 86, Aug. 1, 2008, *available at* http://www.sec.gov/rules/interp/2008/34-58288.pdf.

[616] *See* 1994 Interpretive Release, *supra* note 31; *See also, e.g.*, Securities Act Release No. 9078/Exchange Act Release No.60928, *In the Matter of J.P. Morgan Securities Inc.* (Nov. 4, 2009) (failure to disclose payments of $8.2 million in 2002 and 2003 by respondent to various local firms whose principals or employees were friends of Jefferson County commissioners, who selected respondent as underwriter for bond offerings and affiliated bank as swap provider, violated Section 17(a)(2) and (3) of the Securities Act, Section 15B(c)(1) of the Exchange Act, and MSRB Rule G-17), *infra* note 628.

[617] *See supra* § III.B.3 (Exposure to Derivatives).

[618] *See* G-17 Interpretive Notice, *supra* note 251.

[619] Pay-to-play is considered an inappropriate practice whereby a market participant is expected to make political contributions to elected officials in order to be considered for selection to provide underwriting or other services. *See* definition of "Pay-to-play" in MSRB Glossary, *supra* note 31.

[620] *See* SEC Business Conduct Proposal and CFTC Business Conduct Final Rule (regarding pay-to-play prohibitions on security-based swap dealers, swap dealers and independent representatives in transactions with a state, state agency, city, county, municipality or other political subdivision of a state or any governmental plan).

[621] Market participants continue to call for the MSRB to ban such contributions. In December 2008, public finance executives from the three largest underwriting firms sent a letter urging the MSRB to restrict such contributions. *See* Andrew Ackerman, "Public Finance Execs Urge G-37 Amendments," The Bond Buyer, Jan. 7, 2009, *available at* http://www.bond buyer.com/issues/118_4/-298110-1.html. Municipal advisors made a similar request of the MSRB in comment letters with respect to the MSRB's proposed pay-to-play rules for municipal advisors. *See. e.g.,* Letter from National Association of Independent Public Financial Advisors commenting on proposed pay-to-play rules for municipal advisors (MSRB Notice 2011-004), Feb. 24, 2011, *available at* http://www.msrb.org/Rules-and-Interpretations/RegulatoryNotices/2011/~/media/Files/RFC/2011/2011-04/NAIPFA.ashx. *See also* Letter from WM Financial Strategies commenting on proposed pay-to-play rules for municipal advisors (MSRB Notice 2011-004), Feb. 24, 2011, *available at* http://www.msrb.org/Rules-and-Interpretations/RegulatoryNotices/2011/~/media/Files/RFC/2011/2011-04/WM-Financial-%20Strategies.ashx.

[622] *See, e.g.*, Missouri Revised Statutes § 409.107. "No investment firm, legal firm offering bond counsel services, or any persons having an interest in any such firms shall be involved in the issuance of bonds authorized by an election in which the firm or person made any direct or indirect financial contribution to any campaign in support of the bond election."

[623] *See, e.g.*, "Campaign Finance and Political Conduct Rules for School District Bond Elections" *available at* http://www.orrick.com/fileupload/122.pdf.

[624] *See*, Randall Jensen, "Brokers Gifts That Keep Giving," The Bond Buyer, Jan. 13, 2012, *available at* http://www.bondbuyer.com/issues/121_10/california-broker-dealer-contributions-school-bond-issue1035266-1.html (describing statements by a former California legislator who said that he found many instances where broker-dealers charged the school districts much higher fees for [negotiated] deals [where they had made a contribution to the bond election] compared to typical bond issues). *See also*, WM Financial Strategies, "Election Contributions May Equate to Pay-to-Play," *available at* http://www.munibondadvisor.com/Commentary.htm (accessed on May 23, 2012) ("Permitting local governments to engage underwriters based on election contributions reduces competition and increases bonding costs. Competition is reduced when an underwriter is selected based on the best bond election campaign rather than selected through competitive bidding. Bond costs are increased when an underwriter is engaged based on election campaign contributions (whether direct or indirect) rather than based on ability to provide lowest fees and interest rates").

[625] *See*, MSRB Notice 2010-01 (Jan. 22, 2010) and MSRB Notice 2010-03 (Feb. 1, 2010). The amendment to Rule G-37 also requires dealers to create and maintain records of such contributions to bond elections but, because

these records are frequently handwritten and not required to be word searchable, market participants have complained that such records are of very limited practical use in identifying potential problematic activity and using it as a basis for disclosure or enforcement. The MSRB has indicated to the Staff that they are studying ways to improve the searchability of such records.

[626] *See* 1994 Interpretive Release, *supra* note 31. *See also SEC v. Paul J. Silvester, et al.*, Litigation Release No. 16759 (Oct. 10, 2000); Litigation Release No. 20027 (Mar. 2, 2007); Litigation Release No. 19583 (Mar. 1, 2006); Litigation Release No. 18461 (Nov. 17, 2003); Litigation Release No. 16834 (Dec. 19, 2000); *SEC v. William A. DiBella et al.*, Litigation Release No. 20498 (Mar. 14, 2008); 2007 U.S. Dist. LEXIS 73850 (D. Conn., May 8, 2007), aff'd 587 F.3d 553 (2d Cir. 2009).

[627] *SEC v. Larry P. Lanford, William B. Blount, Blount Parish & Co., Inc. and Albert W. LaPierre,* Lit. Release No. 20545, Case No. CV-08-B-0761-S (N.D. Ala.) (Apr. 30, 2008), *available at* http://www.sec.gov/litigation/litreleases/2008/lr20821.htm.

[628] Securities Act Release No. 9078/Exchange Act Release No. 60928, *In the Matter of J.P. Morgan Securities Inc.* (Nov. 4, 2009), *available at* http://www.sec.gov/litigation/admin/ 2009/33-9078.pdf.

[629] *SEC v. Charles F. LeCroy and Douglas W. MacFaddin,* Lit Release No. 21280, Case No. CV-09 U/B 2238-S (N.D. Ala. Nov. 4, 2009), *available at* http://www.sec.gov/litigation/ litreleases/2009/lr21280.htm.

[630] Exchange Act Release No. 59439, "RBC Capital Markets Corporation" (Feb. 24, 2009), *available at* http://www.sec.gov/litigation/admin/2009/34-59439.pdf; Exchange Act Release No. 60043, "Merchant Capital, L.L.C." (June 4, 2009), *available at* http://www.sec.gov/ litigation/admin/2009/34-60043.pdf.

[631] *SEC v. Henry Morris, et al.*, Lit. Rel. No. 20963 (Mar. 19, 2009), Lit. Rel. No. 21001 (Apr. 15, 2009), Lit. Rel. No. 21018 (Apr. 30, 2009), *available at* http://www.sec.gov/litigation/ litreleases/litrelarchive/litarchive 2009.shtml.

[632] *SEC v. Paul J. Silvester, et al.*, Lit. Release No. 16759 (Oct. 10, 2000), *available at* http://www.sec.gov/litigation/litreleases/lr16834.htm; Lit. Release No. 20027 (Mar. 2, 2007); Lit. Release No. 19583 (Mar. 1, 2006); Lit. Release No. 18461 (Nov. 17, 2003); Lit. Release No. 16834 (Dec. 19, 2000); *SEC v. William A. DiBella et al.*, Litigation Release No. 20498 (Mar. 14, 2008), *available at* http://www.sec.gov/litigation/litreleases/2008/lr20498.htm; 2007 U.S. Dist. LEXIS 73850 (D. Conn., May 8, 2007), aff'd 587 F.3d 553 (2d Cir. 2009).

[633] SEC v. Kwame M. Kilpatrick, Jeffrey W. Beasley, Chauncey C. Mayfield, and MayfieldGentry Realty Advisors, LLC, Lit. Release No. 22362, Case No. 12-cv-12109 (E.D. Mich.)(May 9, 2012), *available at* http://www.sec.gov/litigation/litreleases/2012/ lr22362.htm.

[634] *See supra* discussion of EMMA under § II.B.3.a (Municipal Securities Rulemaking Board).

[635] *See supra* § III.A.4 (Market Participant Observations and Other Commentary). *See also, e.g.*, San Francisco Hearing Transcript at 251(Lehman) ("Taxpayers, investors, and regulators would all benefit from access to timely and accurate information."); San Francisco Transcript at 232-233 (Gill) ("An improved disclosure system is needed that will boost investor confidence and improve access to information about the municipal securities market."); Birmingham Hearing Transcript at 178 (Nolan) ("Investors can no longer rely on bond insurers or bond rating agencies, particularly on the secondary market . . . [Investors] must have access to the data themselves to bring greater transparency to the municipal securities market").

[636] *See supra* § III.B.1.d (Timeliness of Financial Information) (discussing the timeliness of financial information available after an offering).

[637] *See supra* note 196.

[638] *See, e.g.,* San Francisco Hearing Transcript at 58-60 (Colby) (discussing availability of road shows to institutional investors, and not retail investors), 258-259 (Lehman) ("[I]nstitutional investors in the security may have better access to information than retail investors, and we're potentially trading against those institutions. So they have more timely information, and we're getting adversely selected.").

[639] San Francisco Hearing Transcript at 59 (Colby). *But see* San Francisco Hearing Transcript at 59 (McNally) (arguing that institutional investors and retail investors usually have equal access to information and that there are generally no material differences between the electronic road show and the issuer's publically available offering statement).

[640] *See* Birmingham Hearing Transcript at 165 (Johnston) ("[Sometimes,] rating agencies are provided with information that potential buyers are not. This, in fact, just happened a couple of weeks ago when an issuer provided to a rating agency operating results and potential investors were not given this information"). For example, market participants have noted that rating agencies may have better access to issuers' financial information and revenue forecasts than other market participants. The Staff has also heard from market participants that institutional investors generally have greater access to issuer officials, to request additional information that may not be available publicly.

[641] The extent to which government entities use their websites to disclose financial information has been the subject of a few recent studies. One study, undertaken in 2004, surveyed the disclosure practices of the 100 largest U.S. municipalities, and found that 89% provided some form of financial disclosure on their website. James E. Groff and Marshall K. Pitman, *Municipal Financial Reporting on the World Wide Web: A Survey of Financial Data Displayed on the Official Websites of the 100 Largest U.S. Municipalities*, JOURNAL OF GOVERNMENT FINANCIAL MANAGEMENT 20, at 21 (Summer 2004). That same study also found that in terms of the content of disclosure provided, the surveyed municipalities gave more prominence to budget data than to CAFR data, as evidenced by the greater number of entities providing each type of information (88% gave budget data, while only 54% provided CAFR data) as well as a subject determination of the relative accessibility by reference to proximity to the entity's home page. *Id.* at 21. Within the sampled entities, larger cities were more likely to present CAFRs data on their websites, which the authors of the study suggested might be due to the importance that debt financing plays in the administration of such entities. *Id.* at 28. A second study, which surveyed the availability and accessibility of local government financial reports on the Internet by sampling 300 municipalities of varying size, found that "a significant proportion of U.S. cities are harnessing the communicative powers of the Internet as a means to promote financial accountability . . . ." The study also found that overall the provision of municipal reports on issuer websites is higher among municipalities that are larger, have higher income per capita, have higher levels of debt and maintain a healthier financial position. *See also* Alan Styles and Mack Tennyson, *The Accessibility of Financial Reporting of U.S. Municipalities on the Internet,* 19 J. OF BUDGETING, ACCOUNTING & FIN. MANAGEMENT 1, (April 2007).

[642] GFOA, GFOA Best Practice: Using a Web Site for Disclosure (2002 and 2010), *available at* http://www.gfoa.org/downloads/debt-using-web.pdf ("The Government Finance Officers Association (GFOA) recommends that governments and bond issuers use their websites to disseminate information to the municipal securities market regarding their debt, financial condition and other related information. The Internet, in general, and issuers' websites, in particular, provide a powerful tool for communicating with, and disclosing information to, credit analysts, investors, underwriters and other municipal market participants"). *See also* GFOA, "GFOA Best Practice: Using Websites to Improve Access to Budget Documents and Financial Reports" (2003), *available at* http://www.gfoa.org/downloads/caafr-budgets-towebsites.pdf; GFOA, "GFOA Best Practice: Web Site Presentation of Official Financial Documents" (2009), *available at* http://www.gfoa.org/downloads/websitepresentation.pdf ("The GFOA encourages every government to use its website as a primary means of communicating financial information to citizens and other interested parties").

[643] *See* San Francisco Hearing Transcript at 21 (Lockyer) (indicating that in addition to maintaining an investor website, State of California provides monthly financial reports that include cash reports with budget to actual comparisons, as well as updated economic and data information), 32 (Mayhew) (indicating that monthly budget, treasury report and board minutes are posted on the Bay Area Toll Authority website, even though specific investor relations website is not maintained).

[644] While posting information on an issuer website may assist an issuer in meeting its antifraud obligations under the federal securities laws, it does not satisfy an issuer's disclosure obligations under Rule 15c2-12.

[645] Birmingham Hearing Transcript at 56 (Presley).

[646] Birmingham Hearing Transcript at 130 (Scott).

[647] Birmingham Hearing Transcript at 128-129 (Henderson). *See also* Birmingham Hearing Transcript at 129-130 (Presley).

[648] *See* Electronic Media 2000 Release, *supra* note 610.

[649] *See, e.g.*, NABL Comment Letter, *supra* note 391.

[650] *See id.*

[651] A number of individual investors speaking at the Commission's field hearings expressed frustration with the complexity of municipal issuer disclosure. *See* San Francisco Hearing Transcript at 251 (Siminoff), 245 (Lehman); Washington, DC Hearing Transcript (Morning Session) at 29 (Kirkpatrick), 34 (Niewiaroski). *See also* Municipal Market Advisors, "Presentation to House Judiciary Committee, Subcommittee on Courts, Commercial, and Administrative Law," Feb. 14, 2011, *available at* http://judiciary.house.gov/hearings/pdf/Fabian02142011.pdf.

[652] *See, e.g.,* San Francisco Hearing Transcript at 133 (McIntire); Washington, DC Hearing Transcript (Morning Session) at 29 (Kirkpatrick). *See also* San Francisco Hearing Transcript at 245 (Lehman) (noting that the lack of municipal bond standardized terms, means that in order to properly differentiate between securities, investors must read the entire official statement for each issue).

[653] *See, e.g.*, San Francisco Hearing Transcript at 234-35 (Gill), 245 (Lehman) ("I'm an experienced professional investor in complex financial areas, such as credit and equity options, yet even I still feel challenged by the task of picking apart a municipal prospectus. It is questionable whether the average retail investor is equipped to wade through these complex documents").

[654] *See* Letter from Michael G. Bartolotta, Chair, MSRB, to Commissioner Elisse B. Walter, Aug. 8, 2011, *available at* http://www.sec.gov/comments/4-610/4610-69.pdf ("They have also expressed the desire for standardization of disclosure concerning the name of the issuer, the name of any other obligor, the source of payment of debt service, and the sector (*e.g.*, hospital, public power)").

[655] *See, e.g.*, San Francisco Hearing Transcript at 152 (Singer), 239 (Kuhn), 251 (Siminoff).

[656] San Francisco Hearing Transcript at 255 (Siminoff) (suggesting a 100 point scale, with 100 indicating no credit (default) risk and the lower numbers reflecting higher credit (default) risk).

[657] *See supra* note 352.

[658] *See supra* note 164.

[659] *See* Disclosure Roles of Counsel, *supra* note 18, at 65 (noting that in the absence of Commission guidance on transaction-specific municipal disclosure prior to use, SEC enforcement actions provide the principal source of guidance in applying the anti-fraud provisions of the federal securities laws to particular circumstances). Commission action or guidance in this area may also be set forth through Commission reports. *See, e.g.*, Exchange Act Release No. 36761, "Report of Investigation in the Matter of County of Orange, California, as it Relates to the Conduct of the Members of the Board of Supervisors" (Jan. 24, 1996), *available at* http://www.sec.gov/info/municipal/mbonds/publicof.htm. *See also* sources cited *infra* note 661.

[660] *Id.*

[661] *See, e.g.*, *In the Matter of State of New Jersey, supra* note 359 (with assistance of outside disclosure counsel, state instituted formal, written disclosure policies and procedures and implemented a mandatory compliance training program for employees); *In the Matter of the City of San Diego, supra* note 360 (The city adopted certain disclosure controls and procedures, including an ordinance incorporating internal control procedures based upon requirements of the Sarbanes-Oxley Act); Securities Act Release No. 8601, *In the Matter of Utah Educational Savings Plan Trust* (order) (Aug. 4, 2005), *available at* http://sec.gov/litigation/admin/33-8601.pdf (Respondent undertook to retain an independent consultant to assist it in establishing internal controls to address noted weaknesses in its disclosure, accounting and other procedures).

[662] *In the Matter of the City of San Diego, supra* note 360.

[663] Disclosure Roles of Counsel, *supra* note 18, at 73.

[664] Stanley Keller, "Third Annual and Final Report of Independent Consultant of the City of San Diego," 4-5, 15-16, Feb. 24, 2010, *available at* http://dockets.sandiego.gov/sirepub/ pubmtgframe.aspx?meetid=642&doctype=Agenda ("San Diego Final Report") (noting the creation of the Internal Audit Committee and the Disclosure Practices Working Group).

[665] *Id.* at 15-16.

[666] *Id.* at 3 (noting the hiring of a Deputy City Attorney for Finance and Disclosure). The Utah Education Savings Plan also hired new employees including a new director who brought the Savings Plan into line with the College Savings Plan Network's disclosure principles. *See* Utah Educational Savings Plan News Release, "UESP and SEC Enter into Settlement Agreement," Aug. 4. 2005, *available at* http://www.uesp.org/pdfs/Press Release/2005_08-PR-SEC-Settlement.aspx ("UESP News Release").

[667] *See* San Diego Final Report, *supra* note 664, at 6-10 (describing the implementation of a resource planning system called OneSD designed to improve internal controls). The Utah Education Savings Plan also implemented a new computer system designed to improve internal controls with the assistance of outside consultants. *See* UESP News Release, *supra* note 666.

[668] San Diego Final Report, *supra* note 664, at 6-10, 20-21.

[669] *Id.* at 5-6.

[670] One of these participants was Stanley Keller, the independent consultant for the city of San Diego. His comments are reflected above in the discussion of the internal controls implemented in San Diego. *See* San Francisco Hearing Transcript at 195-200 (Keller) for his full remarks on San Diego's controls at the hearing.

[671] *See* San Francisco Hearing Transcript at 190 (Harrington).

[672] San Francisco Hearing Transcript at 188-190 (Harrington). Mr. Harrington also pointed out that the SFPUC reports to several public oversight boards and committees under its voter approved charter. *Id.* at 190.

[673] *Id.* at 192.

[674] San Francisco Hearing Transcript at 198-99 (Keller).

675 Some commenters have expressed concern that Commission rulemaking in this area could be overly burdensome.

676 San Francisco Hearing Transcript at 201 (Keller).

677 *Id.*

678 *See supra* § II.A.1(Municipal Securities Issuers) and II.A.5 (The Secondary Market for Municipal Securities).

679 *See supra* § II.A.2 (Description of Municipal Securities). *See also* Birmingham Hearing Transcript at 270-71 (Lanza) (noting the large and extremely diverse nature of the municipal securities market, the infrequency of trading in most issues, and the impact of these characteristics on price transparency)

680 The state and local tax treatment of municipal bonds often is more advantageous for in-state investors. In fact, there are tax-exempt mutual funds that specialize in the bonds issued by a single, generally high-tax, state. *See, e.g.*, Summary prospectus for "Fidelity New York Municipal Income Fund," *available at* http://www.sec.gov/Archives/edgar/data/718581/ 000088019512000181/main.htm.

681 Some municipal securities are taxable. Some municipal securities are issued as private activity bonds under the Internal Revenue Code and are subject to the alternative minimum tax. Some municipal securities are "bank qualified bonds" and are qualified for the special tax treatment afforded to banks under Section 265(b) of the Internal Revenue Code; generally, a bond is bank qualified if the issuer does not intend to issue more than $10 million in bonds in a calendar year. *See* I.R.C. § 265(b)(3). *See also,* Feldstein and Fabozzi, *supra* note 72. In addition, the ARRA for a limited time period authorized taxable BABs and other new types of municipal securities to be issued. *See supra* notes 58 – 59 and accompanying text. Those BABs and other municipal securities continue to trade in the secondary market.

682 It is important to note, however, that there was increased institutional investor interest in BABs financings. *See, e.g.*, Helen Avery, "Municipal Bonds: Build America Bonds Are Here to Stay," Euromoney, Sept. 2009, *available at* http://www.euromoney.com/Article/ 2296313/Municipal-bonds-Build-America-Bondsare-here-to-stay.html. Market participants credit the short-lived BABs program with expanding the investor base for municipal bonds (for example, they could be sold overseas) and support efforts to expand the investor base for municipal bonds.

683 *See supra* § II.A.3 (Investors in Municipal Securities) (providing statistics describing the investor base of the municipal securities market).

684 *See id.* (also noting that individuals directly hold approximately 50% of the outstanding principal amount of municipal securities). One study has concluded that, while the par value of sales to and purchases from customers is roughly equal, the number of transactions that are sales to customers is almost twice the number of transactions that are purchases from customers. The authors suggest that this is typical of a "retail market" where the intermediaries buy larger quantities at wholesale prices and sell in smaller quantities to retail customers. *See generally* Richard C. Green, Dan Li and Norman Schürhoff, *Price Discovery in Illiquid Markets: Do Financial Asset Prices Rise Faster Than They Fall?,* 65 J. FIN. 1669, 1676 (2010) ("Green, Li and Schürhoff 2010").

685 *See supra* note 103. In centralized markets, each investor can trade with everyone else. In decentralized markets, investors have preferred dealers and dealers trade preferably with counterparties. *See, e.g.,* Dan Li and Norman Schürhoff, Dealer Networks (Working Paper Nov. 2011) ("Li and Schürhoff, Dealer Networks"), *available at* http://papers.ssrn.com/ sol3/papers.cfm?abstract_id=2023201 (estimating average dealer markups for municipal securities to be 1.77%-2.0%).

686 One study of municipal bond transactions executed between 1998 and 2011 concludes that agency trading accounted for 6% of the trades in the sample. *See* Li and Schürhoff, Dealer Networks, *supra* note 685.

687 *See supra* note 105.

688 *See supra* § II.A.5 (The Secondary Market for Municipal Securities) (with graph illustrating Distribution of Customer Trades Traded (based on par amount traded)).

689 We derived this statistic by dividing 15,213 (the average daily number of unique municipal securities traded in 2011, according to MSRB) by 1,048,146 (the number of outstanding municipal securities as of December 31, 2011). Staff generated statistic. Data source: Mergent's MBSD. *See also* GAO Market Structure Report, *supra* note 61 (concluding the same percentage in this manner for 2010).

690 Richard C. Green, Burton Hollifield and Norman Schürhoff, *Dealer Intermediation and Price Behavior in the Aftermarket for New Bond Issues,* 86 J. FIN. ECON. 643, 652 (2007) ("Green, Hollifield and Schürhoff, *Dealer Intermediation*").

691 Richard C. Green, Burton Hollifield and Norman Schürhoff, *Financial Intermediation and the Costs of Trading in an Opaque Market,* 20 REV. FIN. STUD. 275, 282 (2007) ("Green, Hollifield and Schürhoff, *Financial Intermediation*").

[692] While first-day sales account for 73% of the par value of an issue, second-day sales account for 30%; after five days, that figure drops to 12%. *See* Green, Hollifield and Schürhoff, *Dealer Intermediation*, *supra* note 690, at 652.

[693] Broker's brokers act as agents for municipal bond dealers. *See* Harris and Piwowar, *supra* note 103, at 1363. They facilitate information flow in the municipal securities markets by conducting bid-wanted auctions ("bid-wanted") for dealers selling municipal securities. Following a bid-wanted, broker's brokers execute transactions for a fee. They do not typically take securities into inventory. *See* GAO Market Structure Report, *supra* note 61, at 8.

[694] *See supra* § II.C.2 (Alternative Trading Systems).

[695] *See supra* note 61. An analysis of municipal-market data since 1996, however, suggests a relative increase in the trading of municipal bonds. SEC-Generated Statistic. Data Source: SIFMA (calculating at an annual frequency the ratio of average daily trading volume to either the amount of municipal securities outstanding or amount of municipal securities issued).

[696] If a customer – particularly an institutional investor – has relationships with multiple municipal bond dealers, it may request bids directly from all of them. Municipal bond dealers that take municipal bonds into inventory may hold them for varying periods of time, depending on their business model and risk tolerance. Bonds held in inventory may be sold to meet customer or other municipal bond dealer demand. For example, municipal bond dealers may provide liquidity to institutions, such as hedge funds and mutual funds, by purchasing large blocks of bonds from these institutions and selling those bonds in one or more large blocks to other institutions, or in smaller sizes to retail investors or regional municipal bond dealers that have the ability to distribute to retail customers. *See, e.g.* Green, Li and Schürhoff 2010, *supra* note 684, at 1675-76 (noting that municipal bond dealers often provide liquidity to institutions by buying large blocks and selling off in many smaller amounts to retail investors or regional municipal bond dealers and noting that the municipal securities market "has many attributes of a retail market, such as the gasoline market, where the intermediaries buy at wholesale prices and sell in smaller quantities to less sophisticated, retail investors").

[697] For example, a municipal bond dealer could request bids on behalf of its customer by placing the customer order on the "brokers' wire" used by broker's brokers conducting bid-wanteds, or by using ATSs that provide "request for quote," or "RFQ," mechanisms.

[698] *See* Green, Li and Schürhoff 2010, *supra* note 684, at 1676 (noting that such purchases and sales in the municipal securities market occur within minutes of each other).

[699] *See, e.g.*, Li and Schürhoff, Dealer Networks, *supra* note 685 (noting that municipal securities are traded through an "opaque network of financial intermediaries"). *See also infra* § IV.B.1.b (Pre-Trade Price Transparency) (discussing the lack of transparency in quotations for municipal securities).

[700] *See* Washington, DC Hearing Transcript (Morning Session) at 15-16 (Collins) (noting that the financial difficulties faced by banks in recent years impaired their ability to provide secondary credit and liquidity facilities to municipal issuers so that, by late 2010, only 15-17 institutions were actively providing these facilities). *See also* Birmingham Hearing Transcript at 297 (Lessley) (noting how bond insurance simplified the pricing of municipal bonds); Washington Hearing Transcript (Morning Session) at 11 (McCarthy) (expressing the view that bond insurance and credit ratings, by homogenizing the underlying credits, enhanced market liquidity to the benefit of retail investors). *But see* Washington Hearing Transcript (Morning Session) at 7-8 (Doe) (expressing the opinion that the commoditization of the municipal securities market prior to 2008 created hidden risk as higher-quality credits were used to inform valuations of lower credits). In addition, the reliability of credit ratings has been questioned, regulators have been removing references to credit ratings from regulation, and a change in the rating scales has led some to complain that it is now more difficult to differentiate among ratings for municipal securities. *See supra* § I(C)(7) at Nationally Recognized Statistical Rating Organizations ("NRSROs").

[701] *See generally infra* § IV.B.2 (Transaction Costs) (summarizing relevant studies concerning transaction costs in the municipal securities market). Retail municipal securities investors often incur roundtrip transaction costs of 2–3%, and as high as 5%, compared to less than 1% for corporate bonds and significantly below 1% for equities. *See* Andrew Ang and Richard C. Green, Lowering Borrowing Costs for States and Municipalities Through CommonMuni, The Hamilton Project at 6, *available at* http://www.hamiltonproject.org/files/downloads_ and_links/THP_ANG-GREEN_DiscusPape_Feb2011.pdf ("CommonMuni"). *See also* Green, Hollifield and Schürhoff, *Dealer Intermediation*, *supra* note 690, at 291–93 (finding customers simultaneously buying bonds at prices up to 5% over the reoffering price, with most from 2–3%); Harris and Piwowar, *supra* note 103, at 1379, 1382 (evaluating municipal securities transactions through October 2000 and estimating that effective spreads on retail trades of $20,000 are 1.98% for municipal bonds compared to either 1.24% for

corporate bonds or 0.4% for equities). Another study found that it is twice as expensive to trade New York municipal bonds as it was when they were actively traded on an exchange in the 1920s. Bruno Biais and Richard C. Green, The Microstructure of the Bond Market in the 20th Century at 23-25 (Carnegie Mellon University Working Paper, Aug. 29, 2007), *available at* http://wpweb2.tepper.cmu.edu/facultyadmin/upload/wpaper_39493927532128_biasgreen829.pdf ("Biais and Green 2007").

[702] *See generally infra* § IV.B.2 (Transaction Costs) (discussing the differences in transaction costs for retail and institutional investors). For example, one study concludes that unlike in the equity markets where trading costs increase with trade size, in the municipal securities market, small trades are substantially more expensive than large trades. *See* Harris and Piwowar, *supra* note 103, at 1393. Specifically, the authors find that effective spreads in municipal bonds average about 2% of the price for retail-size trades of $20,000 and about 1% for institutional-size trades of $200,000. The authors conclude that the difference in cost between small and large trades is attributable primarily to the lack of price transparency, where large institutional traders generally have a better sense of the value of securities than smaller traders. In making this conclusion, the study considered specifically the impact of fixed costs in the municipal securities market. *Id.* at 1362.

[703] As noted by some, a number of factors affect the price provided to an investor for a particular bond. For example, if a municipal security is rated and its financial information is current based upon filings with EMMA and information obtained by research analysts, the municipal security will generally price more competitively than an unrated security or a security for which little or no current credit information is available. *See, e.g.*, Washington, DC Hearing Transcript (Morning Session) at 8, 18-19 (Doe) (discussing the impact correctness and timeliness of issuer information have on valuation). Prices that investors receive can also vary depending on the market conditions. In a calm market, the difference between the evaluation stated on an investor's monthly statement and the price the investor can obtain in the market may not be markedly different. In a rapidly changing market there can be a large discrepancy between the evaluation of the bonds on the customer's monthly statement and actual market conditions on any given day. *See e.g.*, *id.* at 12-13 (Deane), 19 (Greco). In addition, the MSRB recognized in guidance recently approved by the Commission that customers may receive better prices when liquidating their securities if they can take additional time to do so. This notice urges selling dealers "not to assume that their customers need to liquidate their securities immediately without inquiring as to their customers' particular circumstances and discussing with their customers the possible improved pricing benefit associated with taking additional time to liquidate their securities." *See* MSRB Broker's Broker Approval Order, *supra* note 217.

[704] *See generally infra* § IV.B.3 (Dealer Pricing Obligations to Customers) (discussing legal obligations of municipal bond dealers regarding the pricing and execution of customer orders for municipal securities, including common law best execution obligations). *See, e.g.*, Letter from Michael M. Becker (Nov. 22, 2011), *available at* http://www.sec.gov/comments/4-610/4-610.shtml ("Michael M. Becker Comment Letter") (complaining that he is never shown by his municipal bond dealer the best bids or offers on the other side of the market and that his municipal bond dealer will not display his bid or offer to a broad group of municipal bond investors).

[705] *See* MSRB Rule G-14 Reports of Sales or Purchases, *available at* http://www.msrb.org/Rules-and-Interpretations/MSRB-Rules/General/Rule-G-14.aspx. The municipal bond dealer may employ an agent for the purpose of submitting transaction information; however, the primary responsibility for the timely and accurate submission remains with the municipal bond dealer that effected the transaction. The municipal bond dealer or its agent can modify and cancel previously submitted trade reports and can access reports about the quality of their submissions. *See* MSRB Rule G-14(b).

[706] *See* Exchange Act Release No. 59212 (Jan. 7, 2009), 74 FR 1741 (Jan. 13, 2009) (SR-MSRB-2008-07).

[707] Municipal securities trade data is available at http://emma.msrb.org. *See generally supra* § II.B.3.a (Municipal Securities Rulemaking Board) for a discussion of EMMA.

[708] On March 20, 2012, the Commission approved a proposed rule change by the MSRB that would, in part, reprogram RTRS to calculate a corresponding yield for inter-dealer transactions, thereby eliminating a disparity between information disseminated for inter-dealer and customer transactions. *See* Exchange Act Release No. 66622 (Mar. 20, 2012), 77 FR 17557 (Mar. 26, 2012) (SR-MSRB-2012-01).

[709] Although municipal bond dealers report to the MSRB the exact size of executed trades, the exact dollar amount of a trade is publicly disclosed only if the principal amount is under $1 million. All other trades (i.e., those over $1 million in principal amount) are identified using the indicator 1MM+ for one week after the trade date. That indicator is replaced by the exact trade size after one week. *See* MSRB's EMMA Education Center, Understanding Trade Prices, *available at* http://emma.msrb.org/EducationCenter/Understanding

TradePrices.aspx. The MSRB recently requested comment on the proposal to discontinue the practice of masking the exact par value on transactions where the par value is greater than $1 million and including the exact par value on all transactions disseminated in real-time from RTRS. MSRB Notice 2012-29, "Request for Comment on Elimination of Large Trade Size Masking on Price Transparency Reports," June 1, 2012.

[710] MSRB, EMMA, Market Activity, http://emma.msrb.org/marketactivity/recenttrades.aspx. *See also supra* note 196.

[711] MSRB, Specifications for Real-Time Reporting of Municipal Securities Transactions, Nov. 2009, *available at* http://www.msrb.org/Market-Disclosures-and-Data/Submit-Data/~/media/Files/SystemSpecifications/RTRS/RTRSSpecificationsV221.ashx.

[712] MRSB, Real-Time Transaction Reporting System Web Users Manual (June 2010), *available at* http://www.msrb.org/Market-Disclosures-and-Data/Submit-Data/~/media/Files/User-Manuals/RTRSWebUsersManualv27.ashx.

[713] *See* MSRB Rule G-13 Quotations Relating to Municipal Securities, *available at* http://www.msrb.org/Rules-and-Interpretations/MSRB-Rules/General/Rule-G-13.aspx (prohibiting a municipal securities dealer from distributing or publishing a quotation unless it represents a bona fide bid or offer and is based on the municipal securities dealer's best judgment of the security's fair market value at the time the quotation is made). The Staff understands, however, that market participants display indicative quotes on some ATSs and in practice, executions occur at these indicative prices nearly always. The Staff also understands that dealers may place indications of interest representing the same trading interest in multiple ATSs or other electronic systems. *See also* Letter from Joseph S. Fichera, Senior Managing Director & CEO, Saber Partners, LLC, to Commissioner Elisse B. Walter, Nov. 2, 2011, attached to Memorandum from the Office of Commissioner Walter, Nov. 21, 2011, regarding an October 24, 2011 meeting with representatives of Saber Partners, LLC, *available at* http://www.sec.gov/comments/4-610/4610-78.pdf ("Fichera Letter") (noting that secondary market liquidity for municipal securities is inhibited by the absence of market makers).

[714] ATSs include TMC LLC (f/k/a TheMuniCenter.com), BondDesk Trading LLC, TradeWeb LLC, Knight BondPoint, Schwab Bond Source, Bonds.Com, Inc., and HTDonline. Broker's brokers that provide such electronic access to other municipal bond dealers include Wolfe & Hurst Bond Brokers, Inc. and Regional Brokers, Inc.

[715] The Staff understands that registered ATSs account for approximately 30-50% of all trades reported to the MSRB. Two ATSs informed the Staff that they accounted for 18.5% and 23% of trades in the municipal securities market in a given month in 2010. *See, e.g.,* Memorandum from the SEC Division of Trading and Markets (Sept. 14, 2011), regarding a December 15, 2010 meeting with representatives of TheMuniCenter.com, *available at* http://www.sec. gov/comments/4-610/4610-67.pdf; Memorandum from the SEC Division of Trading and Markets (Aug. 4, 2011), regarding a July 18, 2011 meeting with representatives of BondDesk Trading LLC, *available at* http://www.sec.gov/comments/4-610/4610-63.pdf. However, based on aggregate data available to the Staff, the Staff estimates that in 2011, ATSs accounted for a much smaller percentage of the dollar value of municipal securities transactions (roughly 5%).

[716] *See, e.g.*, Fichera Letter, *supra* note 713, at 8 (stating that the principal ATSs in today's bond market offer only the bonds in the inventory of the dealers that own the platform).

[717] These mechanisms can provide requesting municipal bond dealers with the ability to identify the specific bond and amount to be sold; the time by which any bids should be submitted; and a request that the bids be good for at least a certain amount of time. The system then sends the RFQ or bid-wanted request to participating municipal bond dealers that the selling dealer has approved and is willing to trade with for potential responses; the Staff is aware that at least one system provides all participants with the ability to interact with all other participants. Municipal bond dealers responding to the RFQ or bid-wanted request often send bids that are firm for the requesting municipal bond dealer for some limited period of time. *See e.g.*, MSRB Notice 2010-35 (Sept. 9, 2010) (describing two types of broker's broker activities: "bid-wanted auctions," where a selling dealer wants to obtain the best bid it can without specifying a price at which it is willing to sell; and "offerings," where a selling dealer uses the broker's broker's facilities to specify a desired price or yield for a particular security it would like to sell).

[718] The Staff understands that due to a general difficulty in obtaining current and accurate valuations, those with access to these ATSs and broker's brokers may occasionally resort to submitting an RFQ and using the responses as the basis for a valuation. Concerns have been raised that if liquidity providers suspect that the submitter of the RFQ is not serious about trading, the liquidity providers may not respond at all or respond only with wide, imprecise quotes, which could result in an inaccurate valuation (if the requester indeed intended to use the responses solely for that purpose). The practice may also reduce the usefulness of RFQs for

market participants that truly wish to trade. The Commission recently approved MSRB interpretive guidance regarding duties of sellers that addresses this practice. The guidance states that the use of bid-wanteds solely for price discovery purposes without any intention of selling the securities may be an unfair practice within the meaning of Rule G-17 (Conduct of Municipal Securities and Municipal Advisory Activities). *See* MSRB Broker's Broker Approval Order, *supra* note 217.

[719] The Staff understands that some ATSs also allow direct access by institutional investors.

[720] The Staff understands that ATSs also may provide participating dealers with certain trading and informational features. These features include the ability to do enhanced searches of transaction reports (e.g., searches by CUSIP, maturity, type of bond) and to link efficiently to publicly available information concerning a particular issue (e.g., event notices). Some ATSs also provide transaction prices of comparable municipal securities.

[721] In spite of technology's transformational effect on the municipal securities market and all of the resources offered by the financial industry to invest in municipal bonds, understanding the underlying value of bonds has become even more complex. *See* Birmingham Hearing Transcript at 297 (Lessley).

[722] *See* MMA AAA Median Municipal Benchmark, http://www.mma-research.com/mma/non members/Consensus/consensus.asp.

[723] *See* Thomson Municipal Market Monitor (TM3), https://www.tm3.com.

[724] Examples include Standard & Poor's Securities Evaluations, Inc. (providing opinions on the valuation of fixed income securities using a market approach methodology); Interactive Data's Evaluation Services (below); Bloomberg's Valuation Service (providing, along with a price, a score that is an index number that describes the relative strength of the quantity and quality of market inputs used in calculating the price); and Markit's Evaluated Pricing Service (providing an independent price by aggregating market data from multiple sources). *See* Birmingham Hearing Transcript at 277 (Barasch) (noting that his firm (Interactive Data) provides an independent source of evaluated prices that represents the firm's good-faith opinion as to what a buyer in the marketplace would pay for a security, typically in an institutional round lot position).

[725] An evaluator for a municipal bond pricing service generally will seek to value a bond by comparing it to bonds with similar characteristics for which recent prices are known. Municipal bond valuation has been described as more art than science, and the evaluator must sort through many variables in forming an opinion, including the type of bond (e.g., general obligation, revenue, conduit), type of issuer, credit quality, coupon, tax treatment, credit enhancement, call features, and other specific characteristics of the security. *See* Feldstein and Fabozzi, *supra* note 72, at 504-506. *See also* Birmingham Hearing Transcript at 279 (Barasch) (noting three main data points go into an evaluation: transaction activity, such as primary market new issues and secondary market MSRB trade data; bids, offers, and two-sided markets; and credit information, such as audited financials, default and material event notices, and rating actions).

[726] *See* Feldstein and Fabozzi, *supra* note 72, at 504.

[727] The Staff understands that these capabilities are available through market data vendors and some ATSs.

[728] *See, e.g.*, GAO Market Structure Report, *supra* note 61, at 20-27 (discussing institutional investors' greater access to information and greater ability to make use of that information).

[729] *See id.*

[730] *See id.* at 25.

[731] Commenters at the Commission's Field Hearings expressed the view that the general public should be on a more equal informational footing with municipal bond dealers. *See, e.g.*, Birmingham Hearing Transcript at 290 (Roberts).

[732] *See* Birmingham Hearing Transcript at 318 (Lynch) (noting the need to use a pricing matrix for valuing individual municipal securities);. Washington, DC Hearing Transcript (Morning Session) at 23 (Doe) (noting that retail investors are dependent on prices generated by the two primary evaluation services). Some have expressed concerns that the valuations customers receive on their monthly statements do not reflect what a customer may receive when the customer decides to sell. *See, e.g.,* Washington, DC Hearing Transcript (Morning Session) at 12 (Deane) (describing situations where investors may see discrepancies between monthly statement bond values and prices they are receiving when attempting to sell their bonds). The Staff understands from market participants that evaluation services typically provide municipal bond valuations based on institutional, round lot positions, rather than retail-size positions. *See, e.g.*, Birmingham Hearing Transcript at 277 (Barasch) (noting that evaluated prices typically reflect an opinion on what a buyer would pay for an institutional round lot position). In addition, the Staff understands that some municipal bond dealers provide customers with more frequent valuation information on their websites.

[733] At the Field Hearings, some expressed the view that the MSRB should enhance EMMA's search capabilities, as well as other enhancements. Some suggested that it would be useful for investors to receive overview information in a summary format. For example, one commenter noted that cheat sheets should be provided to investors on certain highlights and that converting PDFs to word searchable formats would be helpful. *See* Birmingham Hearing Transcript at 313 (Lynch). Another suggested broader enhancements to EMMA aimed at making information more accessible to retail investors, including different ways to package information and tools that would be helpful to retail investors, such as ways to make comparables easier to review. *See id.* at 309-10 (Lanza). *See also* GAO Market Structure Report, *supra* note 61, at 24. Based on suggestions received over the last several years, MSRB plans to improve EMMA's search capabilities as well as to make other enhancements to its transparency products aimed at serving the needs of retail investors. *See, e.g.*, MSRB Long-Range Plan for Market Transparency Products, *supra* note 197. The MSRB recently launched an online "investor toolkit" to provide basic information to retail investors about navigating the municipal market. *See* MSRB Investor Toolkit, *available at* http://www.msrb.org/Municipal-Bond-Market/ Investor-Resources/Investor-Toolkit.aspx (accessed on May 31, 2012).

[734] *See, e.g.*, SIFMA, Investing In Bonds, http://www.investinginbonds.com.

[735] *See, e.g.*, www.bondview.com.

[736] GAO Market Structure Report, *supra* note 61, at 22.

[737] The "effective spread" represents the cost that an investor would incur if she simultaneously bought and sold the same security. They are typically measured as twice the difference between the execution price and the midpoint of the best bid and best offer at the time of order receipt. *See e.g.*, Rule 600(b)(4) of Regulation NMS. Due to limited quote transparency for municipal securities, effective spreads have been estimated using various methods, including economic models. *See* Harris and Piwowar, *supra* note 103, at 1364-67.

[738] *See* Harris and Piwowar, *supra* note 103, at 1379, 1382; Amy K. Edwards, Lawrence E. Harris and Michael S. Piwowar, *Corporate Bond Market Transaction Costs and Transparency,* 62 J. FIN. 1421, 1437-38 (2007) ("Edwards, Harris and Piwowar 2007"). *See also* CommonMuni, *supra* note 701, at 6 (stating that retail municipal securities investors regularly incur transaction costs of 2-3%, and as high as 5%, compared to less than 1% for corporate bonds and significantly below 1% for equities). Notably, average trading costs in municipal securities today are twice as large as they were during 1926-1927 when bonds traded on the NYSE. *See* Biais and Green 2007, *supra* note 701, at 23-25.

[739] Effective spreads for institutional-size trades of $200,000 average 0.98% for municipal bonds, but only 0.48% for corporate bonds. *See* Harris and Piwowar, *supra* note 103, at 1379; Edwards, Harris and Piwowar 2007, *supra* note 738, at 1437.

[740] A "markup" generally refers to the amount a dealer charges a customer in excess of the security's prevailing market price when the customer is buying a security from the dealer, and a "markdown" generally refers to the amount a dealer pays a customer beneath the security's prevailing market price, when the dealer is purchasing a security from the customer. *See* NASD Rule 2440 and *infra* §III(B)(3) at Exposure to Derivatives (discussing legal obligations of municipal bond dealers regarding the pricing and execution of customer orders for municipal securities). As used herein, the term "markup" refers both to markups and markdowns.

[741] *See* Green, Hollifield and Schürhoff, *Financial Intermediation*, *supra* note 691; Dan Li and Norman Schürhoff, Dealer Networks (Working Paper Nov. 2011) ("Li and Schürhoff, Dealer Networks"), *available at* http://papers.ssrn.com/sol3/papers.cfm? abstract_id= 2023201 (estimating average dealer markups for municipal securities to be 1.77%-2.0%).

[742] *See, e.g.*, Harris and Piwowar, *supra* note 103, at 1392-93 (concluding that municipal securities trades are substantially more expensive than similar-sized equity trades and attributing this result to the lack of transparency in the municipal securities market). In addition, one study has found that a disproportionately large number of municipal securities prices and yields are rounded off to whole numbers or common fractions. The study's author believes that this is a function of the lack of price transparency and liquidity in the municipal securities market, with dealers tending to round quoted prices to enhance their profits. *See* Dan Li, Rounding as Discrimination—Price Clustering in the OTC Tax-Exempt Bond Market (AFA 2008 New Orleans Meetings Paper, Nov. 2007), *available at* http://papers.ssrn.com/sol3/papers.cfm?abstract id=971074.

[743] *See generally* GAO Market Structure Report, *supra* note 61, at 16-19 (finding that relative to institutional investors, (1) individual investors paid higher prices when buying and received lower prices when selling; (2) municipal bond dealers received larger spreads when trading smaller blocks; and (3) the prices individual investors paid for a security tended to be more dispersed).

[744] Effective spreads average about 1.98% for retail-size trades of $20,000, but only 0.98% for institutional-size trades of up to $200,000. *See* Harris and Piwowar, *supra* note 103, at 1379. Markups average 2.3% for

smaller trade sizes up to $100,000, but then decrease to approximately 1.1% for trade sizes between $100,000 and $500,000. *See* Green, Hollifield and Schürhoff, *Financial Intermediation*, *supra* note 691, at 289 table 7.

[745] Harris and Piwowar, *supra* note 103, at 1362. *See, e.g.,* Exchange Act Release No. 42450 (Feb. 23, 2000), 65 FR 10577 (Feb. 28, 2000) (SR-NYSE-99-48) (Notice of Filing of Proposed Rule Change by the New York Stock Exchange Rule 390; Commission Request for Comment on Issues Relating to Market Fragmentation).

[746] *See supra* note 702 (discussing the findings of Harris and Piwowar on this point); *see also* Green, Hollifield and Schürhoff, *Financial Intermediation*, *supra* note 691, at 280 (citing lack of transparency and dealers' market power for the high trading costs for small transactions).

[747] *See id.*

[748] Green, Hollifield and Schürhoff, *Dealer Intermediation*, *supra* note 690, at 644. In addition, the authors found that prices of newly issued municipal securities traded by retail investors tend to drift upward in the days following the start of trading in a manner that suggests that municipal securities offerings are underpriced. The upward drift is not apparent in interdealer and institutional-sized trades. This leads the authors to conclude that the upward drift is not the result of gradual price discovery or the release of information. *Id.*

[749] *See* Green, Hollifield and Schürhoff, *Dealer Intermediation*, *supra* note 690, at 653 (noting that some retail customers simultaneously buy bonds at the reoffering price while others buy bonds as high as 5% over the reoffering price). *See also* GAO Market Structure Report, *supra* note 61, at 18 (finding that from 2005– 2010, prices for smaller trades tended to be more dispersed, while prices for larger trades tended to be more concentrated).

[750] *See* Green, Hollifield and Schürhoff, *Dealer Intermediation*, *supra* note 690, at 661.

[751] *See supra* § IV.B.1 (Price Transparency).

[752] Paul Schultz, The Market for New Issues of Municipal Bonds: The Roles of Transparency and Limited Access to Retail Investors at 2, 16 (U. of Notre Dame, Working Paper Sep. 2011), *available at* http://ssrn.com/abstract=1988548 or http://dx.doi.org/10.2139/ ssrn.1988548 ("Schultz 2011 Working Paper"). While post-trade transparency did sharply reduce price dispersion, the author found only a small effect on markups. *Id.*

[753] *See* Li and Schürhoff, Dealer Networks, *supra* note 741, at 10. Trading costs increase with the number of intermediaries participating in a transaction. Average markups on single-dealer "split trades" – when a dealer sells the initial block of securities purchased in several smaller blocks – are 2.00%, while they are 1.77% when the block does not need to be split among multiple dealers. *Id.* at 9–10. In extreme cases in which six dealers intermediate the trade before it reaches a customer, the total markup increases to 4.19%. *Id.* at 10. For retail-sized trades (up to $100,000), average split-trade and non-split trade markups are 2.36% and 2.13%, respectively. *See* Green, Hollifield and Schürhoff, *Financial Intermediation*, *supra* note 691, at 289 table 7.

[754] *See* Schultz 2011 Working Paper, *supra* note 752, at 21. *See also* GAO Market Structure Report, *supra* note 61, at 20-21.

[755] *See* Dan Bernhardt et al., Why Do Large Orders Receive Discounts on the London Stock Exchange?, 18 R. FIN. STUD. 1343 (finding that dealers offer better price improvement to more-valued customers—those who give business more regularly and send larger orders).

[756] *See* graph entitled "Distribution of Customer Trades Traded (based on par amount traded)," *supra* § II.A.5 (The Secondary Market for Municipal Securities).

[757] Green, Hollifield and Schürhoff, *Financial Intermediation*, *supra* note 691, at 278 (finding that the dealer's market power is a significantly larger contributor to the size of a markup than the cost of intermediating the trade).

[758] Li and Schürhoff, Dealer Networks, *supra* note 741, at 11.

[759] Green, Hollifield and Schürhoff, *Financial Intermediation*, *supra* note 691, at 278.

[760] *See* Harris and Piwowar, *supra* note 103, at 1362. Note, however, that the data evaluated in this study was of transactions that occurred prior to the MSRB's RTRS system and did not account for the impact that additional post-trade transparency may have on this conclusion.

[761] *See* Harris and Piwowar, *supra* note 103, at 1362. Other reasons may include, for example, that investors may not know which bonds are most liquid and should have lower transaction costs. Alternatively, this could be due to high credit quality bonds being viewed by investors as substitutes, or to dealers taking no inventory risk in inactive bonds. *Id. See also* Michael A. Goldstein and Edith S. Hotchkiss, *Know When to Hold Them, Know When to Fold Them: Dealer Behavior in Highly Illiquid Risky Assets* at 29 (Working Paper, Jan. 2011), *available at* http://faculty.babson.edu/goldstein/research/Dealer-Behavior--2011-0105.pdf (discussing findings

that dealers in corporate bonds actively manage inventory risk in illiquid bonds by actively searching for counterparties, offering slightly lower spreads on these illiquid bonds, perhaps to induce trading).

[762] *See* MSRB Rule G-18 Execution of Transactions; MSRB Rule G-30 Prices and Commissions; *see also* Review of Dealer Pricing Responsibilities, *supra* note 248.

[763] *See id.*

[764] *See* MSRB Rule G-30(a). *See also supra* § II.C.1.b.iii (Fair Pricing and Compensation). As discussed above, municipal bond dealers effect virtually all municipal securities transactions with their customers on a principal basis, with a portion of these principal trades effected on a "riskless principal" basis. Rule G-30(a) applies to all transactions effected on a principal basis, including riskless principal transactions.

[765] *See* MSRB Rule G-30. Rule G-30(a) requires both that the (1) total transaction price to the customer be reasonably related to the market value of the security and (2) mark-up or mark-down not exceed a fair and reasonable amount. *See* Review of Dealer Pricing Responsibilities, *supra* note 248. *See also* Birmingham Hearing Transcript at 275-76 (Lanza) (noting that although customers may have difficulty determining the fair value of their securities, MSRB Rule G-30 requires the municipal bond dealer to obtain a fair and reasonable price for the investor); *Id.* at 306 (Lessley) (suggesting that customers looking for a fair price should have multiple brokers obtain multiple prices). The MSRB has also identified other factors that may be relevant in determining the fairness and reasonableness of prices in municipal securities transactions, such as the availability of the security in the market; the price or yield of the security; the maturity of the security; the nature of the professional's business; the rating of the security; the existence of an active sinking fund for the security; the trading history of the security (including the degree of market activity and existence of market makers), and compensation for services provided. *See* MSRB Interpretive Notice, "Report on Pricing," Sept. 26, 1980 ("Report on Pricing"). FINRA enforces two rules that apply to transactions in non-municipal securities. NASD Rule 2440 applies to customer transactions in non-municipal securities, including corporate debt. For transactions effected on a principal basis, the rule requires dealers to buy or sell at a fair price, taking into consideration relevant circumstances, including market conditions, expenses, and the fact that a dealer is entitled to a profit. For transactions effected on an agency basis, the rule requires dealers not to charge their customers more than a fair commission or service charge, taking into consideration all relevant circumstances, including market conditions with respect to such security at the time of the transaction, the expense of executing the order and the value of any service rendered by reason of the dealer's experience and knowledge of such security and the market therefore. *See* NASD Rule 2440 - Fair Prices and Commissions. FINRA has proposed to amend NASD Rule 2440 to, among other things, note that a dealer is entitled to remuneration rather than profit. *See* FINRA Regulatory Notice 11-08, "Markups, Commissions and Fees" (Feb. 2011) *available at* http://finra.complinet.com/net_file_store/new_rulebooks/f/i/finra_11-08.pdf ("FINRA Markup Proposal"). Additionally, NASD Rule 2440 provides guidance that a markup of 5% or less in most transactions may be considered "fair and reasonable," although this is not a firm rule. *See* NASD IM-2440-1. FINRA has also proposed eliminating this guidance, noting that 5% is significantly higher than markups charged by most firms currently and that the 5% threshold is "based on the execution practices and market efficiencies of nearly 70 years ago." *See* FINRA Markup Proposal *supra*. Second, FINRA Rule 5310 applies a more-detailed "best execution" standard for principal and agency transactions in equities and corporate bonds. *See infra* note 781.

[766] *See* FINRA v. Morgan Stanley & Co. Inc., Letter of Acceptance, Waiver and Consent No. 20060056031-01 (Oct. 28, 2011) (enforcement matter against a municipal bond dealer for charging excessive markups in violation of MSRB Rules G-17 and G-30).

[767] MSRB Rule G-18. A municipal bond dealer's duty under Rule G-18, however, can be more limited in certain agency transactions for sophisticated customers, referred to as SMMPs. *See* MSRB "Restated Interpretive Notice Regarding the Application of MSRB Rules to Transactions with Sophisticated Municipal Market Professionals" (effective Jul. 9, 2012), Exchange Act Release No. 67064 (May 25, 2012), 77 FR 32704 (June 1, 2012) (SR-MSRB-2012-05). The term "SMMP" means an institutional customer of a dealer that: (i) the dealer has a reasonable basis to believe is capable of evaluating investment risks and market value independently, both in general and with regard to particular transactions in municipal securities; and (ii) affirmatively indicates that it is exercising independent judgment in evaluating the recommendations of the dealer. If a municipal bond dealer effects non-recommended secondary market agency transactions for SMMPs and its services have been explicitly limited to providing anonymity, communication, order matching, and/or clearance functions and the dealer does not exercise discretion as to how or when a transaction is executed, the MSRB believes the dealer is not required to take further actions on individual transactions to ensure that its agency transactions are effected at fair and reasonable prices. The MSRB has noted that this

interpretation is particularly relevant to dealers operating ATSs in which SMMPs are permitted to participate. *Id.*

768 The dealer either will need to know the current market value of the security, or will have to use diligence in the attempt to ascertain it in order to meet the requisite level of care in finding a price for the customer that is fair and reasonable in relation to prevailing market conditions. Review of Dealer Pricing Responsibilities, *supra* note 248.

769 MSRB Rule G-18. FINRA and the SEC have brought several enforcement actions against broker's brokers for misconduct in the conduct of bid-wanted auctions. *See e.g.,* FINRA v. Associated Bond Brokers, Inc. Letter of Acceptance, Waiver and Consent No. E052004018001 (Nov. 19, 2007) (settled action finding that a broker's broker violated Rule G-17 by lowering the highest bids to prices closer to the cover bids without informing either bidders or sellers); FINRA v. Butler Muni, LLC Letter of Acceptance, Waiver and Consent No. 2006007537201 (May 28, 2010) (settled action finding that a broker's broker violated Rule G17 by failing to inform the seller of higher bids submitted by the highest bidders); In re. D. M. Keck & Company, Inc. d/b/a Discount Munibrokers, Donald Michael Keck and Patricia Ann Seelaus, Exchange Act Release No. 56543, A.P. File No. 3-12839 (Sept. 27, 2007) (settled action finding that a broker's broker violated Rules G-13 and G-17 by disseminating fake cover bids to both seller and winning bidder; broker's broker violated Rules G-14 and G-17 by paying seller more than highest bid on some trades in return for a price lower than the highest bid on other trades, in each case reporting the fictitious trade prices to the MSRB's RTRS); In re. Regional Brokers, Inc. and Patrick Lubin, Exchange Act Release No. 56542, A.P. File No. 3-12838 (Sept. 27, 2007) (settled action finding that a broker's broker violated Rules G-13 and G17 by disseminating fake cover bids to both seller and winning bidder and violated Rule G-17 by accepting bids after bid deadline); In re. Wolfe & Hurst Bond Brokers, Inc. and Peter J. Debany, Exchange Act Release No. 59913, A.P. File No. 3-13469 (May 13, 2009) (settled action finding that a broker's broker violated Rule G-17 by disseminating fake cover bids to both seller and winning bidder and by lowering the highest bids to prices closer to the cover bids without informing either bidders or sellers). *See* MSRB Notice 2010-35, Request for Comment on MSRB Guidance on Broker's Brokers at n.3 (Sept. 9, 2010) (highlighting these enforcement cases against broker's brokers). The MSRB has recently received approval from the Commission of a rule change to address misconduct in the interdealer brokerage market. The rule, among other things, highlights a broker's broker's existing duty to "make a reasonable effort to obtain a price for the dealer that is fair and reasonable in relation to prevailing market conditions." *See* MSRB Rule G-43(a), MSRB Broker's Broker Approval Order, *supra* note 217. This duty is currently found in MSRB Rule G-18. The rule also creates a safe harbor for broker's brokers: broker's brokers would satisfy their obligations in Rule G-43(a) if they conduct bid-wanted auctions consistent with certain enumerated provisions in the proposed rule. *Id.*

770 MSRB Rule G-30(b). *See also supra* note 765 (discussing MSRB and FINRA pricing and conduct rules).

771 *See* Review of Dealer Pricing Responsibilities, *supra* note 248. The prevailing market price generally is the price at which municipal bond dealers trade with one another. *See* In re. Alstead, Dempsey & Co., Exchange Act Release No. 20825, 47 S.E.C. 1034, 1035 (Apr. 5, 1984). Absent countervailing evidence, a municipal bond dealer's contemporaneous cost is the best evidence of the prevailing market price. *See id.* This standard has been accorded judicial and Commission approval. *See* Barnett v. U.S., 319 F.2d 340, 344 (8th Cir. 1963); Notice to Broker-Dealers Concerning Disclosure Requirements for Mark-Ups on Zero-Coupon Securities, Exchange Act Release No. 24368 (Apr. 21, 1987), 52 FR 15575 (Apr. 29, 1987) ("Zero-Coupon Securities Release"). In the case of integrated market makers, different considerations may be applicable. *See id.* at 15575 (noting that for integrated market makers, the best evidence of the prevailing market price generally is the contemporaneous sales by the firm or other market makers to other dealers). The Commission has noted, however, that "quotations for obscure securities with limited interdealer trading activity may have little value as evidence of the current market." In re. Alstead, Dempsey & Co., 47 S.E.C. at 1036.

772 Review of Dealer Pricing Responsibilities, *supra* note 248. The fair pricing responsibilities of dealers require attention both to the market value of the security and the reasonableness of the dealer's compensation. Excessive markups may cause a violation of the fair pricing standards. Even with a reasonable markup, it is possible to violate the fair pricing standards because of inattention to market value. The MSRB has recognized that a small number of issues each day trade with intra-day price differentials that are abnormally wide. For example, this can occur when a single block of securities moves from one customer to another through a "chain" of multiple-dealer transactions. Because of the interdealer trading, the difference between the price received by the original customer and the price paid by the ultimate customer can be large, sometimes exceeding 10% or more. In these cases, while the dealers effecting trades with customers at each end of the chain may have charged reasonable markups, there is a large intraday price differential due to the price

increases generated by the series of inter-dealer transactions. The MSRB has noted that municipal bond dealers in these transactions nevertheless are responsible for providing customers with prices reasonably related to the market value.

[773] *Id.*

[774] *See* MSRB Notice 2010-10, "Request for Comments on Draft Interpretive Guidance on Prevailing Market Prices and Mark-Up for Transactions in Municipal Securities" (Apr. 21, 2010). The draft guidance is designed to harmonize the manner in which the prevailing market prices for municipal securities are determined with the manner established by FINRA for other types of debt securities. *See* NASD IM-24402, Additional Mark-Up Policy for Transactions in Debt Securities, Except Municipal Securities.

[775] *Id.*

[776] *Id.* Specifically, the prevailing market price presumptively would be established by referring to the dealer's contemporaneous cost as incurred, or contemporaneous proceeds as obtained, consistent with MSRB Rule G-30(a). A dealer's cost would be considered contemporaneous if the transaction occurs close enough in time to the customer transaction that it would reasonably be expected to reflect the current market price for the municipal security. If there is a contemporaneous dealer transaction, that price would be presumed to be the best measure of the prevailing market price unless the dealer can show that (i) interest rates or yields changed after the dealer's contemporaneous transaction to a degree that such change would reasonably cause a change in municipal securities pricing; (ii) the credit quality of the municipal security changed significantly after the dealer's contemporaneous transaction; or (iii) news was issued or otherwise distributed and known to the marketplace that had an effect on the perceived value of the municipal security after the dealer's contemporaneous transaction.

[777] *Id.*

[778] *Id.* A "similar" municipal security should be sufficiently similar to the subject security that it would serve as a reasonable alternative investment to the investor. At a minimum, a market yield for the subject security should be able to be fairly estimated from the yields of the similar securities. Factors that may be relevant to determine similarity include: (i) credit quality considerations (e.g., similar credit rating or credit enhancement); (ii) trading at similar spreads to U.S. Treasury securities of a similar duration; (iii) similar structural characteristics, such as coupon, maturity, duration, complexity, callability, or other embedded options; (iv) technical factors, such as the size of the issue, the float and recent turnover, and legal restrictions on transferability; and (v) similar federal or state tax treatment.

[779] *Id.* These could include discounted cash flow or other models that take into account measures such as credit quality, interest rates, industry sector, time to maturity, call provisions and any other embedded options, coupon rate, and face value; and consider all applicable pricing terms and conventions, such as coupon frequency and accrual methods.

[780] *See, e.g.*, Washington, DC Hearing Transcript (Afternoon Session) at 15 (Hotchkiss) (highlighting the MSRB's attempts to harmonize, where appropriate, markup practices in municipal securities with FINRA's requirements in the corporate debt world); *id.* at 15-16 (Norwood) (expressing SIFMA's opinion that the corporate debt market and the municipal debt market are fundamentally different and that the MSRB's original requirements concerning markup practices are appropriate).

[781] FINRA Rule 5310 applies a more-detailed "best execution" standard for principal and agency transactions in equities and corporate bonds. This rule requires broker-dealers to "use reasonable diligence to ascertain the best market . . . and buy or sell in such market so that the resultant price to the customer is as favorable as possible under prevailing market conditions." Certain factors are considered in determining whether a broker-dealer has exercised "reasonable diligence," including (i) the character of the market for the security (e.g., price, volatility, relative liquidity, and pressure on available communications), (ii) the size and type of transaction, (iii) the number of markets checked, (iv) the accessibility of the quotation, and (v) the terms and conditions of the order. FINRA Rule 5310(a)(1). These requirements apply to any transaction by a broker-dealer acting as agent or principal with a customer or a customer of another broker-dealer. *See* FINRA Rule 5310(a)(1), (e). The duty to provide best execution does not apply, however, when a dealer is simply executing, against its own quote, the order of a customer of another broker-dealer. *See* FINRA Rule 5310, (Supplementary Material .04). In general, the Supplementary Material prescribes best execution obligations when handling orders, including corporate debt orders, where there is limited pricing information available. Furthermore, members have a general documentation requirement that requires members to maintain records sufficient to demonstrate that orders were handled according to the member's policies and procedures. *See, e.g.*, FINRA Rule 5310 (Supplementary Material .01 to .09).

[782] The MSRB has stated that municipal bond dealers currently do not have a duty of best execution under MSRB rules. *See, e.g.,* Exchange Act Release No. 66625, "Notice of Filing of a Proposed Rule Change Consisting of Proposed Rule G-43, on Broker's Brokers; Proposed Amendments to Rule G-8, on Books and Records, Rule G-9, on Record Retention, and Rule G-18, on Execution of Transactions; and a Proposed Interpretive Notice on the Duties of Dealers that Use the Services of Broker's Brokers" (SR-MSRB-201204) (Mar. 20, 2012), 77 FR 17548 (Mar. 26, 2012), *available at http://www.sec.gov/rules/sro/msrb/2012/34-66625.pdf.* For example, a commenter asked whether a broker-dealer using an electronic platform is permitted to screen competitors' bonds from the platform in an effort to have a customer purchase from the broker-dealer's inventory. In response, the MSRB stated that there currently is no best execution standard under MSRB rules similar to FINRA standards and that as long as a customer is provided a fair and reasonable price a broker-dealer is not obligated under MSRB rules to seek the most favorable price for its customer. *Id.*

[783] *See* Newton v. Merrill, Lynch, Pierce, Fenner & Smith, Inc., 135 F.3d 266, 273 (3d Cir.), *cert. denied*, 525 U.S. 811 (1998) ("[T]he basis for the duty of best execution is the mutual understanding that the client is engaging in the trade – and retaining the services of the broker as his agent – solely for the purpose of maximizing his own economic benefit, and that the broker receives her compensation because she assists the client in reaching that goal."). This case also recognized that the duty of best execution does not "dissolve" when an intermediary acts in its capacity as a principal. *Id.* at 270 n.1 (citation omitted). *See also* Regulation NMS, Exchange Act Release No. 51808 (June 9, 2005), 70 FR 37496, 37538 (June 29, 2005) ("A broker-dealer's duty of best execution derives from common law agency principles and fiduciary obligations, and is incorporated in SRO rules and, through judicial and Commission decisions, the antifraud provisions of the federal securities laws."); Exchange Act Release No. 43963 (Feb. 14, 2001) (citing *Newton*, but concluding that respondent fulfilled his duty of best execution). *See also* Payment for Order Flow, Exchange Act Release No. 34902 (Oct. 27, 1994), 59 FR 55006, 55009 (Nov. 2, 1994) (discussing a broker-dealer's duty of best execution in relation to routing orders).

[784] *See* Newton, *supra* note 783, at 269-70.

[785] *See id.* at 270.

[786] *See id.* Intermediaries have the obligation to evaluate customer order practices with changes in technology and the market.

[787] *See generally* Review of Dealer Pricing Responsibilities, *supra* note 248 (noting that a municipal bond dealer "must exercise diligence in establishing the market value of the security and the reasonableness of the compensation received on the transaction").

[788] *See* MSRB Rule G-15 Confirmation, Clearance, Settlement and Other Uniform Practice Requirements with Respect to Transactions with Customers.

[789] *See* MSRB Rule G-15 (a)(i)(A)(5). Specific guidance is given for transactions effected on the basis of a yield to maturity, yield to call date, or yield to put date, as well as for those effected on the basis of dollar price and other discrete scenarios.

[790] *See* MSRB Rule G-15(a)(i)(A)(6)(f). Specifically, if the dealer is effecting the transaction as agent, the confirmation must show the amount of any remuneration received or to be received (shown in aggregate dollar amount) by the dealer from the customer in connection with the transaction, unless such remuneration is determined, pursuant to a written agreement with the customer, other than on a transaction basis. In addition, MSRB Rule G-15(a)(i)(A)(1)(e) requires disclosure of the source and amount of any remuneration received or to be received by the dealer, when acting as agent, from any person other than the customer, or a statement indicating whether any such remuneration has been or will be received and that the details will be provided upon the customer's written request. The scope of the disclosures required under MSRB Rule G-15 parallels the disclosures that broker-dealers effecting transactions in other securities as agents, such as corporate bonds, have to provide to customers under Exchange Act Rule 10b10, including the disclosures related to compensation. *See* Exchange Act Rule 10b-10.

[791] *See, e.g.*, Grandon v. Merrill Lynch & Co., 147 F.3d 184, 192 (2d Cir. 1998) (acknowledging that no requirement to disclose markups exists for debt securities). MSRB Rule G-15 does, however, require municipal bond dealers to disclose to the customer in what capacity they effected a transaction (i.e., as principal or agent). *See* MSRB Rule G-15(a)(i)(A)(1)(d).

[792] *See* Exchange Act Rule 10b-10. Specifically, Rule 10b-10(a)(2)(ii)(A) requires that, if a broker-dealer, after having received a customer order to buy or sell an equity security, buys or sells that security from another person to offset a contemporaneous sale to or purchase from the customer, then the broker-dealer must disclose on the customer confirmation the difference between the price to the customer and the dealer's contemporaneous purchase or sale price. In addition, for principal transactions in exchange-listed securities,

Rule 10b-10(a)(2)(ii)(B) requires the broker-dealer to disclose the difference, if any, between the reported trade price and the price to the customer.

[793] *See* Exchange Act Release No. 33743 (Mar. 9, 1994), 59 FR 12767 (proposing a rule that would have included disclosure of markups for municipal securities transactions); Exchange Act Release No. 15220 (Oct. 6, 1978), 43 FR 47538 (proposing mark-up disclosure for riskless principal trades in municipal securities); Exchange Act Release No. 13661 (June 23, 1977), 42 FR 33348 (proposing mark-up disclosure by non-market makers in riskless principal transactions involving equity and debt securities, but not municipal securities); and Exchange Act Release No. 12806 (Sept. 16, 1976), 41 FR 41432 (proposing mark-up disclosure by non-market makers in riskless principal transactions involving equity and debt securities).

[794] *See* Washington, DC Hearing Transcript at 34 (Niewiaroski).

[795] Comment Letter of Nathan Saks (Mar. 28, 2011). *See also* San Francisco Hearing Transcript at 247-50 (Siminoff).

[796] *See generally supra* § III.A.4 (Market Participant Observations and Other Commentary).

[797] *See supra* §§ III.A.4.c (Continuing Disclosure) and III.B.1.d.iii (Market Participant Observations and Other Commentary Regarding Timeliness of Financial Information).

[798] *See supra* notes 371 - 373 and 398 - 402 and accompanying text.

[799] *See supra* note 404.

[800] *See supra* notes 30, 124 - 126 and accompanying text.

[801] *See supra* § III.A.4.d (Disclosure by Conduit Borrowers).

[802] *See supra* note 438.

[803] *See supra* notes 422 - 421 and accompanying text.

[804] *See* 1994 Interpretive Release, *supra* note 31.

[805] *See supra* § III.B.1.a (Overview).

[806] *See supra* note 418.

[807] *See, e.g.,* §§ III.B.1.d.ii (Interim Financial Information), III.B.1.d.iii (at Interim Financial Information) and III.B.2.d (Disclosure of Pension and OPEB Funding Obligations).

[808] *See supra* notes 383 and 473 and accompanying text.

[809] *See* Section 27A of the Securities Act and Section 21E of the Exchange Act.

[810] *See supra* § II.B.2 (Internal Revenue Service).

[811] Alison McConnell, "IRS: Tax-Exempt Bond Office Would Welcome Looser Disclosure Rules," The Bond Buyer, Oct. 28, 2005, *available at* http://www.bondbuyer.com/news/-233416-1.html.

[812] U.S. Government Accountability Office, Taxpayer Privacy: A Guide for Screening and Assessing Proposals to Disclose Confidential Tax Information to Specific Parties for Specific Purposes, Dec. 2011 (GAO-12-231SP).

[813] *See supra* § III.A.3 (Continuing Disclosure) and III.A.4.c (Market Participant Observations and Other Commentary: Continuing Disclosure).

[814] *See supra* note 404.

[815] *See generally supra* § II.A.4.c (Certain Primary Market Practice: Reporting of Not Reoffered Bonds).

[816] *See generally supra* §§ II.C.6.a (Credit Enhancers: Market Participant Observations and Other Commentary), III.A.4.b (Market Participant Observations and Other Commentary: Initial Disclosure) and III.B.3.e.i (Exposure to Derivatives: Disclosure Issues: Market Participant Observations and Other Commentary).

[817] *See generally supra* notes 371 - 373 and 398 - 402 and accompanying text.

[818] *See, e.g.,* NABL Comment Letter, *supra* note 391 (requesting guidance regarding when remarketings of demand securities constitute "primary offerings" for purposes of Rule 15c2-12). The Staff also receives questions regarding the application of Rule 15c2-21 to underwritten municipal fund securities.

[819] *See generally supra* §§ III.C.1 (Access to Information), III.C.2 (Use of Issuer Websites) and III.C.3 (Presentation of Information and Comparability).

[820] *See supra* note 244.

[821] *See supra* note 197.

[822] *See supra* § III.A.1 (Voluntary Disclosure Initiatives and Disclosure Guidelines).

[823] *See generally supra* § III.C.4 (Disclosure Controls and Procedures).

[824] *See generally supra* § III.B.1.d (Timeliness of Financial Information).

[825] *See generally supra* § III.B.1.d (Timeliness of Financial Information).

[826] *See generally supra* § III.C.2 (Use of Issuer Websites).

[827] *See generally supra* §§ III.C.1 (Access to Information) and III.C.3 (Presentation of Information and Comparability).

[828] *See generally supra* § III.B.3 (Exposure to Derivatives).

[829] *See generally supra* § IV.B.3 (Dealer Pricing Obligations to Customers).

[830] Transparency initiatives are also being pursued in other jurisdictions. For example, the Markets in Financial Instruments Directive (MiFID), which has been in force since November 2007, is currently under review. The MiFID review proposal was published in October 2011, *available at* http://ec.europa.eu/internal_market/securities/isd/mifid_en.htm. Among other initiatives, the European Commission is considering additional transparency requirements in non-equity market asset classes including bonds to increase market efficiency and protect investors.

[831] The Staff understands that, today, the orders displayed on ATSs to more than one person are generally offers rather than bids.

[832] *See* MSRB Long-Range Plan for Market Transparency Products, Jan. 2012, *available at* http://www.msrb.org/msrb1/pdfs/Long-Range-Plan.pdf.

[833] *See* Exchange Act Release No. 55638 (Apr. 16, 2007), 72 FR 20150 (Apr. 23, 2007) (SR–NASD–2003–141).

[834] *See* 17 C.F.R. 240.10b-10. Specifically, Rule 10b-10(a)(2)(ii)(A) requires that, if a broker-dealer, after having received a customer order to buy or sell an equity security, buys or sells that security from another person to offset a contemporaneous sale to or purchase from the customer, then the broker-dealer must disclose on the customer confirmation the difference between the price to the customer and the dealer's contemporaneous purchase or sale price. In addition, for principal transactions in exchange-listed securities, Rule 10b-10(a)(2)(ii)(B) requires the broker-dealer to disclose the difference, if any, between the reported trade price and the price to the customer.

[835] *See, e.g.*, MSRB Rules G-18 and G-30(a);MSRB Interpretive Notice, "Review of Pricing Responsibilities," (Jan. 26, 2004); MSRB Interpretive Notice, "Interpretive Notice on Commissions and Other Charges, Advertisements and Official Statements Relating to Municipal Fun Securities," Dec. 2001; MSRB Interpretive Notice, "Report on Pricing," Sept. 1980.

[836] *See supra* note 782 (noting a recent MSRB statement regarding the lack of a best execution obligation under the MSRB's rules).

[837] *See* FINRA Rule 5310.

In: The Municipal Securities Market
Editor: Michal N. Wilson

ISBN: 978-1-62417-295-3

Chapter 2

STATEMENT OF ALAN D. POLSKY, CHAIR, MUNICIPAL SECURITIES RULEMAKING BOARD. HEARING ON "THE IMPACT OF THE DODD-FRANK ACT ON MUNICIPAL FINANCE"*

Good morning Chairman Garrett, Ranking Member Waters and members of the Subcommittee. I appreciate the invitation to testify today on behalf of the Municipal Securities Rulemaking Board (MSRB). My name is Alan Polsky and I am Chair of the MSRB. I am also senior vice president of Dougherty & Co., LLC, a Minneapolis, Minnesota-based investment banking firm.

The MSRB was created by Congress in 1975 as the principal regulator for the municipal securities market with the mandate to protect investors and the public interest. By adopting a principles-based approach to regulating municipal securities dealers, operating retail-oriented information disclosure systems and establishing professional standards for municipal securities professionals, the MSRB has effectively created protections for retail investors in the $3.7 trillion United States municipal securities market.

The MSRB also acts as an independent resource and expert on the municipal securities market for policymakers such as Congress and the U.S. Department of the Treasury as well as other federal and state regulators including the Board of Governors of the Federal Reserve and the Internal Revenue Service.

The Dodd-Frank Wall Street Reform and Consumer Protection Act (the Dodd-Frank Act) included multiple provisions that affect the municipal market and the MSRB. The provisions relating to the MSRB's rulemaking and related activities became effective on October 1, 2010. Specifically, Section 975 broadened the mission of the MSRB to include the protection of state and local governments, as well as certain private sector obligated persons — such as universities and hospitals — that access the capital markets through the issuance of municipal bonds. The MSRB, of course, also continues to pursue its original mission of protecting investors and the public interest.

* This is an edited, reformatted and augmented version of testimony given on July 20, 2012 before the House Committee on Financial Services, Subcommittee on Capital Markets and Government Sponsored Enterprises.

Section 975 of the statute expanded the MSRB's responsibilities to include the regulation of municipal advisors. Municipal advisors include businesses and individuals that advise municipal entities concerning municipal financial products and municipal securities, as well as businesses and individuals that solicit certain types of business from municipal entities on behalf of unrelated broker-dealers, municipal advisors or investment advisors. Municipal securities dealers performing municipal advisory services were previously subject to MSRB regulation because of their municipal securities dealer activities. Under the new law, however, other municipal advisors are subject to MSRB regulation for the first time.

The MSRB's Board of Directors was reorganized under our amended authorizing statute to be made up for the first time of a majority of public, independent members and to include municipal advisor representatives. Previously, the Exchange Act required that the MSRB be governed by a board with a majority of industry members. Under the new structure, effective October 1, 2010, the MSRB is required by statute to maintain a balance of regulated and non-regulated Board members, with investors, municipal entities, securities dealers, bank dealers and municipal advisors each having representation on the MSRB Board of Directors.

Protection of State and Local Governments

Over the last two years under its majority public Board, the MSRB has acted to enhance disclosure and transparency measures to comply with the new law to protect a broader array of participants in the municipal market. The MSRB has undertaken its expanded mandate to strengthen protections for state and local governments — and the taxpayers who support municipal borrowing.

The role of the MSRB in protecting state and local governments is critical because these entities raise, through the issuance of bonds, notes and other debt obligations, an average of nearly $450 billion in the capital markets each year.[1] The municipal bond market has evolved from one in which states and municipalities offered traditional, general obligation fixed rate bonds to finance specific projects to one that involves the use of various security structures, complex derivative products and intricate investment strategies, and the presence of an ever-expanding group of service and product providers, advisors and sales teams.

Many of the bond transactions undertaken by state and local governments are complex transactions involving sometimes dozens of financial, legal and other players, each of whom represents his or her own interests and often has conflicts tied to an additional and often invisible set of market participants. Moreover, compensation of participants in a municipal finance transaction in almost all cases is contingent on the completion of the deal, creating incentives that put unknowing state and local governments at risk of inappropriate and unsuitable transactions and products — at the expense of taxpayers and ratepayers.

In the vast majority of cases, state and local government officials are unfamiliar with the mechanics of a municipal finance transaction. At the local level, many are part-time staff. As public servants, these individuals are responsible for representing the interests of their communities, their taxpayers and their ratepayers, but in many cases, they lack the experience and/or expertise needed to assess the terms of the structures presented to them by financial professionals recommending structures and products. Transactions involving interest rate swaps and other complex structures further complicate the situation. In cases such as these, state and local governments can hire a municipal advisor or advisors but need to have the confidence that they represent their best interests.

As Committee Chairman Spencer T. Bachus wrote in 2009, "Although local governments frequently tap the municipal finance market to raise funds to pay for long-term projects, conflicts of interest and complexity in the municipal finance market can sometimes trap the unwary, particularly when local officials lack the expertise to independently assess the terms of the financing structures proffered by sophisticated underwriters."[2]

State and local governments are not the only ones who can lack expertise. Unqualified municipal advisors recommending ill-advised or unsuitable transactions to state and local governments can compound the challenges they face. Like underwriters of municipal securities, these advisors can have multiple undisclosed ties to other market participants that can threaten the integrity of the advice given to state and local governments. Until now, many market professionals acting as financial advisors to state and local governments have, by and large, been exempt from meeting any standards of quality, professionalism and expertise.

High profile examples like the Jefferson County, Alabama bankruptcy,[3] municipal bid-rigging convictions obtained by the U.S. Department of Justice,[4] unsuitable derivative transactions sold to local governments[5] and guarantees provided by localities for corporate projects that have defaulted[6] illustrate the price of gaps in regulation of the municipal securities market. Local governments, rather than being able to turn to a trusted financial advisor to help defend against questionable advice, practices and complex products, in these cases instead received advice of questionable quality from unregulated financial advisors.

Many states, counties and communities across the country face this same alignment of professionals that, rather than serving the best interests of their state or local government clients, can serve to provide an avenue for taking advantage of financially less sophisticated public servants.

With a Congressionally mandated role to protect state and local governments, the MSRB has assessed and is amending its existing regulations for banks, broker-dealers and municipal securities dealers to explicitly protect state and local governments. These changes are intended to ensure that dealers follow rigorous fair-practice and other standards, and that state and local governments have the information they need to make appropriate decisions.

The MSRB has also developed the framework for a principles-based regulatory regime that would establish regulations for municipal advisors and protect state and local governments. These include draft rules on conflicts of interest, including pay-to-play.

I'd like to go in to some more detail about these draft rules so the Subcommittee has an understanding of the philosophy and consistency of the approach to municipal advisor regulation compared to that of dealers, and how the MSRB's draft rules would establish fair practice and other rules for the two groups of financial professionals with arguably the most extensive influence and contact with state and local governments.

DRAFT MUNICIPAL ADVISOR RULES

The MSRB is directed by statute to adopt rules for municipal advisors in a number of areas, including, among other things: (1) prevent fraudulent and manipulative acts and practices, promote just and equitable principles of trade, enhance mechanisms of a free and open market, and protect investors, municipal entities, and obligated persons; (2) prescribe means reasonably designed to prevent acts, practices, and courses of business that are not consistent with a municipal advisor's fiduciary duty to its municipal entity clients; (3) prescribe professional standards; (4) provide continuing education requirements; and (5) provide for periodic compliance examinations. The MSRB is directed to not impose a regulatory burden on small municipal advisors that is neither necessary nor appropriate to the public interest and the protection of investors, municipal entities and obligated persons, provided that there is robust protection of investors against fraud.

Beginning in October 2010, the MSRB undertook an extensive outreach effort to solicit input from market participants and the public on the type and nature of regulations needed to protect state and local governments. At the same time, the MSRB conducted extensive analysis of its existing rules for municipal securities dealers and studied the nature of the professional services provided by municipal advisors.

Following this outreach and analysis, the MSRB began to lay the foundation for municipal advisor regulation under our expanded statutory mandate. As one of the MSRB's initial municipal advisor rules, the MSRB extended its fair dealing rule, MSRB Rule G-17, to cover the actions of municipal advisors.

MSRB Rule G-17 provides that, in the conduct of its municipal securities and municipal advisory activities, each dealer and municipal advisor must deal fairly with all persons and may not engage in any deceptive, dishonest or unfair practice. This "fair dealing" rule is key to defining the relationships of dealers and municipal advisors with investors and issuers, serving as the core to the MSRB's principles-based approach to regulation and as the basis for numerous enforcement actions to address misbehavior in the marketplace.

Also, since October 1, 2010, Section 975 of the Dodd-Frank Act has imposed a federal fiduciary duty on municipal advisors to state and local governments when providing financial advice. Specifically, the MSRB proposed a new rule and an associated interpretation covering the details of an advisor's fiduciary duty.

The proposed regulation would, consistent with the obligations of other types of fiduciaries under federal or state laws, require municipal advisors to act consistent with the basic duties of loyalty and care by, among other things, acting in the best interests of their state or local government clients and disclosing all material conflicts of interest. The proposed regulations would address these basic duties in the context of the relationships and activities between state and local governments and their municipal advisors. The proposed rule notes, for example, that municipal advisors must not undertake an engagement when an unmanageable conflict exists, must not charge excessive compensation, and must review reasonably feasible alternatives to proposed products and transactions when advising their state and local governments of a particular financing.

Prohibiting conflicts of interest on the part of financial professionals that can undermine the integrity of the municipal market is an important aspect of many MSRB regulations. One form of conflict of interest in the municipal market can arise if financial professionals seek to influence the award of business by state and local government officials by making political contributions to those officials or soliciting contributions on their behalf. This activity can have a negative impact on market fairness and public confidence in municipal capital markets. In 2011, the MSRB proposed a rule that would regulate so-called "pay to play" activities of municipal advisors, as well as firms and individuals that solicit certain business from municipal entities on behalf of others.

Modeled after MSRB rules in place since 1994 for municipal securities dealers doing business with state and local governments, the proposed rule seeks to sever any connection between political contributions to municipal officials and the awarding of advisory service business to municipal advisors. Like municipal securities dealers, municipal advisors would be prohibited from engaging in business with municipal entities for two years if the firm or their municipal professionals make certain political contributions to state or local government officials with authority to hire such municipal advisors.

The proposed rule would also institute requirements designed to prevent circumvention through indirect activities and would require quarterly disclosures of certain information concerning municipal advisor political contributions to the MSRB, which would make the information available to the public through its website, at www.msrb.org.

The MSRB proposed several other rule changes designed to ensure that state and local governments are protected from potentially unfair conduct on the part of municipal advisors.

These draft rules include: (1) restricting the use of gifts to curry favor with employees controlling the award of municipal business; (2) establishing basic standards of fairness and accuracy in advertising and other promotional materials; (3) providing guidance on fair practice duties toward obligated persons; and (4) establishing basic supervisory requirements for municipal advisors based in part on existing municipal securities dealer supervisory requirements but simplified and appropriately tailored in recognition that most municipal advisors are small firms with less complex structures.

Finalization of the MSRB's proposed municipal advisor rules have been put on hold pending completion by the Securities and Exchange Commission (the SEC) of its pending rule proposal to more clearly delineate the breadth of professionals covered under the new statutory definition of municipal advisors. The MSRB expects to complete its initial phase of municipal advisor rulemaking outlined above following resolution of the definition by the SEC.

PROFESSIONAL QUALIFICATIONS OF MUNICIPAL ADVISORS

In addition developing draft rules for municipal advisors to implement Section 975 of the Dodd-Frank Act, the MSRB began the process of establishing minimum professional qualifications for municipal advisors.

This work started in October 2010 when the MSRB began conducting outreach events and focus groups to gather input from municipal advisors and others about the development of a professional qualification examination for assessing the competency of entry-level municipal advisors. The MSRB subsequently organized a municipal advisor examination working group to consider all comments received by the MSRB, assess commonalities in municipal advisory activities, provide additional input and assist in the drafting of a content outline for an examination.

Prior to finalizing the initial qualification exams after final SEC rulemaking on its definition of municipal advisor, the MSRB will survey registered municipal advisors about the proposed examination content to ensure it is properly tailored to their functions in the marketplace.

EXPANDED OBLIGATIONS FOR UNDERWRITERS

As part of the MSRB's implementation of Section 975, the MSRB also reviewed the existing obligations of underwriters of municipal securities to state and local governments. As a result of this assessment, the MSRB determined that additional protections for state and local governments were necessary. These important new protections, in the form of a new interpretive notice to MSRB Rule G-17 on fair dealing, take effect August 2, 2012.

The interpretive notice significantly clarifies the different roles, responsibilities and relationships of the financial professionals involved in municipal bond deals, and highlights for state and local governments the risks and characteristics involved in complex municipal financings.

Beginning August 2, 2012, an underwriter must disclose to its state or local government client that an underwriter's primary role is to purchase securities for distribution in an arm's-length commercial transaction and that it has financial and other interests that differ from those of its client. While the nature of this relationship may be clear to some, state and local governments that are not in the capital markets on a regular basis may not be aware that an underwriter and an issuer have an arms-length relationship. On the other hand, municipal advisors have a fiduciary duty to act in the best interests of their state and local government clients.

As part of the MSRB's effort to clarify the difference in these relationships to the issuer, the interpretive notice requires an underwriter to disclose that, unlike a municipal advisor, it does not have a fiduciary duty to its state or local government clients and, therefore, is not under a duty to subordinate its own financial or other interests to those of its clients. The underwriter must also disclose to the state and local government client any third-party relationships that may introduce conflicts of interest, including payments or profit-sharing arrangements with third parties, as well as the issuance or purchase of credit default swaps on the issuer's securities.

The new interpretive notice also requires underwriters to disclose the material financial characteristics and risks of complex municipal securities financings to help ensure that state and local governments understand the features, risks and characteristics of transactions recommended by an underwriter so they can make the best decision for their particular situation.

The MSRB continues to reevaluate other existing dealer regulations in light of the explicit mandate to protect state and local governments, and is considering changes where necessary. This effort includes addressing rules related to ensuring that underwriters honor the intention of state and local governments in selling certain portions of their bonds to retail investors and also to improving the availability of current information about initial offering prices or yields of new issues of municipal securities, among others.

MARKET TRANSPARENCY, EDUCATION AND OUTREACH

Part of the MSRB's effort to safeguard state and local governments over the last two years has been to make them aware of information that helps them make appropriate decisions. The MSRB's Electronic Municipal Market Access (EMMA) website, at http://emma.msrb.org, has dramatically improved the availability of information about the municipal market. This free, public website operated by the MSRB is the official source of municipal market documents and data, helps state and local governments evaluate trading activity, and provides them with a free and centralized avenue for disseminating disclosure documents and related information on their municipal securities to their investors, taxpayers and other stakeholders.

The EMMA website houses offering documents for almost every municipal security issued in the United States, secondary market disclosures that provide valuable information about the issuer of a bond throughout its life, real-time trade prices, interest rates and liquidity documents for variable rate securities, and other relevant information, including current credit ratings from rating agencies agreeing to make such information freely available to the public. EMMA provides enormous benefits to investors, state and local governments, and other market participants because it ensures free, convenient and easy access to information that is essential for making investment and other decisions related to municipal securities. EMMA has been embraced by all categories of municipal market professionals, including regulated municipal securities dealers and municipal advisors, state and local governmental issuers, institutional and retail investors, other professionals that support issuers, and the general public. EMMA has been recognized broadly by the national financial press as a critical tool for retail investors who seek to be self-directed investors or who simply want more information about their investments or a way to check on the quality of service their brokers or investment advisors are providing.[7]

In 2011, the MSRB also began expanding its online tools for state and local governments, including videos and fact sheets about what to expect when working with municipal securities dealers and advisors, the continuing disclosure obligations of state and local governments, and using the EMMA website to communicate with investors.

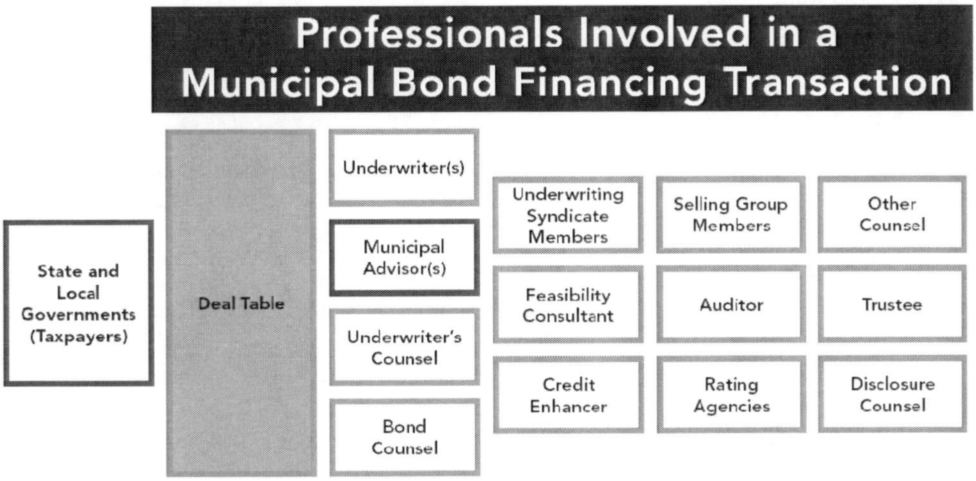

The chart illustrates the complexity and number of professionals[#] involved in a municipal bond financing transaction. In almost every case, compensation of these professionals is contingent on the closing of the bond deal. In the vast majority of cases, state and local government bond issuers are unfamiliar with the mechanics of the financing transaction.

[#] Description of responsibilities follows.

The MSRB has also engaged in a proactive effort to communicate with state and local government issuers regarding the development of rules for municipal advisors and how the MSRB can effectively protect state and local governments through regulation and market transparency.

This type of outreach by the MSRB has encouraged further discussion of the most efficient and effective means of ensuring the fairness and transparency of the municipal market for all participants.

RESPONSIBILITIES OF PROFESSIONALS INVOLVED IN A MUNICIPAL FINANCING TRANSACTION

State or Local Government Issuer

Municipal entity that sells its securities to the public.

Underwriter(s) (also known as Senior Manager, Lead Manager or Bookrunner)

Forms a syndicate to distribute securities to the public. The underwriter allocates securities among other firms in the group but is itself generally responsible for the largest share of the issue.

Municipal Advisor

Retained by an issuer in a fiduciary capacity to assist in executing a municipal bond transaction, purchasing a financial product or other activity.

Underwriter's Counsel

Acts as the legal advisor to the underwriter, underwriting syndicate and selling group members.

Bond Counsel

Represents the interests of investors in a bond transaction and issues an opinion as to the legality of the bonds.

Underwriting Syndicate

A group of investment banking firms that purchases a new issue of securities from the issuer and distributes them to investors.

Selling Group

Assists in the distribution of a new issue of securities but does not participate in the profits or liabilities of the underwriting syndicate.

Feasibility Consultant

Writes the feasibility report prepared for revenue bond sales, which is generally included in the preliminary and final official statements.

Credit Enhancers

Companies that provide a substitute for or a support — such as bond insurance or a letter of credit — to enhance an issuer's credit, in exchange for a fee or premium.

Auditor

Is responsible for examining the issuer's financial records and reports, and delivers an opinion on those financial records.

Rating Agencies

Companies that grade securities so as to indicate the quality of the securities for the investors.

Trustee/Paying Agent

An appointed institution that manages assets for the benefit of the bondholders according to the terms of the trust indenture.

Disclosure Counsel/Other Counsel

Takes responsibility for preparation of the preliminary and final official statements. Other counsel may include special tax counsel, bank counsel and borrower's counsel.

End Notes

[1] Thomson Reuters SDC Platinum database on new municipal issuance from 2007-2011

[2] Federal Policy Responses to the Predicament of Municipal Finance, Congressman Spencer T. Bachus, Cumberland Law Review, 2009.

[3] In re *Jefferson County, Alabama* Chapter 9 Case No. 11-05736-TBB-9, U.S. Bankruptcy Court for the Northern District of Alabama (November 9, 2011) ("Jefferson County Bankruptcy").

[4] *See, e.g.*, U.S. v. Carollo, 10-cr-00654, U.S. District Court, Southern District of New York (July 27, 2010); U.S. v. Rubin/Chambers, Dunhill Insurance Services Inc., 09-CR-01058, U.S. District Court, Southern District of New York (October 29, 2009). Allegations regarding bid rigging have been raised in other venues as well. *See also* SEC Complaint 1, SEC v. J.P. Morgan Securities LLP, Case No. 2:11-cv-03877 (D.N.J. July 7, 2011) (alleging fraudulent bidding practices by J.P. Morgan Securities in at least 93 municipal bond reinvestment transactions); SEC Litigation Release No. 21956, Securities and Exchange Commission v. UBS Financial Services Inc. (May 4, 2011) (alleging fraudulent bidding practices by UBS Financial Services in at least 100 municipal bond reinvestment transactions); In the Matter of Banc of America Securities LLP, Exchange Act Release No. 63451 (December 7, 2010) (alleging fraudulent bidding practices by Banc of America Securities in at least three municipal bond reinvestment transactions).

[5] Jefferson County Bankruptcy.

[6] *See, e.g.*, Report of the Missouri House Interim Committee on Government Oversight and Accountability Mamtek Report, (February 2012) and Yvette Shields, *Lombard Draws on Reserves*, The Bond Buyer (January 5, 2012).

[7] *See, e.g., Forbes Magazine*, "Finally, An Easy Way To Get Timely Municipal Bond Data," July 9, 2012; *Smart Money*, "Muni Bonds Require More Attention Nowadays," July 10, 2012; *Wall Street Journal,* "A Site to Check Municipal Bond Ratings," November 19, 2011; *New York Times*, "In Uncertain Times, Municipal Bonds Call for Caution," October 18, 2011; *New York Times*, "Fresh Air in the Muni Market," August 20, 2009.

INDEX

D

E

F

G

H

R

S